PAL

THE SMILE OF A RAGPICKER

The Life of Satoko Kitahara

Convert and Servant of
the Slums of Tokyo

IGNATIUS PRESS   SAN FRANCISCO

First Published by
Marist Fathers Books, Hunters Hill, N.S.W., Australia
©1992 by Paul Glynn
All rights reserved

Cover design by Riz Boncan Marsella

Published 2014 by Ignatius Press, San Francisco
All rights reserved
ISBN 978-1-58617-881-9
Library of Congress Control Number 2014905849
Printed in the United States of America ⊗

THE SMILE OF A RAGPICKER

CONTENTS

PART THREE
FIRST FRUITS

PART FOUR
THE NEW JERUSALEM

FOREWORD
TO THE FIRST EDITION

The small Christian community of Japan has given the world many remarkable Christians. In the late sixteenth century, the Twenty-six Martyrs were crucified together in Nagasaki because of their refusal to renounce their faith. Successive shoguns were concerned that Japanese Christians gave their real allegiance to a foreign authority.

In his companion book *A Song for Nagasaki,* Paul Glynn brought us Dr. Nagai, a Christian convert of remarkable courage and compassion particularly after the atomic bomb attack on his city. The bomb took from him his wife, who had introduced him to Christianity. Now in *The Smile of a Ragpicker,* Paul Glynn brings us the heroic and moving story of Satoko Kitahara-san. In nine remarkable years at Sumida Park in Tokyo, she showed through her commitment and serenity how the lives of so many people could be changed. Importantly she helped them recover their self-respect and dignity.

In finding Christ, Satoko-san found herself. The journey was not easy, and she got no guarantees in advance except that Christ would be with her. Satoko-san experienced the "dark night of the soul". She was challenged so directly by her associate Matsui-san, "surely you don't imagine that you are a follower of Christ just because you give to the poor what you do not need at Christmas and Easter." A restless, young, rich woman, dabbling in good works, was led by the Holy Spirit to forget her reservations and pride and became one with the ragpickers. She plunged into the life of the poor, regardless of the consequences. The Lord heard the cry of the poor, and he sent them Satoko-san. She became known as Ari no Machi no Maria—Mary of Ants Town. She inspired all those she touched. Despite their poverty, her children helped lepers and the homeless. The clever and the rich passed by, but not the urchins of Sumida Park.

Little did they all know that garbage collection and sorting would one day become a major world issue and an industry in itself. But the few yen that Satoko-san and her young friends earned, helped them feed themselves and their families, provide some repairs for their shanties, build a refectory, a bathroom and a plain church.

Every day Satoko-san encountered Christ in some new and challenging way. She was calling the Church back to identification with the poor. She showed the strength of her internal faith. It didn't depend on external disciplines and ceremonies. And like Dr. Nagai, she expressed her faith through the sensitivity and beauty of her own culture. She was a "Christian without the Western baggage". Satoko-san died a young woman, in physical poverty in a Tokyo slum. Yet her death matched her triumphant life. One senses that she knew beyond any doubt that Christ was on both sides of death—that death was only a short journey.

We are now [1992] remembering the events of fifty years ago—Pearl Harbor, the fall of Singapore and the bombing of Darwin. This book is a wonderful story of reconciliation, not between countries, but between people of different social and religious backgrounds, inspired by a frail young woman.

Saint Elizabeth of Hungary, in the thirteenth century, spent out her life for the impoverished sick. Satoko-san took Elizabeth as her baptismal name. Mary of Ants Town lit a light that still burns and this book spreads her light. We owe Paul Glynn our gratitude for bringing this remarkable young woman to us.

Sydney, March 25, 1992
John Menadue
Australian Ambassador to Japan, 1977–1980
Chief Executive of Qantas, 1986–1989
N.S.W. President of the Literature Committee
Saint Vincent de Paul Society

INTRODUCTION

The Tribe of the Setting Sun

It was the cool spring morning of March 10, 1947. Satoko Kitahara passed through a ticket gate at Shibuya Railway Station and almost tripped over a man without legs. He "sat" on a piece of straw matting, propped up against a wall and in a weak voice almost lost in the city din pleaded: "Don't forget us who lost everything just two years ago tonight." The eyes lacked luster; the face was unshaven and drawn. A thin grubby hand rattled a chipped enamel mug containing several coins. Satoko stopped, slipped in ten yen, gave a bow and hurried away. She walked very quickly as if trying to get away from the terrible memories of that night but they caught up with her.

Those memories began with the look on her father's face on this very night two years ago. A sharp wind had chilled Tokyo that morning, turned gusty in the afternoon and was howling like a spring cyclone by nightfall. Her worried father muttered: "It will be a bad night if the bombers come!" Even as he said that, General LeMay's B-29s had already taken off from fields in the Marianas and Carolines: 333 huge bombers, loaded with incendiaries!

Pathfinders flew in first and lit a big X with napalm incendiaries to mark the center of downtown Tokyo. Just before midnight wave after wave of B-29s arrived and bombed around that X at will. So many families and records were totally wiped out that night no one is sure how many died. City officials at the time put the number at 130,000, almost the same as the death toll in the raid on Dresden, February 13, not quite a month before.

Her father had gone with other district air-raid wardens to visit the bombed-out area the next day. His voice was husky when he came home and described the horror to his wife, probably not realizing young Satoko could hear. Block after block of the wooden suburbs had vanished leaving only heat-whitened steel safes standing incongruously in the ashes. Piles of charred bodies lay everywhere like cords of charcoal. The great Buddhist temple complex dedicated to the Merciful Kannon, a haven in the fires that followed the 1923 earthquake, had simply disappeared. Its grounds were littered with thousands of incinerated bodies. The tortuous labyrinths of Asakusa's red light district were a vast charnel house. A huge crowd had sought shelter in the Meijiza Theater and had been roasted alive. Everywhere open pools of water, dug in front of public buildings for the use of firefighters, were awash with bodies. The Sumida River was clogged with bloated corpses. Two years later to the day the limbless man staring sightlessly into the crowd and whimpering "Don't forget ...." had set running again the horror movie locked in Satoko's memory.

Early for her appointment with a fellow university student, she slipped into a restaurant popular with students and ordered tea and castera cake. Students at the next table were noisily discussing the avant-garde writer Osamu Dazai. Interested both in literature and several of Dazai's themes, she listened in. Dazai was a young quasi-aristocrat who believed that Japan was doomed. He coined a malicious phrase to describe postwar Japanese as the "tribe of the setting sun". Some months before he had summed up this mood, this despair with a brilliant short story, *Tokatonton* (*A Sound of Hammering*). That so many students had read it—and those at the table alongside Satoko were discussing it passionately—showed how many of them resonated with Dazai's pessimism.

The subject of Dazai's story is a man gone to seed. He was working in a munitions factory in 1945 but, drafted into the army in the last months of the war, he was furiously digging fortifications on the Chiba coast near Tokyo when the unimaginable surrender came. With deft, evocative words Dazai portrays the young man's sense of disillusionment and meaninglessness.

A woman student at the table next to Satoko's was reading from Dazai's book in a pinched voice. "Everything appeared absurd.... I went to my room, crawled under a quilt and fell asleep. When someone called I refused to get up. I wasn't feeling well—that's all I said. I felt sluggish and morose ... living in a trance, like an inert minnow near the bottom of a goldfish bowl. A vast emptiness lay before me.... I went to Aomori City and saw a workers' demonstration and felt akin to despair—the leaders (as all our leaders now) were seeking power for themselves,... gesturing and roaring about how disaster will come if they are ignored.... But then, as has happened so often, their favorite prostitutes will give them the cold shoulder and they will cry desperately for the abolition of whores."

One of Dazai's antiheroines appears, a young woman without moral values. The man falls for her but as abruptly he loses interest. He realizes he has become a nonperson with only "a passion for nothing". Is suicide the one logical escape? He sets out on a sake-drinking bout with an uncle. His courage fueled by alcohol he asks the older man if there's any meaning to life. "I don't know about life", replies Uncle, "but the world's nothing but sex and greed."

The idealist Satoko shuddered as if someone had walked over her grave. Half in anger, half in despair she stood up, paid her bill and went outside to wait for her friend from

Yokohama. Their rendezvous was a favorite meeting place for young Tokyoites, the larger-than-life bronze of the dog Hachiko outside the Shibuya Station.

Her friend was late and, as she looked vacantly into the crowds swirling by, Satoko found her thoughts turning to the famous canine hero that has been so often photographed and written up in Japanese children's storybooks and junior school texts. Hachiko was a sturdy male Akita, a species of dog first bred in Akita prefecture high up on the eastern coast of Honshu. Back in 1923 Hachiko, just over a year old, used go to Shibuya Station early every evening to meet his master, Professor Uno, who always returned from his university on the same train. One day the professor collapsed at his work place and died, but the dog continued going to the station late every afternoon to look for his master. The grieving widow, distressed by the daily ritual, took the mournful dog to acquaintances in the distant suburb of Asakusa, by the banks of the Sumida River. She was sure the dog would be quite disoriented by the tortuous trip through the maze of Tokyo's winding streets and short cuts. To be doubly sure, they tied Hachiko up.

Hachiko chewed through the rope and escaped. Days later he turned up at Shibuya Station, footsore and bedraggled, but eyes alert as he looked for his master among the crowd streaming from the station. For the next ten years he appeared there daily at the same spot where the statue now stands.

When arthritic limbs made Hachiko's walking slow and painful, the stationmaster built a kennel in the goods shed and cared for him. The sick dog still dragged himself out each evening punctually to meet that train. One night a station hand noticed he was missing, went to Hachiko's kennel and found him dead.

The story touched something deep within the Japanese heart. Though the Pacific war had begun to bite into Japan's preciously scarce supply of gunmetal, and ancient temple bells were being collected and melted down for weapons, the authorities cast a larger-than-life bronze statue of Hachiko, "the dog who served his master faithfully till death". The statue was unveiled in 1943 in front of Shibuya Station. When Satoko heard the story as a small child, she cried and prayed that Hachiko would find his way to *Jodo*, the Pure Land, and she made a special place for him in her heart.

It was now almost dark and she stared through the gloom at the indistinct faces, looking for her friend's. Were she and her tardy friend like Hachiko? she mused sadly. They used to spend hours together discussing "philosophy", looking for a meaning to life. Was Dazai right, was it all pointless? Were they doomed, like Hachiko, to wait for something that would never turn up?

This young woman Satoko, who felt so dissatisfied with life, was a twenty-year-old student at the Showa Women's Pharmaceutical University and a member of the privileged class. Her father was Professor Kinji Kitahara, a recognized academic who held prestigious degrees from three universities. The Kitaharas traced their family tree back a thousand years and also to a Kyoto aristocrat, Michizane Sugawara, who was a Shinto priest serving an imperial minister of state at the close of the ninth century. This ancestral line of Shinto priests was unbroken until the last quarter of the 1800s when Satoko's grandfather, Yoshimatsu Kitahara, left the Shinto priesthood. He became a very wealthy land speculator in Hokkaido, Japan's last frontier.

Satoko would graduate from Showa University, never hold down a regular job, not marry or even have a boyfriend, and die penniless in a Tokyo slum at the age of twenty-eight. One of Dazai's anti-heroines? No—the major Japanese newspapers would carry glowing articles and even editorials about her when she died, and within a year of her death Japan's top movie company would screen a movie on her short life, with the famous star Kakuko Chino in the role of Satoko. Books would be written about her amazing life that would become radio and stage productions. The nationally popular Takarazuka Revue, mostly famous for chorus girls and glitzy extravaganza, would recount her life in a top-billing production called *The Town Where Stars Fall*—and reduce audiences to tears.

In February 1990, one of Japan's most prestigious monthlies, *Bungei Shunju*, would publish an article on the fifty Japanese women who "moved the nation most" during Emperor Hirohito's sixty-two-year reign. Satoko would be one of that select band.

Chief Justice Kotaro Tanaka, the second Japanese judge to sit on the international bench at the Hague, observed that overnight this young woman became both a folk heroine for the hoi polloi who read pulp magazines and also the topic of deep discussion among Japanese intellectuals. He wrote a short piece about her stating that she achieved such wide-ranging fame simply because she possessed one all-important secret. That secret answers the question on so many modern lips: what is wrong with our enlightened age that gives almost everyone a scientific education but leaves so many people discontented?

To tease out her secret it will be necessary to leave her waiting for her young university friend for awhile and study the unique times that did much to form her character and temperament.

PART ONE

The Waters of Chaos

. . . formless and void, with darkness over the surface of the waters.

Genesis 1:1

Chapter 1

Doolittle and Tokyo Rose

Unfortunately for Satoko and her fellow citizens of Tokyo the Japanese militarists made many miscalculations in planning the Pacific War. One of them was not preparing for fire raids from the US Air Force. The militarists thought Tokyo, and indeed all of Japan, was well shielded from serious air raids. The non-aggression pact with Russia neutralized the skies due north. Japan's occupation of Manchuria protected the northwest, while her armies in Korea, Burma, eastern and southern China protected her western flank. Vast stretches of ocean made air attack from the northeast, east and southeast highly improbable if not impossible. Japan's powerful Pacific fleet would prevent US carrier planes getting close enough to attack. Japanese aviation experts calculated that enemy planes could bomb Japan only from carriers at least 400 miles away. They were wrong, not knowing the range of recently developed US B-25s. On April 18, 1942, Colonel Doolittle—an aeronautical scientist as well as a daring and skillful pilot—led sixteen B-25 bombers off the decks of the US carrier *Hornet*, 550 miles due east of Tokyo. Thirteen of the planes bombed Tokyo while the other three hit Nagoya, Osaka and Kobe.

The raid did little physical damage. The United States had hoped it would boost American morale and disturb the Japanese psychologically. It did far worse. The light damage encouraged the Japanese to believe that air raids would not be a serious problem. The government offhandedly told citizens to dig some holes on the streets in case they were

3

caught out-of-doors in an air raid. Otherwise they were to remain at home during raids, ready to put out fires quickly! It was suggested they barricade one room with bedding as a measure against bomb concussion! Unlike London's underground railway, Japan's Chikatetsu Line was too shallow to provide any real shelter from the bombs soon to rain from the skies.

At Midway, June 3–5, 1942, in one of the greatest sea battles in history, Japan lost four aircraft carriers in almost as many minutes. A staggering three hundred planes and the Japanese Navy's most experienced air crews went down with the carriers. US intelligence, having cracked the enemy code, had lured the Japanese into a giant steel trap. The debacle destroyed Japan's naval control of the whole western Pacific Ocean won at Pearl Harbor on the previous December 8 (December 7).

In November 1942 the beginning of Japan's all-conquering thrust south toward Port Moresby and Australia was halted. In a three-day sea battle off Guadalcanal Japan lost two battleships, one heavy cruiser, three destroyers and eleven transport ships. The transports went down with eight thousand seasoned soldiers, and almost ten thousand tons of provisions meant for the beleaguered Japanese garrisons on Guadalcanal and the northeastern coast of New Guinea. The US Navy had lost as many fighting ships in that action but the gathering momentum of American production lines made US naval losses sustainable. Japan's shipping, harried more and more by the swelling shoals of US submarines and attacked repeatedly by land and carrier based planes, was unable to keep the southernmost bases in supplies. The mauled, lean and malaria-ridden Japanese forces pulled out of the southeastern tip of New Guinea at the end of 1942. Just a month later they evacuated Guadalcanal. The painful retreat back to Japan had begun. Satoko was thirteen years old.

By 1943, US shipbuilding yards were launching a carrier a month. Longer range and vastly improved planes, submarines and warships were being turned out in increasing numbers and manned by eager graduates from US training camps. The Japanese military, on the other hand, were restricted by dwindling supplies of raw materials reaching their own shipbuilding yards and airplane factories. The more realistic grew apprehensive as they watched American forces creep ever closer. Every Tokyo household was now told to dig an air-raid hole in the yard. The holes were shallow, often without a roof. Satoko's family dug one, ignorant of how ineffectual and even dangerous these holes would be.

In late 1943 a confident group of US and British top brass met in Cairo. Hitler's Sixth Army faltered at Stalingrad in a colossal military debacle and Russian armies had commenced driving the Germans back. MacArthur's Pacific counter-attack was moving forward but was criticized for taking too long. The Cairo planners decided that the Japanese Home Islands would be crippled by B-29 bombers, taking off from some scattered Micronesian islands east of the Philippines and north of the equator—the Gilberts, the Marshalls, the Carolines and the Marianas. About the same time, Satoko's father, a gentle university professor whose three degrees included absolutely nothing about warfare or air raids, suddenly found himself commissioned as a high-ranking officer in the air-raid defense of the Suginami area of Western Tokyo. He would soon learn the grim significance of these Micronesian islands, and so would the residents of Hiroshima and Nagasaki.

The Japanese garrisons on these outpost islands had built formidable concrete bunkers but relentless US naval and aerial bombardments systematically cracked them wide open. US communiques detailed how "fanatically" the Japanese fought to the very last man. However, without a real navy or air force to help them, the Japanese positions fell like dominoes before the juggernaut. The island of Tarawa was in US hands before the end of 1943. By June 6, 1944 (D-Day in France), a huge US force was steaming for Saipan. It was a small place about twenty-five miles long and only six miles wide in most places, but absolutely vital to Japan's air-raid defence. The B-29 bombers could reach Tokyo from Saipan.

On June 11, 1944, 216 US carrier-based planes hit Saipan and Tinian, shooting down the outmoded Japanese fighters that flew up to meet them and destroying over 100 planes on the Japanese airfields. Following that, twenty-one battleships and twenty-two smaller US warships moved in unopposed and unleashed a horrendous bombardment. The next day eight more US battleships, six heavy cruisers and five light cruisers joined in. On June 14, at night, 128,000 US troops, mostly Marines, were making last-minute adjustments to their equipment. Suddenly Tokyo Rose beamed into their radios: "I've some swell recordings for you", purred the nisei graduate from the University of California at Los Angeles. "Enjoy them while you're alive. We will be ready for you when you hit Saipan tomorrow at O six hundred." She both fascinated and unnerved them, but her pathetic propaganda was about all the Japanese militarists had left.

Chapter 2

Golden Hawks from Old Black Hens

On June 15, 1944, US troops landed on Saipan. The Japanese fought without thought for life or limb, contesting every square yard, but they were hopelessly outnumbered by more than four to one. Furthermore they were without air or sea support. Two Japanese aircraft carriers which had rushed in to give support were soon sent to the bottom, with 364 planes. Although US naval and air attacks cut huge holes in the defence lines, the Japanese knocked fourteen thousand US troops out of action before all but a few of the entire Japanese garrison of thirty thousand soldiers were killed. Twenty-two thousand Japanese citizens, which was two-thirds of the civilian population, also perished, many of them choosing to die by their own hand rather than surrender. Quite a few mothers, their babies strapped Japanese-style on their backs and other children clinging or roped to them, jumped to their deaths on the rocky sea coast below Marpi Point.

Back in Tokyo, Satoko and her high school classmates began government sponsored training with bamboo spears. Saipan was only a small island, relatively easily blasted and overrun. Japan was a nation of ever receding mountains; Satoko and her companions were convinced it would never be subdued if they fought with the utter commitment of their compatriots on Saipan. This psychology, incomprehensible to most Westerners, is an essential part of Satoko's story and needs some explanation.

Satoko's generation was only one lifetime away from Japan's seven-hundred-year-long history of Bushido, the Way of the Bushi (or samurai), and Satoko was still very much influenced by this ancient code. Bushido as such began in 1192 when warrior Yoritomo Minamoto became shogun, or generalissimo of Japan, setting up his military headquarters at Kamakura. The heart of Bushido is absolute loyalty to one's *shukun* or liege lord. Since the late nineteenth century Meiji Restoration, the shukun was the emperor. Dedication to one's shukun and his honor must be absolute, precluding any thought of surrendering to his enemies! The fourteenth-century classic *Tsurezure-gusa,* read by Satoko and every Japanese middle school student, expressed this ideal succinctly: "Only if a man accepts death calmly when his sword is broken and his arrows spent, to the end refusing surrender, does he prove himself a hero." Japanese soldiers and even civilians of Satoko's day could recite by heart the *Senjin,* Japan's Code of Battle Ethics: "I will never suffer the disgrace of being taken alive." On Saipan almost every Japanese soldier and most civilians obeyed this code. Taking the concrete example of one Saipan civilian, a young woman almost the same age as Satoko, will illustrate how profoundly Bushido influenced the Japanese people before the 1945 surrender. The self-sacrificial ideals held by this young woman were cherished as dearly by Satoko. An understanding of these particularly Japanese ideals will help in comprehending Satoko's life, then and later. The story is well told in John Toland's Pulitzer Prize winning classic, *The Rising Sun.*

Shizuko Miura, eighteen years old, was nervously watching steel storm clouds of battleship-gray gathering on the Saipan horizon. She jumped for cover when made-in-USA steel began raining red hot all around her. Running through the burning, exploding town of Garapan she only just made it to the safety of a cave in the hills. She watched a pitiful line of Japanese tanks move sluggishly toward the hordes of US Marines landing on the beaches. The light tanks were quickly and unceremoniously knocked out as if they were made of plywood. She was doubly horrified—her older brother was in one of those tanks. She shouted out "Goodbye, big brother", and a firm resolution took hold of her. She scurried out of the cave and across the uneven terrain to the Mount Donnay military hospital on the other side of the island. Hospital? There were no buildings left. Row after row of wounded, groaning soldiers lay on the ground. There must have been 1,000 wounded but there were only three doctors and seven orderlies, all male, to tend to them. She volunteered her services as a nurse and the head doctor put her straight to work. Without any nursing experience she trembled at first as she helped a doctor get chunks of shrapnel from a soldier's back. Next she was told to hold a leg while the doctor hacksawed a man's foot off without anaesthetics. The smells were nauseating.

She bent over a bloodied, almost naked lieutenant who clasped a grubby photograph. "Let me help you, soldier. My brother died in the tanks. I've volunteered to nurse you all." Tears coursed down the man's cheeks as he showed the nurse the photograph of a young woman in a kimono. "Your wife?" she asked. Lieutenant Shinoda nodded: "When I was hit all I could think of was her. I wanted to live for her sake. But I shall die...." She refused to believe it but, over the next fifteen days, his life and that of scores of other wounded slipped through her fingers.

On June 30 the Americans at last broke through what they called Death Valley, putting the field hospital at risk of being overrun. At dusk the Japanese commander sent a message to the chief surgeon. The latter mounted a rise to break the news to the wounded lying on the ground below him: "We have orders to evacuate to a village over five miles to the north—with patients who can walk! To my great sorrow I must leave you others behind.... You will be given grenades. Die with honor like Japanese soldiers." Shizuko jumped up and said she would die with the ones who couldn't walk, but the head doctor ordered her to accompany the walking wounded.

Doomed men crawled over for a few final words with this vibrant young woman who had given herself unstintingly for the last two weeks, bringing back memories of mothers, wives and sisters. She listened to each with all her attention, promising to give last messages to their families if she survived. A young soldier on this strange death row made a halting request—that she sing "Kudanzaka". It was an emotional song about a feeble mother from the country, coming to Yasukuni War Shrine in Tokyo, clutching the medal her son was awarded posthumously for valor. Shizuko understood the implications of his request. Without hesitation she began, her voice filling the field like a last blessing from five hundred mothers.

> *I've become impatient finding my way in*
> *the huge city, hobbling along with my walking stick.*
> *I am a black hen who gave birth to a hawk!*
> *That was a grace I did not deserve.*
> *I've come to greet you, my son, in Kudanzaka*
> *And show you your Medal of the Golden Hawk.*

The chief surgeon set off with three hundred walking patients and staff, to a chorus of *arigato* and *sayonara* from the cripples. When they reached the end of the field she heard someone shout "Goodbye, Mother." Then a succession of grenade blasts. The Japanese mother, who for several years will carry a baby strapped to her back, talking and singing to the child while she does her household chores, holds a central place in the psyche of most Japanese for the whole of their lives.

Staff officer Major Hirakushi, who would later be found wounded and unconscious by US medics, was preparing for the suicide charge of the last remnant of the Japanese garrison. It was July 7, 1944, just before dawn. He went down to the beach, peeled off his clothes, and dived into the reef-tamed surf. Japanese have a special feeling for the sea, so cleansing, so teeming with life. The complex ideograph for sea contains the simple ideograph for mother. The major began to cleanse his body in preparation for death. The clear salt water washed away his weariness and stung his eyes. Suddenly alert, he was struck by the shape of the moonlit clouds above that looked "like a mother carrying a child strapped snugly on her back". For a moment he had left the stinking hellhole of Saipan and was a boy back in Japan with his mother. Then he said the cloud formation altered and he could see the likeness of his wife. With a wrench of willpower he forced himself back to his grim duty, ran out of the surf and donned his filthy uniform for the suicide charge.

The moon had now paled with the swift tropical dawn. Lieutenant Colonel O'Brien, exhausted, dirty, light years away from those wonderful "soft mornings" of his beloved Ireland, rubbed his bloodshot eyes. He could scarcely believe what he saw. A red flag was slashing the pale horizon sky. Behind it came about one thousand roaring Japanese soldiers. Behind them was double that number of civilians. As they rushed toward the US positions he could see they brandished a wild assortment of guns, swords, clubs and spears. Some were heavily bandaged, others could barely hobble, but on they came, cheering, into the murderous American fire. Though they went down in hundreds their lines did not break and now they were crossing the US forward positions.

O'Brien kept firing until he was hit, one of the 650 American casualties of that charge.

That same dawn Shizuko peered cautiously out of a foxhole in Jigoku-dani, The Valley of Hell, where all that was left of the field hospital personnel were gathered. The chief doctor had told her he would do his duty as a soldier and take his life when the attack came. She, he said, must hold aloft a white cloth and surrender. Suddenly American grenades rained on the Japanese positions and shouting US soldiers came racing toward them. The head doctor whipped out his pistol and shot himself, his assistant slashed his throat savagely and tumbled over Shizuko. She took a grenade, went cold all over and tried to call out "Mother". Her throat was so constricted that no sound came out. She activated the grenade and tried to throw herself on top of it. In the tangle of writhing bodies the blast only knocked her unconscious. A long time later she came to, with a solicitous American officer speaking to her in Japanese. She recovered from her wounds and returned to Japan to tell the story after the war.

By July 8, 1944, the battle for Saipan was over. US casualties had been high—fourteen thousand, mostly Marines—but the spoils were priceless. A one and a quarter mile airstrip, Isley Field, could be built on a low expanse in the southeastern sector of the island. The specially developed B-29, the biggest bomber in existence and aptly named the Superfortress, could operate on a runway that long. When US engineers had laid down the airstrip Tokyo would suffer a new kind of bombing that would eventually clutter its docks with sunken ships, wipe out over half of the factories and production plants—and turn Satoko's life into a nightmare. However, before that, the powerful Japanese army garrison in the Philippines plus the potentially lethal remnant of the Japanese fleet stationed from Singapore to Formosa (Taiwan) must be neutralized.

The Japanese High Command thought the Americans would attack the Philippine Archipelago from the southernmost island, Mindanao, and concentrated their forces there. In a daring strategy (which he was to repeat brilliantly at Inchon in the Korean War) MacArthur struck at Leyte, in the middle of the Philippines. His invasion armada of almost six hundred ships carried over two hundred thousand combat personnel. They landed almost unopposed in Leyte Gulf and sliced deep into the island. It was October 20, 1944.

If the Philippines fell, only Formosa, Iwo Jima and Okinawa stood in the way to Japan itself. Japanese strategists quickly drew up plans for "a final decisive battle". The Imperial Navy must muster from Singapore, Cam Ranh Bay and Formosa to attack the US fleet off Leyte. Despite their chronic lack of air cover the Japanese threw themselves at the Americans in the biggest naval battle in history and were all but annihilated. In the space of four days Japan lost four carriers, three battleships, six heavy cruisers, three light cruisers and ten destroyers. US strategists were now ready to begin their plan of bombing the Japanese mainland into submission.

On the first day of November 1944, a Mariana based B-29 flew over Tokyo. An apprehensive Professor Kitahara and his air-raid warden colleagues discussed the huge silver plane that passed over without dropping bombs. They would have been stunned to have heard the US planners back on Saipan, discussing the Tokyo data the B-29 crew brought back.

Chapter 3

More Flowers of Edo

It was now November 1944. Where chrysanthemums had once waved showy heads in a celebrated public park near Satoko's home, there was now only dark earth and rice stubble from a crop harvested the month before. The food situation was acute because most rice from Japanese farmlands went to the wide battlefronts or military storehouses in Japan. Though areas like city parks had been ploughed into paddies the rice ration was just a third of what civilians needed. Fish, once the staple protein diet, had all but disappeared from most kitchens. Since the Japanese naval debacles, US submarines and aircraft carriers controlled the sea lanes. Fishing boats that risked going any distance from the Japanese coast usually went to the bottom and US planes were systematically sinking small boats at their moorings. French journalist Robert Guillain, caught by the war in Tokyo, writes that a citizen's ration was one dried sardine every two or three days! The north winds blowing from wintry Siberia had frozen the growth of most green vegetables by November and Satoko and fellow Tokyoites had grown thoroughly sick of their new staple diet, sweet potatoes.

The omnipresent neighborhood associations tried to bolster morale with spartan slogans like *yase gaman* (Grow thinner to endure!). Many could not endure. Infant mortality was now three times higher than in Great Britain or Germany. Hunger lowered people's physical resistance to tuberculosis, intestinal problems and all manner of viruses and diseases.

Women had been called into the workforce to replace the men who were in the armed services and tens of thousands of them now worked in coal mines. Sixteen-year-old Satoko was put to working a lathe in the Nakajima airplane factory in Tokyo. Since September, 1943, when the military government grew alarmed at the navy losses and the US thrust northward, all-out aircraft production had been decreed, with factories working herculean shifts, twenty-four hours a day. Production was doubled but at a tragic cost to the workers' health. Satoko soon showed the first signs of lung trouble. A number of her school friends had already died of tuberculosis.

Tokyo had once been the most colorful and interesting city in the Orient. Now everything was deadly drab. Men wore an economy uniform of dark and austere synthetic fiber, topped by an equally dull soldier's cap. Women wore rough *monpe*, skirt pantaloons tied at the ankles, made from kimono material dyed dark. Frivolity was frowned on. Travel by train, bus and tram was almost totally restricted to that essential for the war machine. Public vehicles had thoroughly deteriorated— fittings stayed broken, smashed windows went unrepaired. It availed little to have a car as there was no gasoline. With rubber tires and tubes now irreplaceable, many Tokyo citizens rode bicycles with permanently punctured tires. Soap, stationery, thread and similar household items vanished from shop shelves. Heating fuel had also disappeared, and the coldest winter in years had begun—over the next months, forty-five days would record a temperature below freezing. The highly artistic Satoko missed the colorful kimonos, music and stage plays that she loved passionately. But not a word of complaint escaped her lips. That would be unpatriotic, and treason to the soldiers risking their lives at the front.

The fear of fire had always been a preoccupation for the people of Tokyo, a city built of wood because Japan's frequent earthquakes made stone structures too dangerous. There had been many fearful conflagrations in the crowded city's three-century history. In 1657, when the city was still called Edo, 108,000 had died in one fire. Since Satoko's parents had come to live in the city, there had been three terrible fires. The 1923 earthquake had struck just before lunchtime and charcoal cooking pots were overturned, starting wide-ranging fires that claimed tens of thousands of lives. After that, Tokyo citizens used roof tiles instead of traditional thatch or cedar bark roofs, but this did not stop the devastating fires of 1925 and 1932. Tokyoites, noted for quick-wit and for coining phrases, named their fires "The Flowers of Edo". Edo was the name of the capital until Emperor Meiji changed it in 1868 to Tokyo, meaning Eastern Capital, vis-à-vis Kyoto, the old capital in the west. Now Tokyoites were told to expect Flowers of Washington! Already ugly scars crisscrossed the city's most crowded sections where lines of houses had been torn down in July and August of 1944 as firebreaks. They would prove of little help against the napalm flowers that B-29s would deliver in aluminium vases!

Many of the city's full-time firemen had been called up into the services and their places were taken by young women. They lacked nothing in courage and commitment but their equipment would prove utterly inadequate—bamboo ladders, antiquated hand pumps for when water mains burst, tins of sand for incendiaries, straw mats soaked in water, and lists of housewife volunteers for water-bucket brigades!

There had been no Tokyo air raids since Doolittle's foray in 1942. US bombers from North China had struck western cities like Nagasaki and Kokura but could not reach Tokyo. On November 1, 1944, a B-29 from a newly constructed field in the Marianas flew leisurely over Tokyo. At thirty thousand feet it had no fear of antiaircraft fire or Zero fighters. It dropped no bombs, content to take aerial photographs.

Millions of apprehensive eyes looked up at it from holes in tiny gardens or footpaths. After the all clear, their sense of beauty overcoming their fear, many discussed the breathtaking sight the huge silver body made against a peerless blue sky! B-29s appeared daily after that, still content to collect photographic details of the sprawling capital. The government responded by reiterating previous instructions: in a raid, stay in a hole close to your home, ready to dash out to extinguish fires. A few fireproof buildings were erected, air-raid "equipment" was increased, drills were held regularly and many children were sent to country areas.

Suddenly the real bombers came. On November 24, 111 Superfortresses from Mariana airfields set out for the Musashino airplane factory in Tokyo. Only thirty-five managed to drop bombs near the target. Some B-29s developed engine trouble on the way and turned back, others dropped bombs on unconnected targets, some even on the countryside! The raid was a dismal failure and Tokyoites breathed a sigh of relief. Three days later eighty-one B-29s returned to bomb the Musashino and Nakajima airplane factories. Satoko, just turned sixteen, was working in the latter factory, making plane parts on a lathe. The factories suffered no hits. Two days later the bombers returned, this time attacked by some stripped-down Zeros that just managed to climb thirty thousand feet to ram several B-29s. The Japanese press excitedly lauded the heroism and skill of these "Wild Eagles". The B-29s then bombed Yokohama and Nagoya but again the results were paltry.

When General Curtis LeMay was brought from North China to take charge of the Marianas-based B-29s, Admiral Nimitz gave him a simple job description: knock out aircraft factories and airstrips. A new phenomenon, the *kamikaze*, had suddenly appeared, threatening Nimitz's navy with horrifying possibilities. LeMay obeyed and on February 25 he sent

172 B-29s, assisted by carrier-based fighters and bombers, to hit aircraft factories in Tokyo. Despite the number of planes, the raid was another failure. Satoko and her workmates began joking about the B-29s.

LeMay seriously considered the situation. Since November 24, 835 bombers had dropped twenty-three hundred tons of high explosives on Japan but only one airplane factory had been destroyed. The much targeted Musashino factory had sustained a mere 4 percent damage! He jotted down reasons for the failure that was now drawing sarcastic comments from Washington. First, the altitude of thirty thousand feet. That was five thousand feet higher than the range of antiaircraft guns and out of the range of most Japanese fighters. However the altitude reduced the bomb load significantly and winds up there blew at 125 mph and more, making precision bombing impossible! Furthermore US intelligence knew that Japan's famous "cottage industries" decentralized production. Minor factories all over the city, employing thirty workers or less, made parts that were merely assembled in the big plants. The high-explosives bombing that was effective on Germany's concentrated workplaces was proving a failure in Japan. Washington was demanding explanations from LeMay. Why had he lost over one hundred of the much vaunted Superfortresses and done so little damage to the Japanese war industry?

He came to a simple decision. On March 9 he assembled the aircrews of 333 Superfortresses and stunned them with his new plan. They would coordinate takeoff from the neighboring islands of Saipan, Tinian and Guam before dark that same day. Previously they had bombed Tokyo in the daytime when they could see the city. The almost 3,000 mile round trip, however, meant they either took off or landed in the dark on dangerously short airstrips and crashes were mounting up. Enough of the new napalm type incendiaries had now arrived in the Marianas for every one of the

333 planes to carry a full load. Special pathfinders would hit Tokyo at just about midnight marking a big X with M47 incendiaries, delineating a clear target area. Japanese ack-ack guns were effective between ten thousand and twenty-five thousand feet. Tonight all B-29s would go in between five thousand and eight thousand feet, rendering antiaircraft guns useless! As the Japanese had no night fighter, he continued, the nose, top and belly cannons and their gunners would be taken off each B-29, the rear cannon providing enough protection. Eliminating three gunners and their heavy cannon and ammunition, on planes that no longer had to carry extra gasoline to get them up to 30,000 feet, would increase the load of incendiaries over 65 percent!

The airmen were stunned. The almost 3,000 mile trip made fighter escorts an impossibility. Many shook their heads in disbelief at the risk they were ordered to take. Though externally he manifested the confidence of a man supremely sure of himself, LeMay was also apprehensive. He was taking a huge risk. If his intuitions were wrong, many planes would go down, seasoned aircrews perish and his career end in disgrace.

Chapter 4

The Night Tokyo Burned

Satoko's father, an officer in Air Raid Defence because regular army officers could not be spared, was spending a very troubled March 9. It was Army Day in Japan and that morning he had heard Major General Matsumura's radio speech with its ominous admission that the citizens of Tokyo might have to fight the US Army in the Kanto Plain. He had been told that many small factories in Tokyo were furiously making hand grenades. The grenades would be primed in army-supervised factories and distributed to Tokyo citizens if (when?) the invasion came.

A northerly wind had sprung up early in the morning and was gale force by evening, tearing down radio antenna and ripping off galvanized roofing. Since November 29 there had been a number of night raids by B-29s. This more random night bombing was hard on citizens who had to huddle in freezing holes in the ground, often up to their ankles in water. Colds, influenza and the loss of sleep were seriously harming many people's health. With a gale blowing tonight, the air-raid warden-professor shuddered to think of what could happen if the "Bees" came in force. He tuned in to the 10:00 P.M. weather report: "Winds gusting between 60 and 70 mph." He told Satoko to get her infant sister Choko straight into their shelter hole if there was a raid. There was fear in his voice, which Satoko picked up. She was ready to move at a moment's notice—the whole family no longer changed into night attire but slept in street clothes.

The trailblazers arrived just after midnight, flying low and undetected at 300 mph. With the skill and daring that had made them top airmen they sowed clusters of M47 incendiaries on the Kiba docks area. Thirty meters above the ground the one-hundred-pound missiles burst open, scattering a shower of small napalm canisters that exploded on impact and flung burning jellied gasoline in all directions. The planes crisscrossed the target neatly and left a giant burning X as the marker for more than three hundred bombers coming up from the south. The first of them arrived ten minutes later and by 12:30 P.M. an area that housed four hundred thousand residents was clearly doomed. The swirling winds had whipped the flames into waves of wildfire.

French journalist Guillain was watching the conflagration with mixed feelings. He wanted the Americans to destroy Japan's military potential so that he could go home but shuddered at the possibility of the B-29s hitting his suburb. In his book *I Saw Tokyo Burning* he commented on the discipline of the citizens that night and on how their famous sense of wonder came to the fore in this veritable hell. "All the Japanese near me were out of doors in their gardens or peering out of holes, uttering cries of admiration—so typically Japanese—at the grandeur of the almost theatrical spectacle." An outstanding spectacle, especially in the realm of nature, be it beautiful or terrible, will evoke in most Japanese an "Ah!" response. Gilbert and Sullivan got at least this right about Japan when the formidable Katisha sings in *The Mikado*: "There is beauty in the bellow of the blast, There is grandeur in the growling of the gale." The poet Gonsui expressed this sense of wonder in a seventeen-syllable haiku that can be translated approximately as "A bleak gale howls itself out over a roaring surf."

Toland notes this same phenomenon and quotes as typical a Tokyo woman's comments: "(The huge B-29s) sailed like shoals of pearly fish riding the seas of the universe.... Their splashing of earth with showers of incendiaries in rhythmic rumble was like ocean breakers.... On every run the Americans brought new kinds of bombs and shells.... The unaccustomed noises increased the terrors and the thrills."

This kind of comment came from people in the safety of outer suburbs. Dwellers on either bank of the lower Sumida River, the main target area, had little leisure to admire the bellow of the blast! For some minutes they had stayed in their holes, ready to leap out and smother fires in their homes. Suddenly they realized everyone's home was doomed, and they would be, too, if the hurtling walls of fire closed in on them. They ran for open spaces like Sumida Park but were soon gagging on hot smoke. They had to dodge dangling electric wires and often crashed into people racing out of side streets. Sometimes a tongue of flame leapt onto the road and fleeing people crumpled to the ground with hair and clothing on fire. Mothers would suddenly scream upon discovering the quilting over the baby on their backs was ablaze.

Crowds jammed into Sumida Park pushing people already there into the water. Many escaped death from the asphyxiating pall of smoke by getting on all fours and crawling to cleared or burned-out areas, panting like dogs. The eleven steel bridges over the Sumida River became clogged with people. Many choked on the smoke and tumbled dizzily into the river. The congested industrial suburbs bordering the Fukagawa docks, Honjo and Mukojima, now burned out of control. The west bank suburbs of Asakusa, Shitaya and the edges of Kanda and Nihonbashi were fast disappearing in a sea of flames.

The extensive grounds of the ancient Temple of Mercy dedicated to Asakusa Kannon had safely sheltered thousands in the 1923 earthquake fires. A huge crowd gathered there again seeking sanctuary, but the blasphemous flames violated the sacred ground and incinerated everyone. Fireballs bounced about like tormented spirits from Gehenna, scattering burning napalm that set people alight. Concentrated firestorms spawned sudden whirlwinds that spiralled one hundred feet high, sucking flimsy houses up with them and spewing out burning tatami mats and red-hot planks.

A huge crowd surged into the ultra-modern Meiji Theater for shelter but the roof collapsed under a hail of incendiaries. The walls caught fire and everyone perished, "as if cooked in a casserole". The fame and wealth of the geisha houses in Susaki were no protection against the charging, goring bulls of flame. The high coiffures and many-layered kimonos of the geisha became their tragic funeral pyres. The iron gates of Yoshiwara, the Nightless City of the Floating World, had been bolted at the beginning of the raid to prevent prostitutes escaping. Everyone perished—madams, procurers, patrons, geisha and prostitutes, all reduced to indistinguishable carbonized blobs.

The B-29s kept coming in, sometimes being tossed thousands of feet by thermal winds howling up from the burning city. About 3:00 A.M. the last B-29 sowed its incendiary seed in the fire-ploughed fields of southeast Tokyo and left.

Thousands of burned victims below groaned for the dawn. When it came both the wind and the fires died down. It was as if they were slinking away, shocked and guilty at seeing in the light of day the twisted, naked bodies and the wholesale destruction caused by their mad orgy with the foreign airmen during the night. People crawled out from storm pipes along the Sumida's banks, or clambered over corpses as they waded to shore from the lukewarm shallows of the river. Others hobbled away from scorched streets or pockets of cleared ground, sometimes with "burnt feet swollen three times their size like big tennis balls".

The macabre sights stunned air-raid wardens who came to study the results the next day. There were charcoaled mothers shielding charred babies and husbands and wives fused into carbonized embrace. Thousands of bloating corpses floated in the Sumida River, the wind and tide piling up bodies on banks like fat logs in a grotesque timber yard. Many groping survivors were sightless, their eyes glued shut from conjunctivitis contracted in last night's hot, soot-filled air.

Over the succeeding weeks city authorities estimated that one hundred thirty thousand died in that first incendiary raid. Some who studied the catastrophe at a later date put the figure lower, but certainly above one hundred thousand. The figures varied because almost every suburban census book had been consumed by the flames. Whole families disappeared, with no one to report their deaths. Many bodies vanished out to sea when the tide turned in the Sumida. Sixteen square miles of eastern and northeastern Tokyo, including 261,000 houses, were burned to the ground and a million people were left homeless in this first of LeMay's firebomb raids.

LeMay was ecstatic, almost like a man possessed. He told his staff he would "burn Japan out of the war by October". The very next night he sent 313 napalm-loaded bombers to give the same treatment to Nagoya. Massive incendiary raids on Osaka and Kobe followed in quick succession. By March 17, seven days later, his B-29 incendiary raids had wiped out forty-five square miles of Japan's cities.

Some of the Allies were having serious second thoughts about this carpet bombing of cities. Dresden had no military value and one hundred thousand of its citizens had died in the ugly fires of mindless revenge, they complained. True, these critics conceded, the Japanese had bombed Chinese civilians and the Nazis had tried to obliterate Coventry. But didn't retaliation bombing of innocent citizens make the Allies share in the very evil they went to war to destroy? The US Jesuit weekly *America* doubted whether mass raids on cities were consistent with "either God's law or the nobility of our cause". The carpet bombers hotly retorted that only mass destruction could halt the total-war machine unleashed by the Axis. Long after the war had finished, when the obstinate shadow of the mushroom cloud still refused to go away, many thoughtful people commented that war's first casualty is truth and the second is morality. Combatants who are long at the front become capable of doing those very things they once called the enemy brute animals for doing.

Tokyoites had little sleep on that night of fire, March 9–10. In the late morning of March 10 a bone-weary Professor Kitahara went with other air-raid wardens to study the bombed out eastern areas. The sights and smells turned their stomachs and made one of his party retch bile. Just past Midori cho in Sumida Ward, close to where the Sobu railway crosses the river, they came across what had been a bike shop. The twisted bicycle frames told them that. Three charred bodies stood leaning against a stone wall, reminding him of descriptions of the grotesque larva-encased bodies left in ancient Pompeii after Mount Vesuvius erupted. He surmised that the tall carbonized corpse was the proprietor of the shop and the two corpses were his children, whose sex it was impossible to tell. The smallest, maybe four years old, clung to the father's knees. An older child, maybe ten, clung to the father's waist, its charcoaled flesh and the father's actually melted together. The professor had a terrible presentiment that he was looking at himself, soon to be incinerated with Satoko beside him and little Choko clinging to his knees.

Shaken, he walked in silence through the eerie moonscape of burned-out buildings and streets piled high with strange-smelling, coal-black corpses. He boarded the train for home, not twenty minutes away. As he entered the *genkan* and his wife greeted him, O-*kaeri-nasai*, Welcome home, he experienced a terrible urge to gather this good woman and the children and flee north to their extensive land holdings in Hokkaido. There, in some snowbound mountain lodge that the B-29s could not find, they might be safe!

Chapter 5

Naught for Your Comfort

I tell you naught for your comfort,
Yea, naught for your desire,
Save that the sky grows darker yet
And the sea rises higher.

G. K. Chesterton,
The Ballad of the White Horse

Typhoons that ravaged the Philippines had once seemed very remote to Satoko, but not so this new kind of typhoon that she heard about. Her father would always explain the news when his children asked him to. He now told Satoko that the fall of Manila on February 5, 1945, meant that a huge fortification protecting Japan had been destroyed. The censored news did not elaborate on the Battle of Leyte Gulf but Professor Kitahara correctly surmised that the Japanese navy had fared badly. Otherwise how had the Americans destroyed Japanese army opposition all the way up to Manila? The radio announcer's enthusiasm for the heroism and skill of the new breed of fliers born in November of 1944 and called kamikaze, did little for his confidence. Such desperation tactics told him how superior the US Air Force was.

The professor's—and Satoko's—fears were terribly justified by the invasion of Iwo Jima on February 15, 1945. Meaning "Sulphur Island", Iwo Jima was utterly barren and looked insignificant, being about a mere five miles long and

26

two and a half miles wide, but it would be a formidable base for the Americans. Only 656 miles from Tokyo and less from Okinawa, it would be an ideal staging area for the attack on the latter, the last barrier between the Americans and Japan. Furthermore, its three airstrips meant US fighters and small bombers had a base close enough for raids on Japan.

The Japanese garrison of twenty-one thousand were grimly determined to hurl the invading Marines back into the sea and fought fiercely and effectively under Lieutenant General Kuribayashi. Their cause was doomed however because US warships shelled them at will and planes from the new US strips in the Marianas bombed and strafed them unopposed. The Japanese fought until their food, water and ammunition were spent and there was hardly an able-bodied man left in the honeycomb caves where they made their last stand in the south of the island. General Kuribayashi had sent tender but resolute letters of farewell to his wife and children before the landings began. Now he radioed a final message to Imperial Headquarters in Tokyo, apologizing for being unable to stop the Americans. He praised his soldiers. "Even the gods would weep", he cabled, "at the heroism of my officers and men." In samurai spirit he concluded his "everlasting farewell" with three short poems he composed in the heat of battle, proclaiming willing acceptance of death for his liege lord, the emperor. On March 27, the badly wounded Kuribayashi stood at attention with difficulty, got down on his knees to face the Imperial palace due north, bowed low three times and plunged a short sword into his lower abdomen. The US flag was flying proudly on the top of Mount Suribachi but 5000 US families were mourning their dead.

All of Japan was shocked by the fall of Iwo Jima. Satoko's school principal gathered as many of the scattered students as she could and addressed them gravely. "General Kuribayashi and his men died gallantly. In his last message to Imperial

Headquarters were the beautiful words: 'When I think of all that I have received from my country I go to my death without regret.' Girls, that is *Yamato-damashii*, the Japanese spirit that has made our land pure. *Yamato-damashii*, and the kamikaze wind from heaven, drove off the Mongol hordes that invaded our land in the thirteenth century. The soldiers on Iwo Jima gave their lives for us. Let us gladly prepare and give of ourselves, utterly, and save our pure homeland."

Satoko and her young friends had already commenced regular bamboo spear practice, readying for the invasion. That night she knelt *seiza* style before the family altar and vowed to her ancestors and the Shinto gods that she would fight with her bamboo spear and willingly give her life for her sacred homeland. She had only one request—that the lives of the others in her family be spared.

Chapter 6

Cherry Blossoms That Exploded

Should someone ask you what is the Yamato-damashii,
you can reply: The fragrance of wild cherry blossoms
in the morning sunlight.

Shinto poet Norinaga Moto-ori, 1730–1801

Okinawa is about 373 miles south of Kyushu. Japanese are apprehensive when Okinawa is mentioned on weather reports in late summer and autumn because the typhoons spawned there can hit Japan with devastating force. Satoko began hearing of an even more terrible kind of typhoon brewing there, one that rained red-hot steel. She listened with growing distress to the persistent rumors that the Americans planned to invade Japan, kill every male and destroy *Yamato-damashii* forever—by raping the women to create a bastard race!

On April 1, 1945, the invasion of Okinawa commenced. After weeks of bombardment from sea and sky one hundred eighty thousand US troops in thirteen hundred transports, aircraft carriers and fighting ships bore down on the narrow, forty-three-mile long island.

The Japanese commander, Lieutenant General Ushijima, was every inch a professional soldier. He knew his army would be annihilated if he met the Americans on the beaches. He had deployed his one hundred ten thousand men in defensible lines behind the narrow coastal area, erecting powerful perimeters and anchoring his bigger guns in block-houses, fortified caves and pillboxes. Behind him were miles of natural caves too deep to be destroyed by US shelling or bombing. His men could retreat into them and the enemy would find it hard to take them.

Sixty thousand Americans had landed on the beaches by nightfall of Okinawa's D-day, April 1, "without being shot at, without getting our feet wet" reported famous war correspondent Ernie Pyle. If the Americans were surprised, the homeland Japanese were stunned. The militarists in Tokyo unleashed their anger by dismissing Koiso, the prime minister.

Professor Kitahara, like many of the intelligentsia in Tokyo, knew Japan's military forces were spent and the war lost. But he also knew the militarists would refuse to surrender. Japan would be invaded and the whole population would be dragged into a guerrilla warfare that could end in national annihilation! The prospect haunted him. It was with some relief therefore that he learned the new prime minister was retired Admiral Kantaro Suzuki. The latter was seventy-eight years old, stooped and quite deaf—hardly one to inspire confidence! But he was a man of strong will and nerves to match, and he was not a militarist. He had been one of the "impure" political figures that militarists had gunned down on February 26, 1936. He had been struck by four bullets, one actually passing through his heart, and yet he had survived.

Suzuki named Shigenori Togo as his foreign minister and immediately began covertly suing for peace, secretly encouraged by the emperor and some senior statesmen. The militarists still controlled the army, navy and the police, however, and regarded any talk of surrender as treason. An all-out kamikaze counterattack on American positions in Okinawa was ordered.

All that was left of the Japanese navy was the sixty-three thousand ton superbattleship *Yamato*, one light cruiser and eight destroyers. Carrying enough oil for a one-way trip to Okinawa, the ten warships set out from the Inland Sea on the night of April 6, without plane protection! They hoped to smash into the ring of enemy boats off Okinawa and take many to the bottom, maybe even beaching themselves and firing on the Americans behind and in front of them! The *Yamato's* huge guns had a range of twenty-five miles.

About noon US planes discovered the kamikaze fleet, still hundreds of miles from Okinawa. Attacked by several hundred planes that came in three waves over two hours, the mighty *Yamato* went down, directly hit by many bombs and at least twelve aerial torpedoes. Captain Ariga, ordering all survivors to abandon ship so they could fight again, lashed himself to the compass post and went down with his ship. Of the crew of 3,332 there were only 269 survivors. The cruiser and four destroyers joined *Yamato* on the bottom of the sea. A badly scorched and tiny remnant limped back to Japan.

Japanese navy and army planes began a concerted series of strikes against Okinawa that same day. During April 6–7, 341 conventional bombers and 355 kamikaze sank six US ships and heavily damaged ten. The Zero kamikaze carried a 250 pound bomb under each wing. The *Ohka*, meaning Cherry Blossom, was a 20 foot one-way wooden glider carrying a 2,646 pound bomb in the nose, with gunpowder-fired rockets in the tail. A Mitsubishi ("Betty") bomber carried it under its belly and released it when the glider pilot decided he was close enough for a strike. When the bomber set him flying free, the pilot would fire his rockets and steer his glider-bomb at bullet-like speed at an American ship.

It took the Americans a full three months to subdue Okinawa. During that time kamikaze airfields in Kyushu launched ten major attacks on the invaders. They sank twenty-six ships and badly damaged another fifty. Nearly four thousand Japanese airmen perished off Okinawa, 1,450 being kamikaze pilots. The majority of the latter were between eighteen and twenty years old; some being only seventeen. In his perceptive historical study, *The Rising Sun*, Toland writes of the inability of Westerners to comprehend the kamikaze rationale. In Toland's words there was "a welter of theories and rumors about the kamikaze: They went into battle like priests in hooded robes; they were drugged; they had to be chained to their cockpits; they were trained from youth to suicide". "Not true", writes Toland. "They were average young Japanese who were volunteers. Their goal was to die a meaningful death, convinced this was the only way to overcome Japan's inferior productivity vis-à-vis America's."

The extraordinary kamikaze offensive brought some temporary respite from air raids on Tokyo. Admiral Nimitz grew so alarmed at the physical and psychological damage the kamikaze were doing that he halted the B-29 raids on Tokyo and the other cities, ordering concentrated bombing on the kamikaze airfields in Kyushu, located in Kanoya, Chiran, Miyazaki, Shibushi and Usa. The kamikaze also had a profound effect on Satoko and her generation, firing them with a peculiarly Japanese idealism and even romanticism. The kamikaze epic is an essential chapter in the story of the Japanese people, and therefore of Satoko. Any attempt to explain her to Westerners demands some attention to this *Nihon-teki* (particularly Japanese) phenomenon. One name given to kamikaze operations, *Kikusui*, is a key to unlocking what is regarded as an Oriental mystery by many in the West.

Every Japanese had learned at school that *Kikusui*, meaning chrysanthemum-on-water, was the family crest of the heroic Kusunoki clan. In 1333 the first ashikaga shogun (supreme generalissimo) drove Emperor Go-daigo into exile from the capital city, Kyoto. A total loyalist, Masashige Kusunoki unhesitatingly took to the field in the emperor's name, despite the overwhelming strength of the enemy. A brilliant strategist, he gave the emperor's cause a fighting chance until numerically superior forces annihilated his army at Minato-gawa, Kobe, in 1336. Escaping with his brother to a farm-house, he took off his coat of mail, exposing eleven wounds. The brothers decided that death with honor was preferable to life in a land where treason had conquered. They ran one another through with their swords.

Masashige had a young son, Masatsura, whom he had ordered away from the fateful battle "to look after his mother". With the dedication of Tennyson's Gareth prepar-ing to be a knight of King Arthur's Round Table, the son trained himself in all the martial skills he would need to fulfil his "sacred duty" of restoring the emperor's and his father's honor. In 1348, aged twenty-three, he raised and led an army of one thousand loyalists and unfurled the emperor's standard against usurper Ashikaga and his huge army. He repulsed the attack on his small castle in the mountains above Nara and moved south to defend the emperor in Yoshino. The equiv-alent of Tennyson's Lynette appeared in the person of a court lady, Ben no Naiji, whom Kusunoki rescued from moun-tain brigands. The emperor offered her to him in marriage. He refused; it would be unfair to her because his untimely death seemed the certain price of uncompromising loyalty to the emperor. His foreboding proved true. Defeated and wounded in the battle of Shijo Nawate, he escaped with his brother. Rather than keep on running like cowards, he and his brother chose to die as their father and uncle had, piercing one another with their swords.

The Kusunoki father and son have become two of the nation's greatest heroes in popular Japanese sentiment. Both of them were "failures", thoroughly defeated in battle. But they were utterly faithful to *makoto*. No one English word translates *makoto*. The authoritative Kenkyusha dictionary defines it: "Sincerity, faithfulness, honesty, a true (single) heart, fidelity, constancy, devotion". A *makoto* person uses none of those stratagems and compromises that lesser people employ to gain mundane "success". *Makoto* people devote themselves to what they see as the noblest cause without any thought of selfish gain. In the Japanese mind the very impracticability or hopelessness of their cause enhances their heroism and even holiness.

Essays and books have been written on this Japanese phenomenon that is sometimes referred to as the "cult of noble failures". Among the half-dozen most famous examples of heroic failure are Michizane Sugawara, with whom Satoko's ancestor went into exile over one thousand years before, and the two Kusunoki. Satoko venerated them and was stirred to her depths when the Floating Chrysanthemum crest of the Kusunoki fluttered proudly again to lead the noblest of causes. Like the younger Kusunoki the kamikaze renounced romance and marriage so that *makoto* and the Japanese race might survive. Their single-minded commitment fired Satoko's patriotism and her determination to give her life for the same cause.

That, like most people, the kamikaze wanted to live is obvious if you read their last letters at the Yasukuni shrine in Tokyo or in the numerous books written about them. Many kamikaze were university arts students who, unlike engineering students, could be sacrificed! On their last flight they often carried their favorite book of literature or poetry in one flying-suit pocket and a photo of their mother in the other. Almost all left farewell letters that move readers still. A typical example is Ensign Teruo Yamaguchi's farewell letter to his father—he had lost his mother early in life: "On learning my time had come I closed my eyes and saw your face, mother's and grandmother's.... It is an honor to be able to give my life in defence of lofty and noble things.... During my final plunge on an enemy ship I will be thinking of all you have done for me and, though you will not hear it, I will be calling *Chichi-ue!* (Revered Father)."

Some letters console parents by reminding them they will die beautifully, like the cherry blossoms that fall several days after blooming. "Like cherry blossoms in the spring, falling clean and radiant", became the kamikaze motto. The glider-bomb, called *Ohka* after the cherry blossom, often had blossoms painted on its nose of sky blue.

One series of photographs featured in the *Mainichi* newspapers early in April affected Satoko and many of her friends deeply. It showed kamikaze fighters taxiing for takeoff from the Chiran airfield near the southern tip of Kyushu. Bowing schoolgirls wave them off to death with branches of cherry blossoms.

The militarists decided that if Okinawa fell, Operation Ketsugo, "Conclusion", would go into effect. To prepare for American landings in Kyushu and Tokyo Bay ten thousand planes, including trainers, were being transformed as kamikaze. 2,350,000 soldiers were deployed, backed up by 4,000,000 auxiliaries recruited from all walks of life. The Citizen Militia Law was passed on April 13. All males between fifteen and fifty-five years of age, and females between sixteen and forty-five, became soldiers, some of them having only muzzle-loading rifles, ancient samurai bows and arrows or bamboo spears. Every Kitahara except little Choko was now a soldier!

The Professor groaned inwardly at the reckless madness but dared not speak out for fear of the *kenpeitai* police. Satoko, however, believed that the "pure" sacrifice of so many *kamikaze* would win heaven's blessing on Japan and ultimate victory. Having been trained in the ancient martial art of *naginata* (halberd), she was confident of giving a good account of herself with a bamboo spear. She eagerly attended lessons on the fundamentals of judo, learning how to throw an assailant who rushed her. Her father looked at her thin body and pale complexion, at the dark half-moons under her eyes and felt like weeping.

Mile after mile the American advance continued in Okinawa. The Japanese had to concede that the enemy were not as "soft" as they had been led to believe. By the end of June, General Ushijima knew he had lost the battle. He wrote a farewell poem: "Autumn is distant but the grass has already disappeared—only to clothe our Motherland next spring."

By July 2 the last Japanese rifles had been silenced. It had cost the Americans twelve thousand five hundred dead and thirty thousand casualties. Almost a third of these were navy men, a commentary on the grim success of the kamikaze. One hundred ten thousand Japanese soldiers and seventy-five thousand Okinawa citizens had died—many of the latter jumping off cliffs or clustering in a circle and detonating hand grenades.

Professor Kitahara had little time to speculate on what the American army would do next. US bombers had returned with a vengeance, dropping thousands of tons of incendiaries. By May 25, 1945, fifty-six square miles of Tokyo had been destroyed—which was just over half of the city. His house had not yet been hit, though one bomb, the size of a small boy, had crashed into the house next door and failed to explode.

Yokohama, Kobe and Osaka—indeed any city of any consequence—were suffering Tokyo's fate. By the beginning of June, two million Japanese buildings had been destroyed and thirteen million people made homeless. The militarists, however, still controlled the cabinet and hectored the people about final victory "if all do their glorious duty. *Tenno Heika, Banzai!*"

Chapter 7

1945, August 15:
Bearing the Unbearable

Satoko's health had deteriorated to a dangerous degree, especially after she had begun working longer shifts on a lathe in the Nakajima Airplane Factory. She commuted from their fine two-story house in Matsu no Ki, in the suburb of Suginami, about seven and a half mile due west from Tokyo Station. Their spacious grounds had been planted with so many trees, shrubs and flowers that the locals called it "The Gardens". The beautiful setting, however, was little protection against huge bombs and incendiaries. Satoko was now spending much of the night in the air-raid hole with little Choko and working most of the day in the Nakajima Airplane Factory—which was often attacked during the day. There was no adequate shelter and the workers had to dive into holes dug in a bamboo grove. US fighter planes were now machine-gunning the city. On one occasion low-flying fighters were almost over the factory before the siren sounded. She dived under her lathe just as bullets stitched a pattern across the work floor. Her steel lathe saved her from certain death. She crawled out and looked transfixed at the yellowish smoke rising from where hot bullets had scorched the lathe. The acrid smell lingered in her memory like the stink of a vase of withered flowers on a grave!

Her older brother Tetsuhiko was a university student but for the last year had worked full-time in a munitions factory. When his shift ended he would race home to don a steel helmet and uniform and help his father down at the Air Warden's office. Tetsuhiko "sniffed the battle with delight" and read with excitement the colorful accounts of the "Sky Eagles" who rammed B-29s and kamikaze who crashed into US Navy ships. The fall of Iwo Jima and Okinawa did not dampen his conviction that the Americans could never take Japan. They might land but would be repulsed as surely as Kublai Khan's hordes were in 1281. On August 6 and 9, however, the fate of Japan's militarists was sealed when B-29s from the Marianas devastated Hiroshima and Nagasaki with a weird new bomb. The emperor, having consulted Prime Minister Suzuki, made his lonely decision. On August 15, 1945, at noon he broadcast to the nation for the first time. Tetsuhiko and Japan's adult population crowded around radio sets and were stunned to hear the high-pitched voice from the Chrysanthemum Throne telling them "to bear the unbearable". Unconditional surrender! Tetsuhiko wept bitterly.

Tetsuhiko accompanied his father on a journey to the center of the city and was silent as they surveyed a scene of hopelessness. 46 percent of Tokyoites had lost their homes. He saw tens of thousands of them living like rats in lean-tos made of scorched beams and pieces of tin. Most had no blankets, no cooking utensils nor tableware and were eating and drinking from cracked chinaware or tins. Father and son returned home and Tetsuhiko broke the silence: "All we suffered and to end up like this! I wish I had been killed in the raids!" Satoko wished she could console him but could not find the words.

The food ration was less than two small cups of rice a day. The defeat had been the last straw. Now morale slumped, discipline cracked. People began to steal and set up black markets. The young man's gloom deepened. In September a sudden cold front swept over Japan. The professor and his son were among the many who went down with pneumonia. Tetsuhiko had lost the will to live and let himself die.

Satoko was in poor shape physically but her mental and spiritual fiber was tougher than her brother's. More conscious of Japanese history and of her family's, she drew strength from this. She had listened well on those not infrequent occasions when her professor father spoke with feeling about the resilience of the Kitahara family over a millennium of often turbulent history.

Satoko's father, Kinji, could trace the family back to the days of Michizane Sugawara, about whom every Japanese student learns in middle school. He is the patron saint of study, especially calligraphy, and students pray to him in one of his twelve thousand Tenmangu shrines for help in exams. Sugawara was the most famous scholar in the Kyoto Imperial Court of the late ninth century, a master of literature, Chinese poetry and calligraphy. Under the emperor's orders he wrote the two hundred volume *Nihonki* and compiled the *Newly Selected Manyoshu*, an anthology of Japanese poetry. He was responsible for Japan becoming culturally independent from T'ang China in A.D. 894. During the centuries since the historic moment when Chinese ideographs and Buddhism had been introduced into Japan via Korea about A.D. 550, Japanese scholars and monks had almost worn an ocean path to the Flowery Middle Kingdom, China, their cultural and religious mother. With that unique Japanese ability to assess, adapt, and assimilate they began creating a new Yamato culture. Sugawara believed that now, 350 years after the first contacts, it was time for independence from Chinese sources. A master of Japanese-style writing, he encouraged others to adopt it. An amazing literary flowering resulted, one unique feature being the appearance of brilliant writers among ladies at court. Two of the latter, Murasaki Shikibu and Sei Shonagon, wrote books that have become classics of world literature—*Genji Monogatari* and *Makura No Soshi*. It would be almost a thousand years before Western women wrote the equivalent.

Sugawara was an able administrator and eventually became the emperor's favorite and most trusted minister. The tremendously powerful Fujiwara family, from whom most empresses were chosen, decided he had become a threat to their position. In a typically underhand maneuver they had Sugawara condemned "for aspiring to overthrow Emperor Daigo" and exiled to a place in distant Kyushu near the Bay of Hakata. One loyal Sugawara retainer, who was both a Fujiwara and a *kannushi* or Shinto priest, went with Sugawara into exile. In a profound gesture of solidarity with his disgraced lord he relinquished his Fujiwara lineage and changed his name. This *kannushi* began a proud family line of Shinto priests that lasted one thousand years. Satoko's grandfather Yoshimatsu broke the tradition. In charge of a Tenmangu shrine in Kumamoto in western Kyushu, he took an active part in the armed struggles immediately preceding Emperor Meiji's accession. He returned to his shrine wounded and confused about Japan's future and his own.

A return to Shinto mythology and emperor worship had accompanied the Meiji Restoration that broke the 265-year dictatorship of the Tokugawa shoguns. Buddhism and the resurgent Christian religion in Nagasaki were denounced as alien imports. Shinto shrines across the land were put under the government-controlled State Shinto, an organ of right-wing nationalism. Yoshimatsu Kitahara gave up his shrine and his priesthood to try his fortune in untamed Hokkaido. He delighted in the new freedom in that last Japanese frontier, speculated in land and became a rich man with extensive properties.

Satoko's father Kinji was born in Hokkaido, March 26, 1899, the *chonan* or Number One son. He inherited his Shinto ancestors' love of learning. For centuries they had run shrine schools where local children could come to learn *kana*, the Japanese syllabary, Chinese ideographs and the poetry and rich literature born from *kana* and ideographs. Number One Son Kinji's passion for study burned all the stronger for living in the quiet land of Hokkaido where snow lies on the ground from early autumn to late spring, a period of five to six months. As World War I was ending and Kinji was finishing high school, his father told him he would now work with him on the extensive land holdings with a view to taking over one day. Kinji quietly replied No, he was taking the entrance exams for Hokkaido Imperial University. His father barked: "Your studies are over. You will begin your duty as Number One Son and heir." The son reiterated his determination to go to university. The father, furious at this open rebellion from a bookworm who had given no trouble until now, stomped off to the university and told the examiners to fail Kinji.

These professors, however, were of a tough pioneer mold. They had to be, to leave the comforts of the civilized main islands of Japan and come to frontier Hokkaido. Its Imperial University began in 1876 as the Sapporo Agricultural School with strong-willed William Smith Clark of Massachusetts Agricultural University helping to shape its academic ideals. He had a saying that is still quoted fondly by Japanese university students: "Boys, be ambitious." The father's high-handed demand that Kinji be failed in the exams fell on deaf ears. The son was enrolled in the School of Agriculture—to be promptly disinherited by his infuriated father.

His future looked precarious until a shrewd matchmaker made a bold proposal to the Matsumura family. The head of the family had been a comfortable lawyer in Kyoto when the call of wild Hokkaido got the better of him. He moved up with his wife and children and bought heavily treed mountains. When timber prices rose dramatically as railways and frontier towns were built, the Matsumura financial fortunes soared. They had a spirited Number Two daughter called Ei. The matchmaker suggested she meet the gifted student Kinji who could trace his ancestors back to the Fujiwaras of ninth century Kyoto. They were happily married on January 31, 1922. Twenty-year-old Ei brought a healthy dowry. She was skilled at fine needlework which became a main source of income, allowing Kinji to continue his studies. Their first child Kazuko (Child of Peace) was born shortly before Kinji received his degree in agriculture. But he wasn't yet ready to get a job. Gaining a doctorate he then transferred to the School of Law, becoming a doctor of law in 1928. Kinji's mother had died and his father's second wife worked on her husband until he accepted his son back into the fold as Number One Son and heir. Kinji was now free to fulfil his ideal—study at Tokyo University, the best in the nation. In the spring of 1928 he enrolled in the Economics Department. Satoko was born on August 22, 1929, and in 1931 Kinji was awarded his third doctorate and began a highly successful career as a university professor.

His father's death left him a very wealthy man. He bought a home in a Tokyo that boasted a population of six million. The World Depression had forced many Tokyo businesses into bankruptcy. He shared the anger of most Japanese when America and the British Empire, their Allies in World War 1, began trade discrimination against Japan. It struck the young economist, Kinji, that the West had begun a deliberate policy, aimed at preventing Japan from becoming the first non-Western economic force on the world scene. The new laws restricting Japanese from migrating from their overcrowded islands to underpopulated western lands struck him as blatantly racial. However, he did nothing about it. Instead of getting involved in political parties he immersed himself in his beloved books.

Chapter 8

Ninomiya, the Peasant Academic

In 1935 the Kitaharas bought a large property in the western suburbs of Tokyo, built a fine two-story house and covered the grounds in trees, shrubs and flowers. On clear days Mount Fuji was visible on the western horizon, "as beautiful as the moon". Satoko began primary school that year and one day on her way to school was sent sprawling by a bus that swerved to avoid a tram. The bus driver leaped out and rushed into her home carrying the small child in his arms. If the accident was reported he would lose his job—a terrifying thing in a Japan not fully out of the Depression. Her parents decided she wasn't badly hurt so the accident would not be reported. The driver took a long while to reach the front gate—he kept stopping to bow profoundly. Quite some time later in a routine school X ray a bone fracture was discovered. The accident had done more harm than was realized. Perhaps that was the reason why she didn't play as vigorously as her friends; she was happy caring for the small ones, leaving friends her own age to more boisterous activities. From the day of the accident, a limousine took her to and from school each day.

Everyone in her home was keen on learning. Satoko had two older sisters and the one who was a few years older began teaching her *kanji* before she started school. When the sister died—child mortality was still high in Japan—a sad little Satoko used take her copy book and solemnly practice ideographs before her sister's *ihai*—the black-lacquered mortuary

43

tablet on their family altar. It had a new name for her sister written in gold lettering. Bemused Satoko was told it was her sister's name "on that Other Shore" where the Pure Land welcomed the dead.

When Satoko was six and began school, her parents had a teacher come to the home to give her special lessons in writing Chinese ideographs, the ciphers to learning in Japan. The ideograph for her own name had been carefully chosen by her father. Containing the ideographs for "heart" and for "order born of the ancient laws" the combination meant love of law and order—which the professor regarded as the foundation of wisdom. To emphasize the point he used a freedom that is confusing to Westerners unfamiliar with ideographs, bypassing the normal pronunciation "*Rei*" and choosing "*Sato*" clearly referring to "Satorf", the hallowed Zen word meaning enlightenment, which is the highest wisdom. In Satoko, the "ko", which is found in so many Japanese female names, means "Child".

When she finished her six years of primary school, receiving a certificate for never having missed a single day, her parents chose an expensive private middle school for Satoko, Oh-in. The school was begun by a group of graduates from Japan's best girls' school at the time, a public school called Ochanomizu. The founding mothers wanted a private establishment where discipline would be the guardian of a real love of learning. They also wanted it to be a school imbued with specifically Japanese culture so they called it Oh-in, meaning "in the shade of Cherry Blossoms". The woman chosen as its first principal had tutored the empress when the latter was a child.

Someone has said Japan's only natural resources are water, rich mountain soil and a tradition of learning. The great importance accorded to literacy goes back fourteen centuries to the time when Chinese ideographs were introduced. A unique Japanese difference in those ancient times was that learning was not the prerogative of the male aristocracy as was usually the case elsewhere. The earliest popular anthologies of poetry, the *Manyoshu*, first published about A.D. 750, contained poems by ordinary commoners, farmers and rankless soldiers, alongside verses by nobles and court ladies. Even in the turbulent period of continual nationwide warfare, 1467–1615, many samurai wives read and wrote well and taught their small children *kana* syllabary and ideograph rudiments before sending them off to schools run by Buddhist temples and Shinto shrines.

Japan's greatest strength, which the Meiji Reform made compulsory in the 1860s and which continues today, is a strict education system profoundly influencing every level of society. There are literally no normal Japanese who are illiterate. Mastering Japanese is no mean feat. Webster's English dictionary has thirty-five thousand entries while an equivalent Japanese dictionary has forty-five thousand. According to UNESCO, Japanese read more newspapers per capita than any other nation today, which goes a long way in explaining the nation's economic strength and also her cultural output.

Satoko's parents saw ideograph study as a fine arts form in itself, as well as the door to learning, poetry and aesthetics. They made sure Satoko continued to receive supplementary calligraphy lessons even after she entered prestigious Oh-in. The Kitaharas were wealthy but not ostentatious and spent their money wisely. The expensive German piano they installed was not for show. When Satoko was ten she began formal lessons under a good teacher named Hayashi. Satoko soon fell helplessly in love—not with her teacher but with the new world he led her to.

It was now 1939, two years since full-scale war had begun in China. The Japanese militarists, determined that Japan would win at any cost, had turned Tokyo into a drab war city.

Plays, concerts and movies, branded frivolous and unpatriotic
by the fanatical ultranationalists, almost disappeared. Music
became Satoko's golden thread leading her from the capital's
dreariness toward bright and stirring possibilities.

In the winter months of late 1940 as she finished middle
school Satoko decided she wanted to enter one of the *senmon*
high schools specializing in music. She planned to become
a great concert pianist! In her child's imagination she saw
herself as the cynosure of crowded concert halls, with hushed
audiences bursting into ecstatic applause as she finished a
concerto! However her absorption in music disturbed her
parents. It might have been all right for the father to walk out
on his father's plans, spurning the life of the landed gentry in
Hokkaido to force his way into academia, but Satoko was a
girl, who would find it one thousand times harder to defy
convention and find fulfillment as a professional musician.
They were delighted by her love of music but felt sure she
would find true happiness in the traditional roles of a Japanese woman, as wife and mother. Accordingly they said no
to the music school and, as the cherry trees exhaled their
pastel pink mists of blossom at the beginning of April, 1941,
she entered high school at Oh-in.

Now, six years later, in February 1946, her parents asked her
what university she wished to attend. She answered: "Tetsuhiko died of pneumonia. I want to honor Eldest Brother by
studying ways of helping the sick. I'd like to try for Showa
Women's Pharmaceutical University." Her parents were
very happy with the choice. She passed the exams and commenced university studies at the beginning of April 1946.

In a book he wrote some years later Professor Kitahara
made some observations about the city at that time: "Destitute Tokyo of 1945–1946 was full of war casualties. It was
an unbelievable desert of ashes. You would meet people
who had lost every single family member and close relation,

wondering out aloud: 'Was I lucky to have come through the war alive, or was I unlucky?' Many university students were battling against desperate odds to keep attending class."

The professor began planning ways of helping other young people who had a fierce desire to get into university but lacked the means. Remembering his own youthful struggles he was full of sympathy for these bright young folk who believed that scientific tertiary education was their, and Japan's, only chance of rising from the ashes. More universities were desperately needed, so he accepted an invitation to be a member of a board planning a new university. It would begin with two-year tertiary courses in economics, food technology and Japanese culture. He and his wife decided to risk a considerable amount of their money in the venture.

There was an added personal reason for risking a lot of their money, illustrated in the epic experience of a civil servant who lived in Kyoto with his wife and their only child, a boy in primary school. The father was an amateur painter who used go out on Sundays to places like beautiful Arashiyama, Storm Mountains, less than an hour to the west of the city. His small boy loved to go with him and while his father painted the famous cherry blossoms or autumn maples, the child would happily paint in his exercise book. The child was killed in an accident. Long after the period of mourning was over the father still brooded badly. The wife worried about him and coaxed him to start painting again. He did and began to find solace out alone in the silent mountains. After he had painted a nature scene for his own satisfaction he would do another painting "for the boy". Such was his intensity in painting for the boy that he became, almost unwittingly, a great artist whose paintings were exhibited around Japan. He saw these paintings as more his boy's than his own. Professor Kitahara and his wife decided that wholehearted commitment to educating youth was a way of consoling their son's spirit and, in a sense, making him live on, in the students they helped to reach university.

Satoko's university had been hit badly in the B-29 bombing. When she began classes in April 1946, water pipes, gas mains and electric cables were only partially restored, with tables, desks, test tubes, beakers, Bunsen burners, etc. and basic chemicals in pitifully short supply. The president spoke to his students about Sontoku Ninomiya, well known to them all. His statue in bronze or stone stood outside most prewar primary schools and portrayed an impoverished peasant walking with a heavy load of firewood on his back, determinedly reading a book! Ninomiya made up for the lack of educational opportunities in his remote village by educating himself, seizing every scrap of spare time, even when carrying firewood down from the mountains. By the time he died in 1856 the former peasant had become one of the most influential thinkers in Japan. Now, the university president suggested, they had the wonderful chance to imitate him.

The teaching staff and students at Showa did imitate Ninomiya in his thrift, industry and determination to study. They would go out on foot to distant factories that manufactured the chemicals they needed for experiments, and buy them wholesale. To raise cash for desks and equipment, teachers and students began making soap and Baelz lotion in their spare time and hawking it around the suburbs. Satoko threw herself energetically into all this as she had into the war effort, with that especially Japanese ability to sublimate personal interests for a common goal. Gradually the place came to look like a university and hard study made up for deficiencies in equipment.

Satoko became friendly with a fellow student who came from her father's birthplace, Hokkaido. This girl had been orphaned as a child and been taken in by relatives who, like many in that cold frontier land, were none too well off. The girl was bright and her guardians managed to scrape enough money together to put her through high school. She did well and begged to be allowed to sit for university entrance exams in Tokyo, the Mecca of learning. She sat for the same Showa exams as Satoko and passed.

Her foster relatives admired her determination and ability but told her they could not support her financially in Tokyo. If she went she would be on her own. She bowed low, told them she would never forget them for taking her into their home and giving her the chance to get to university, and promised to return with a degree. They gave her the fare for the boat and train journey to Tokyo, a few cooking utensils and enough money for several weeks' board.

She found a cheap room not too far from the university and immediately set out tramping the streets, calling on homes that might need a private tutor. Japan has a fiercely competitive school system, in some places even beginning in kindergarten! Students can gain entrance to a better primary, middle and high school only if they score higher marks. Getting into a top university is the ultimate goal—graduating from that usually secures one for life. Many parents therefore will send their children to *juku* (coaching schools) or engage a private teacher to tutor their children at home. Devastated Tokyo of April 1946 was not very welcoming to the eighteen-year-old "tutor" with the heavy Hokkaido accent and country ways. The meager fees she earned barely paid lodging, university tuition, and text books. She had little money for food.

Satoko had been attracted by the girl's blunt, uncompromising Hokkaido ways. They became firm friends and when Satoko visited her lodging room she was appalled at its bareness. She realized why her new friend who had a healthy, ruddy complexion when the first term began, was now looking sickly. She cajoled her parents into allowing the girl to live with them "for a few weeks" while they helped her find better-paying patrons and gave her nourishing meals. Unfortunately, better patrons were scarce, and the few weeks became three months!

More Kitahara relatives arrived, the Saito family from Manchuria. They had to flee carrying almost nothing, like hundreds of thousands of other refugees returning from liberated Manchuria, Korea and Taiwan. Satoko's father found it hard to tell the girl she had to go. Satoko argued with him, even stating that she herself was eating far more than she needed and could do perfectly well on half the government ration! The refugee relatives, however, had undernourished children who needed every spare grain of rice they could get. The Kitaharas had property in Hokkaido but money was scarce there as it was everywhere and it would have been very bad business to sell land at that time. The tertiary college that Satoko's father was in the process of cofounding was consuming every cent he could afford, and to Satoko's undisguised chagrin the young classmate had to go back to her spartan lodging.

Chapter 9

War Trials and a Withered Moor

On a journey, ailing.
My dreams roam a withered moor.

The last haiku of Matsuo Basho

At this time there was something that began to disturb Satoko far more than the poor Hokkaido student and shortages of food and laboratory equipment. The "heroic and pure" Japanese soldiers, to whom she had sent comfort parcels during the war and whom she had been ready to imitate in fighting until death, were put on public trial—or rather, their leaders were. In May 1946, coinciding with her commencement of university studies, ex-General Hideki Tojo and twenty-seven other "A-class" Japanese leaders were arraigned as war criminals. Their fate would be decided by ranking judges from eleven Allied nations—the United States, Britain, China, India, the Union of Soviet Socialist Republics, France, Holland, the Philippines, Canada, Australia and New Zealand.

Ironically the hearings took place in a huge three-story building in Tokyo that had been War Ministry Headquarters and the nerve center of Japanese military operations. A reinforced concrete structure, it had survived the bombing—even though on Ichigaya Hill, less than a mile from the Imperial Palace. Today it is the headquarters of the Japanese Self Defense Force.

At first Satoko was too preoccupied with settling in at her war-torn university to give the War Crimes Trial much attention. Furthermore it took some months of legal maneuvering before the prosecution and defense could make their real moves. The twenty-eight suspected war criminals had been provided with a formidable defense team—three Japanese and three US lawyers assisted by fifteen attorneys flown in from America at US expense. These defense lawyers immediately and strenuously demanded more time to prepare their briefs and were granted a recess by Chief Judge Webb. The trial was to prove an exhaustive one, running from May 3, 1946, until November 12, 1948.

MacArthur ordered the Japanese press to cover all sessions and print continuing and full-length reports. As the trial increased in intensity Satoko and her university friends began to read the daily newspapers and grow more and more disturbed. Evidence of unbelievable atrocities committed by the Japanese military between 1929 and 1945, mounted up sickeningly. There were two hundred seats for spectators in the large auditorium-become-courtroom and many Japanese university students were in the audience. There would be spirited and usually depressing discussions with fellow students when they returned to campus.

Satoko and her fellow students had believed that wartime Japanese soldiers were chivalrously following a very wise and courageous emperor's call to fight for the emancipation of Asia's colonized masses. Now they received terrific shocks as Japanese of the highest rank testified that the army had gone to war recklessly and wantonly, against the express wishes of the emperor and some of his most trusted advisers and politicians. Seventy-nine year old ex-Admiral Okada, for instance, twice Prime Minister and twice Navy Minister, gave devastating evidence against the army clique that had flouted the imperial will and used assassination to silence pro-peace politicians.

Okada had a score to settle. The militarists had attempted to kill him when he was prime minister in the famous and bloody "2-26 Incident", February 26, 1936, because of his plainspoken stand for peace, shooting and killing his brother-in-law through mistaken identity.

Okada gave the war trials judges chapter and verse of the murder of Chang Tso-lin by Japanese militarists in Manchuria in 1928. He told how young Emperor Hirohito heard about it and, shaken and incensed, told Prime Minister Tanaka "to take strong disciplinary action" against the murderers. With arrogance the army thumbed its nose at these clearly expressed directions—while proclaiming to the nation they were motivated by "pure" devotion to the emperor. The army became progressively more powerful and callous, he continued, until the disobedience and betrayal of the 1931 "Manchurian Incident" which inevitably plunged Japan's sixty million people into a war with China's four hundred million ... and finally into war with the West. The army generals in the dock glowered contemptuously at Okada. The ex-Admiral took note of it. He was testifying against the militarists, he said coldly, precisely because he was a patriot! He felt dutybound to expose the false leaders who were guilty of grave injustices against the emperor and his people.

The prosecution read from the confiscated diary of Marquis Kido, Keeper of the Privy Seal and trusted adviser/confidant of the emperor, which corroborated Okada's testimony. The diary clearly implicated the army clique that "became indignant" when the emperor tried to rein them in. They destroyed all political parties opposing them and set up their own dictatorship. They, not the parliament nor the emperor, ruled the nation and sent it to war. The defense's efforts were hardly convincing and journalists began betting that the generals' last march would be to the hangman's trapdoor! At this juncture the Nuremberg judgments were handed down: of the twenty-two Nazis tried, twelve were sentenced to the gallows and seven imprisoned. The families of the Tokyo accused were stunned and begged the defense to elevate their performance.

The defense lawyers were not a deficient team, however. They used every legal ploy and put up a spirited fight that won admiration around the legal world. Alongside a crushing weight of evidence of the militarists' guilt, moreover, there were glaring inconsistencies in the prosecution's case and the defense pursued them vigorously. The twenty-eight Japanese were being tried, they argued, for the crime of "beginning an aggressive war" and invading other nations against their will. Western nations had done precisely this in colonizing every Asian nation except Japan and Thailand. Indeed some of the very judges on this war crimes bench came from western nations that still practiced blatant colonialism! Indians, Indonesians, Vietnamese, and many in North and South Africa applauded this counterargument. One of the eleven Allied judges, Radhabinod Pal of India, took their side. Judge Pal was a man of considerable legal standing. Before the war he was a joint president of the International Law Association, a lecturer at the University Law College and a member of the High Court of Calcutta.

Another contradiction sat on the very bench in the person of Russian Judge I. M. Zarayanov. Russia had signed a 1939 treaty with Hitler's Germany and ruthlessly divided up Poland and the Baltic states. The USSR had also signed a nonaggression treaty with Japan in 1941. In the interval between the Hiroshima and Nagasaki A-bombs, however, the USSR broke this treaty and attacked debilitated Japan. Troops poured into Manchuria and took an estimated four hundred thousand Japanese prisoners of war—the majority of whom were still living in slave labor camps in Siberia! Many had already died there from brutal work hours and inadequate food, clothing and shelter in often freezing temperatures. USSR armies had

violently repressed the call for free elections in every eastern nation they had occupied—and still occupied! Didn't the
presence of a judge from the USSR make the Tokyo tribunal
a farce? Was not the arraigning of only the Japanese generals a
flagrant case of cynical double standards?

Be this as it may, witness after witness and page after page
of signed and sworn documents began telling the story of
the militarists' atrocities. After the gut-wrenching evidence
of the Rape of Nanking, the prosecution submitted seventy-
two other large-scale massacres.

These terrible indictments, revealed daily, utterly depressed
Satoko. She began to lose confidence in Japan and in the
Yamato-damishii that her tradition-loving father and Oh-in
teachers had taught her to love.

The president of the panel of judges, Sir William Webb,
read the judges' findings on November 12, 1948. All twenty-
seven were found guilty. In summing up the 1,001 pages of
the judges' report Webb stressed that they had tried only
the militarists, not the people of Japan. The latter were not
being blamed for the excesses of the military clique who had
usurped power. This did not help Satoko much. Nor was she
old enough to realize that the history of every nation that has
become powerful contains dark chapters. She would have
received spirited testimony to this if she had asked Aborig-
inals from Webb's Australia, Indians from North and South
America, or those of African descent in the United States.
Japan's black period began when it colonized Korea and
started a war against China under the militarists. Satoko was
yet too young to have any real sense of history; all she saw
was her beloved country put on trial by a world court and
found horribly guilty.

She felt betrayed. She had believed the militarists' propaganda, applauded their hectoring, cheerfully lived on half-
rations, given up a year of high school to labor in an airplane

factory and been ready to die fighting with a bamboo spear. She thought of her many young friends who died from tuberculosis or in air raids, and of countless soldiers and civilians who perished on the Asian mainland and the Pacific islands. It was especially painful to think of her "heroes", the tragically young kamikaze. They had believed they died for a most noble cause. Instead, it was for a lie, foisted on the people by robber generals. Three million Japanese and countless non-Japanese had died for a lie.

She was now in touch with her older brother's anger, disillusionment and bitterness and began to understand why he had lost the will to live. The misery and wretchedness of it all filled her with a painful emptiness she had never known before. Was this Sartre's "existential despair"? Was this what drove Dazai, a kind of Japanese Sartre, to drugs, debauchery and finally to suicide in June of that same year, 1948?

Satoko, like nearly every Japanese who had been at least to high school, loved poetry. The greatest of the haiku poets, late seventeenth century Basho, who lived from 1644 to 1694, was her favorite. He had written with a rare combination of feeling, delicacy and depth. She found his poetry profound, hopeful and encouraging—and yet there was that terrible final poem. Basho had been a lifelong walker, spending long periods of his life on the open road, looking for inspiration from the countryside, the seasons and the stirring historical sites throughout Japan. His last poem was written after he became ill on a journey. Probably realizing he was dying he wrote: "On a journey, ailing. / My dreams roam a withered moor." Was that his conclusion after a lifetime of searching for truth and beauty? Do our lives vanish like a despairing cry lost in the winds on a trackless, desolate waste, heeded by no one?

Were the beautiful dreams of her youth mere illusion? Was she trapped, like Sartre and Dazai, in "the cosmic nightmare"? She longed to talk about it to her parents, especially her father. But they had suffered too much already in losing their only son. It would be heartless to burden them further with her dark questions.

She had several university classmates with whom she could share, however. Going for long walks in quiet places like Yoyogi Park they glumly agreed they could find little ultimate meaning to life. Their future and their motherland's looked utterly bleak. Japan had lost most of her shipping and half of her factories. She had almost no raw materials. How could she rise again? Were not many of their university friends reading Osamu Dazai's dark novels because he had the honesty and courage to spell it out with his bitter phrase "the tribe of the Setting Sun"! He ended up committing double suicide. His female companion in death was a chance acquaintance he met in a bar. He left behind a wife, two small children—and a pregnant mistress! Had Japan become a bleak moor where common humanity and hope had withered?

PART TWO

The Spirit Brooding

... and the Spirit of God brooded over the deep.

Genesis 1:2

Chapter 10

A Plaster Statue on Yokohama Bluff

In either March 1947 or June 1948—it is unclear from the account she wrote a number of years later—Satoko made a very eventful visit to Yokohama to see a fellow student, one of those with whom she used to have very serious discussions about "the fundamental question", the meaning of life.

They met at Sakuragicho station and walked along Kaigan Dori, the main road skirting Yokohama Harbor, and through Yamashita Park. This park is a testimony to human resilience and ability to make good out of catastrophe. Japan's worst modern earthquake struck here at noon of September 1, 1923. Half the buildings in the city were shaken to the ground. The quake, coming as Yokohama housewives were preparing midday meals, overturned their portable pottery stoves, scattering burning charcoal and starting fires, Yokohama was almost wiped out and over forty thousand citizens died. Yet the refugees returned as soon as the fires had gone out and began to rebuild. They carted the rubble to the nearby shores and filled in the shallows of the bay to create beautiful Yamashita Park. Within two years 405,000 people were living in the city again. Satoko and her friend began discussing this 1923 death-and-rebirth of Yokohama, wondering if the fire-bombed cities of Japan could rise again.

They continued the animated discussion as they climbed the Yamate area that foreigners call The Bluff. This is the hilly section of Yokohama where many Westerners built homes after Commodore Perry signed a US treaty of friendship with the last shogun in 1854. Reaching the Foreigners' Cemetery they decided to go in, becoming silent as they observed how different Western tombstones were from those that Japanese erected, though the sentiments that built them were surely the same. They sat on a seat, content to listen to those nameless voices in old cemeteries that evoke deep emotions in all people.

They eventually got up and walked out the gate near the Union Church with its stolid Norman tower and locked doors. They continued walking in silence, taking in the Western architecture of houses on either side of the street, and passed a Marianist brother robed in his severe dark habit. His face was Japanese, softening the foreign atmosphere that pervaded The Bluff. Further along the road they came to an iron fence leading to heavy stone gates. A notice told them that this was the Church of the Sacred Heart, built in 1862 and rebuilt after the earthquake of 1923. A Japanese passed through the gates and into the church. Satoko looked at her friend, inclined her head toward the open door and raised her eyebrows. The friend nodded and they went in.

Neither had been inside a Christian church before. This one was hardly an architectural gem. Erected on the site of the church destroyed in the earthquake, it was a somewhat ponderous quasi-Gothic building in concrete, functional rather than aesthetic. Inside, the pair moved about quietly, trying to take in the unfamiliar atmosphere created by struggling Gothic arches, a rotunda-like pulpit and a large, dominating statue of the Sacred Heart in the wall behind the altar.

Moving to the left-hand nave they came upon a small shrine with a life-size statue of a woman standing above a small altar. Painted on a panel to the left was a foreign girl dressed as a peasant and gazing up at the statue. Satoko would later on learn the girl was Bernadette of Lourdes. On a panel to the right was a matching painting of a Japanese woman wearing the court dress of medieval Kyoto, pointing out the statue to her small children. Satoko would one day come to love this sixteenth-century noblewoman, Gracia Hosokawa, grossly caricatured as Mariko in Clavell's novel *Shogun*.

This statue of Our Lady of Lourdes was of plaster and certainly no great work of art. It paled into artistic insignificance beside Buddhist statues Satoko had studied in school books, world-renowned images like the Moonlight Bodhisattva in Nara, or Kyoto's Miroku, "the Savior-to-come". Yet this decidedly inferior statue of Mary of Lourdes moved Satoko as no other statue had ever done. It touched something deep within her, she was to write, and revived memories of a happening when she was hardly seven years old.

"This was the very first time I had seen a statue of the Blessed Mother. Drawn, I know not why, to enter that church, I gazed on the statue, sensing the presence of a very attractive force that I could not explain. I had always experienced a vague but strong yearning for the Pure. It was not something I could describe in words but it was definitely with me from childhood. The very first time I remember glimpsing what seemed a worthy object of this deep longing was in Meiji Shrine when I was about seven years old. My parents had taken me along for the religious festival called *Shichi-Go-San*, and I had my first glimpse of *miko*, the shrine maidens who serve in Shinto sanctuaries. I was only a child but those *miko* in their brilliant red skirts and white cotton blouses are vividly etched in my memory to this day. I suppose my heart was conditioned for that experience by a long line of Shinto priest ancestors."

Chapter 11

Shinto, the Feminine and the Holy Spirit

With warm breast and Ah! bright wings.

G. M. Hopkins, *God's Grandeur*

Satoko, like most Japanese, was deeply affected by Shinto, Japan's original religion that predates recorded history. The *Shichi-Go-San* liturgy she referred to [at the end of the last chapter] is a festival literally meaning Seven-Five-Three. Girls in their third and seventh years and boys in their fifth year are taken by their family to a Shinto shrine where prayers of thanksgiving are offered because the children have safely arrived at these ages of transition. To mark the event, seven-year-old girls are given an obi—that broad sash of silk brocade wound around a kimono at the waist to keep it neatly in place. Three-year-old girls have their hair put up for the first time and the boys are dressed in manly hakama, stiffly pleated kimonos. The children's kimonos for this transition liturgy are of gorgeous colors and quality. The Shinto priests who chant prayers of purification, thanksgiving and petition wear robes that are almost plain in their simplicity, designed in prehistoric times by people with a sure taste for the naturally aesthetic and symbolic.

What first caught the child Satoko's eye was the dress of the shrine maidens, the *miko*: cotton blouses of sheer white, set off by full skirts of brilliant scarlet reaching down to cotton *tabi*, the stiff white socks that always go with a kimono.

Satoko found herself enthralled by their graceful obeisances and slow liturgical dances of extraordinary reverence.

The Shinto religion is primitive in the sense of predating writing. Original Shinto possessed neither scriptures nor written code. Even in today's sophisticated Japan, Shinto thrives not so much as a developed, clear-cut theology but as Matsuri, those word-scarce festivals that were created to express awe and thanksgiving before the great natural phenomena that surround us. Shinto is both a source and an outlet for the much discussed Japanese sensitivity to the four seasons. It is essentially optimistic because it perceives nature as essentially benevolent. Japan's harsh winter always yields to the bright blossoms of spring; her fierce summer culminates in the fruits and grains of a glowing autumn. Storytellers in prehistoric Japan expressed this core faith in highly symbolic mythology.

The Amaterasu myth, for instance: two powerful *kami* (a word translated as gods, but more correctly rendered as spirits) dwelt in the Plain of Heaven. They gave birth to Japan and to three other *kami*, the most important of which is Amaterasu, "Illuminatrix of the Sky", significantly a female spirit. The second *kami* is not very important but the third is Amaterasu's brother, Susuno-wo ("Swift Impetuous One") who dwells in the wild Plain of the Sea. Of a violent and chaotic temperament he tried to destroy the rice fields his sister tended so carefully. A fierce battle ensued in which order struggled against chaos, light against darkness, growth against dissolution. Amaterasu prevailed and her destructive brother was driven away. Consequently Amaterasu's most important festival is celebrated at the autumn rice harvest.

G. K. Chesterton, while confident that he had found the fullness of the truth in the Gospels, rejoiced in the lodes of spiritual gold hidden in many ancient myths of our race. Commenting on the many forms of the darkness/light, winter/summer myth he wrote in his extraordinary book about Christ, *The Everlasting Man*, "Who does not feel the death and resurrection of the growing things of the earth as something near to the secret of the universe?"

The repertoire of *miko* liturgies includes a dance that acts out this heroic and encouraging myth. You can witness it at Nara's Kasuga shrine, for instance, in the small dark hours of December 17–18, "when the winter sun is furthest away from the earth". Despite the bleak hour large crowds attend—a kind of people's vote on Chesterton's affirmation that "the mighty and branching tree called mythology ramifies around the whole world.... Myths stir up the deep things of the soul".

The opening of this Nara Shinto liturgy is suggestive of the primitiveness of human beginnings. Ancient bamboo wood-winds begin hesitantly and disharmoniously, piercing the winter darkness like the disconsolate cries of aimlessly wandering plovers. The congregation, left to its own resources, stumbles uncertainly down a lightless path to an altar as stark as Shinto altars were two millennia ago.

After offerings from the mountains and the sea have been placed in the makeshift sanctuary, *miko* perform dances of exquisite gracefulness, beseeching the sun to return to the winter-bound land. In a short time the first light of dawn appears in the east.

Many Japanese Christians rejoice to find adumbrations of Genesis 1 in the ceremony: "The earth was without form and void, and darkness was upon the face of the deep. The Spirit of God brooded over the chaos." Catholic bishops have told them to discover the work of the Holy Spirit here. Mother Teresa, having lived alongside non-Christian faiths in India, has gone on record saying: "I am in love with my own religion but I love all the religions of God."

Psalm 29 was originally based on a Canaanite myth poem and Psalm 104 an Egyptian one—which surely reveals to the believer in the Bible something wonderful about the Holy Spirit who took ancient religious myths, purified and completed them and made them part of his scriptural revelation. As an adult, Satoko wrote gratefully of her first consciousness of transcendental purity, experienced as she gazed at *miko* serving at a Shinto sanctuary.

Shinto, unlike Judaism, Christianity and Islam, has no clear idea of a single and unique Supreme Being. Shintoists never sought the Unmoved Mover of Greek philosophers or the unique Source of order, beauty and goodness of the monotheistic religions. Shinto is drawn to worship wherever the numinous is sensed—in the mystery of the sun, in the miracle of clear running streams, in the life force within huge trees, even in the awesome strength of great rocks. Shinto responds to what Chesterton called "sacramental feeling". In believing that Japan was sacred, created by a special divine intervention, Shinto arrived at a truth adumbrated in Isaiah and taught explicitly by Christ—the call of every nation to intimacy with the Father who created all. In declaring dead heroes and heroines to be sacred *kami*, Shinto was close to the New Testament's "children of God" who share the very life of God in heaven. Shinto, seeing spirits everywhere in nature, is in sympathy with the great Christian poet Francis Thompson:

> The angels keep their ancient places—
> Turn but a stone and start a wing!
> 'Tis ye, 'tis your estrangèd faces,
> That miss the many-splendour'd thing.

Francis of Assisi, the possessor par excellence of that gift of the Holy Spirit called "filial piety" by theologians like Thomas Aquinas, wrote poems about Brother Sun and Sister Moon and Sister Water, who is so useful and so humble.

Shintoists understand that. Were he alive in Japan today Il Poverello surely would have engaged in a respectful dialogue with Shinto.

The psychologist Carl Jung made the startling statement that Pius XII's 1954 definition of the dogma of the Assumption of Mary, body and soul into heaven was "the most extraordinary religious event since the Protestant Reformation". Jung was a Protestant, but was appalled by the overemphasis on the merely rational in the Christian West of his day. The West had become all too masculine, he said, and Nazism was the logical result of the overemphasis on masculine power, practicality, hard efficiency, scientific knowledge and quick results that can be priced! He regarded the Assumption of the prayerful Virgin to a very special place beside God as a healing symbol for a society sick with "practical" masculinity.

Gerard Manley Hopkins, a poet appalled by the materialism of the scientific West, wrote in *God's Grandeur:*

> And all is seared with trade; bleared, smeared
>   with toil;
> And wears man's smudge and shares man's smell;
>   the soil
> Is bare now, nor can feet feel, being shod.

But he concludes his poem:

> And for all this, nature is never spent;
>   There lives the dearest freshness deep down
>   things....
> Because the Holy Ghost over the bent
>   World broods with warm breast and with ah!
>   bright wings.

Chapter 12

Loving Providence or Cruel Fate?

Satoko was not sure what to make of her experience before the statue of Mary on the Yokohama Bluff. She returned to Tokyo silent and thoughtful but was immediately caught up in the maelstrom of exam preparation. She sat for a series of difficult papers, passed and in March of 1949 graduated as a qualified pharmacist. She applied for two positions in Tokyo and was accepted for both—one as science teacher in a high school and the other as pharmacist in a hospital. Like father, like daughter—she declined both! She told her parents she was not ready to choose a career yet. She was "still searching" and wanted more time.

The Kitahara home was now back to normal; the refugee relations had gone, and the financial situation was good. Her parents were happy to let her make up her mind in her own time. The professor had only one request: "I've always told you, your mother and I don't mind what you do in life. We will never oppose the path you choose, so long as you walk it well."

Satoko's parents were impressed by what they heard of a private girls' school in nearby Koenji, run by a Spanish order of nuns called Mercedarians, and enrolled their youngest daughter Choko in first year primary. Satoko accompanied Choko and her mother to the commencement ceremony and was impressed by the speech made by Mother Carmel, the principal. The Spanish nun handled Japanese well and said with great self-assurance: "God in his good providence has

69

brought your children to this school." *Mi-setsuri*, the word for
providence was rarely used by non-Christian Japanese. The
ideograph is a combination of "hand", which signifies positive action, and "three ears", which signifies intense listening:
heaven is forever listening closely to the prayers of honest seekers and responding with positive action. Satoko had
always used the word *shukumei*, the close-to-impersonal and
somewhat frightening "Fate". Satoko was intrigued and hoped
to learn more about "God's good providence" if an opportunity arose. Having been betrayed by the false promises of state
Shinto that bowed to the militarists and promised victory in
the recent war, she was somewhat wary of organized religion.

Two months later on a Sunday in May, seven-year-old
Choko announced she was going off to "Mass". Satoko
decided to see her to the church and on the way they encountered a Japanese Mercedarian nun who answered their greeting and replied she was returning from teaching catechism.
Satoko said that, as she looked at the serene face of this bright
young nun, her mind sped back to Meiji shrine when she was
just Choko's age, where the shrine *miko*, dancing so grace-
fully and reverently, evoked a strange yearning ... an experience that was intensified before the statue of Our Lady in the
Yokohama church.

She deposited Choko at the church entrance and went
home with a disquieting realization that she really didn't
know where she was going or what she wanted. Over the
next five or six weeks she attempted to submerge her uneas-
iness by going to more movies and plays. Her older sister
Kazuko smiles as she reminisces about Satoko's passion for
movies. She would go six times a week and, running out of
money and hesitant to admit this to her parents she would
"borrow" movie money from this married sister.

Satoko loved beautiful kimonos. Tall and willowy she
knew she looked well in them. Her parents thought so too

and encouraged her; it enhanced her chances for a fine marriage. Already a marriage proposal had come from a doctor who ran a hospital. Satoko came to the conclusion, however, that movies, kimonos and marriage possibilities were peripheral if she had no peace of heart. She decided on a bold step. It might lead nowhere but it would be better than just doing nothing but escape in diversions.

On a humid day in July she marched off to her sister's school and asked to see a sister. A Spanish nun, Mother Angeles, appeared and Satoko hesitantly explained her restlessness. What is life all about? The no-nonsense nun replied: "Well, why don't you sit down and hear what we Christians believe is the answer to that?" Satoko agreed and began there and then. After that she arrived at the convent at ten o'clock every morning to go systematically through the essentials of Christian teaching, mostly with Mother Angeles Aguirre from Spain, at other times with an American or Japanese nun. A new passion entered her life—she developed an almost fierce desire to get to the very bottom of this "faith that could induce foreign nuns to give up precious things like family to serve the people of a very alien land", as she put it.

The professor and his wife grew alarmed. The warning bells that rang when she wanted to become a concert pianist sounded again! Religion was all right as an accessory but with Satoko it was becoming an all-consuming thing. She was now rising early to join the Sisters at 6:00 A.M. Mass. Maybe she even had ideas of becoming a nun herself! The thought disturbed them deeply. The way to normality and happiness was marriage and a family. Her father knew that direct opposition would be counterproductive so he chanced a different approach. He took out some books from a university library, read up on Catholicism and one day began an apparently casual conversation at the dinner table:

"Catholicism did remarkably good things in Medieval Europe. It gave the people of its day cohesion and a culture suited to the times. The magnificent Gothic cathedrals built mainly by common folk, as well as the convents and monasteries that helped the poor, the sick and the lepers were great achievements. The art of Italy and the music of southern Germany are indications of the inspiration and vitality that Catholic religion gave a world that was without our modern advances in science, medicine and universal education. You find similar phenomena in Japan's history. Buddhism and Shinto ran *terakoya* schools to educate the poor. Every town and village had temples or shrines that were inspiring examples of architecture, places where people were drawn together to share hopes, ideals and talents, dynamic centers of culture and learning. Buddhist monks discovered effective herb medicines and pioneered all kinds of arts and crafts that benefited the people. But that is the past. We live in a new age where stable governments can provide education for everyone.

"Science", he continued, "can explain natural mysteries like lightning, cyclones and epidemics that gave rise to religious superstitions because the peoples of primitive ages interpreted them as punishments from heaven. A non-scientific age sought physical healing through prayers, charms and incantations. I'm not ridiculing the people of those ages. That's all they had to turn to. But we live in an age where medical science solves medical problems. We have a responsibility, an obligation to continue this process of betterment by using our minds intelligently and imaginatively. I share your worries about postwar Japan. However, the solution will be good economics, not a new theology."

He paused as his wife replenished their pot of *O-cha*, the ubiquitous light-green tea. Satoko took up the challenge. "*O-to-sama* (Revered Father) I've just had a long discussion with Mother Angeles who speaks French and has been to investigate Lourdes, a place of pilgrimage in France. There is a scientific bureau there with piles of doctors' sworn statements, reports and X rays on physical healings that go against all the laws of medical science. Mother Angeles showed me a quote from a Dr. Alexis Carrel who won the Nobel Prize for medicine earlier this century. He went to Lourdes with a young woman who had advanced tubercular peritonitis and was close to death. He didn't believe in miracles but wanted to study Lourdes as a psychological phenomenon. He said that during the blessing of the sick he saw her badly distended stomach flatten to normal size in front of his eyes. The young woman got up, instantaneously cured. The same kind of miracles Jesus performed can be scientifically investigated in Lourdes today," added Satoko enthusiastically, thinking that her father was at last interested.

She concluded the story. "The sequel of the story impressed Carrel almost as much as the physical miracle. He told the young woman he knew her case history, and how she had been sick all her teenage years. Now that she was restored to health what was she going to do? She replied quite simply that she was going to become a nun so that she could nurse the sick as the nuns had nursed her." Satoko looked at her father, hoping the story had moved him as it had moved her.

"Satoko," her father said gently, "every religion claims miracles. Remember the story of blind Sawaichi being restored to life and sight after O-Sato's tears before Kannon-sama at Tsubosaka Temple in Nara? You were very excited when you saw the Kabuki play about it. That miracle and your Lourdes miracles have a scientific explanation, either now or in the future. It just takes longer in some cases for scientists to discover the cause." The professor showed the discussion was over by reaching for his glasses and the newspaper. Despite his deliberate casualness, however, he was quite perturbed. Satoko was too intense and impulsive. She was likely to rush off, get baptized, and announce she wanted to become a nun. Perish the thought!

Satoko continues the story of her own journey: "My interest did not flag and by the end of October I had finished the whole course on Catholicism. I was convinced I had found the truth and asked to be baptized. As a rule priests made adult catechumens wait a full year before the lifelong decision of baptism. I talked earnestly enough to convince everyone I was fully ready. I was baptized Elizabeth on Sunday, October 30, which that year was the feast of Christ the King. Two days later I was confirmed, taking the confirmation name of Jesus' mother, Mary."

In the book he wrote, with mixed and sometimes confused feelings after Satoko died, the professor comments on the momentous future significance of the baptismal name she chose, Elizabeth of Hungary. In 1221 Elizabeth, daughter of King Andrew II of Hungary, married Prince Louis of Thuringia. Six years later, when she was the mother of three children and still deeply in love with her husband, Elizabeth was devastated by news of his death while fighting for Emperor Frederick II. Not long before, Francis of Assisi had held his famous *Chapter of Mats* where he had asked for volunteers to go to war-torn Germany to preach the Franciscan ideal of reconciliation and peace. Twenty-five Franciscans had gone, some of them ending up in Thuringia, now ruled by the grief-stricken widow Elizabeth from Wartburg Castle. She took her political obligations very seriously and summoned Brother Rodeger, the superior of the newly arrived Franciscans, demanding an account of what they were doing in her lands. He told her of the extraordinary man Francis who was turning Assisi and half of Italy on its head. She listened, fascinated. Elizabeth was sorely in need of good news—her husband's death and his relatives' bitter campaign to seize her castle and lands had left her despondent.

With Brother Rodeger as counsellor and her own powerful family in Hungary solidly behind her, she established a hospital for the poor. Deeply impressed by the story of Francis embracing a leper and exchanging clothes with him, she opened a place for lepers in her hospital and eventually began nursing these abandoned wretches herself. She died in 1231, not yet thirty, having burned herself out for the impoverished sick. She was canonized just four years after her death.

Satoko's parents were totally opposed to her baptism. The problem was that the professor had promised his children he would respect their freedom to do whatever they wanted to in life, "as long as they did it well". He and his wife let Satoko know how wrong they thought she was but in the end agreed she was free to choose for herself.

When Satoko explained to her bemused parents the un-Japanese custom of a baptismal name, and the story of Elizabeth whom she had chosen, the economics professor quipped: "Were she my pupil I would have to fail her on the way she wasted her family's money!"

Satoko replied: "There are far more important things in life than money!" The professor had meant it as banter to relieve the tension but the sharpness in her voice left him humorless.

Chapter 13

The Sumida, Thames of the Orient

Satoko continues her story in an account she was persuaded to write several years later. "From when I was baptized I experienced a desire, amounting almost to a necessity, to 'serve', which seemed to be a natural accompaniment to being a follower of Christ. I joined a women's group that met regularly at the Mercedarian convent. We used to visit orphanages as far away as Yokohama, draw Bible pictures for children's catechism classes etc. but there was something missing." Was God calling her to be a nun? She hoped he was and staggered her parents by asking permission to go and stay awhile in Hagi where the Mercedarians had a convent for postulants. It was in Kyushu, not far from Yamaguchi where Francis Xavier worked in Japan exactly four hundred years before. Her father still remembered the pain his own father caused by trying to stop him going on to university. He was deeply disappointed at Satoko's decision to be a nun but grudgingly said she could go.

Satoko knew that Mercedarian nuns dress as brides when they take their vows. That is why when she was baptized she did not wear one of her beautiful kimonos, as she loved doing on any kind of special occasion. She wore a bridal dress and veil. It was her secret promise to Christ to serve him as a Mercedarian sister. Now that the secret was out this young woman who loved symbolic actions startled her family by her farewell photo. She had it taken in her classical black kimono, the one that she, like every well-to-do woman, kept

exclusively for funerals! The family were aware of the meaning and it did nothing to lighten their gloom. She was praying they would all be led to baptism and felt sure this would
happen. Then they would rejoice in her choice of life and be
proud of her. She packed all she would need in one suitcase
and bought a one-way ticket to Hagi. Her sister remembers
how she put that ticket under her pillow at bedtime, as a
fiancée would put her engagement ring.

She woke during the night feeling unwell. Her mother
heard her moving about and insisted on taking her temperature. It was a startling 104°F. The family doctor was alarmed
when he saw her next day and ordered her to bed, "doing
absolutely nothing but rest for three weeks". He had her
x-rayed and grimaced as he saw the shadows beginning in
both lungs. Like so many Japanese whose health had been
impaired during the grim wartime and postwar years, she had
contracted tuberculosis. He isolated her in her bedroom and
began treatment. She responded well but the nuns told her to
postpone her postulancy indefinitely.

She used the time in bed on two large volumes she had
long planned to read: *A Compendium of Japanese Literature*
and *A Compendium of Western Literature*. She devoured them
from cover to cover, feeling very much at home in the world
of intuition and journeys of the spirit. Her own education
at Oh-in had given her a special feeling for Japanese haiku
poetry.

Her father was burning the midnight oil as he and several
colleagues labored at bringing the new university college to
birth. He was unwell with a cold one Sunday but came to the
living room to meet a visitor. They sat around a *kotatsu*, the
artificial hearth that was found in well-to-do homes in Japan
until recently, and is still found in rural homes. A *kotatsu*
is a square pit in the floor, with a solid cover over it like a
low table. There is room for four people to sit on the tatami

floor with their hands or elbows on the table-like cover, and their legs in the pit under it. A thick blanket spreads out from the lower edge of the table covering everyone's legs and stopping the warmth escaping. Slow combustion charcoal in the bottom of the pit provides the cosy heat. Unfortunately carbon monoxide can sometimes be generated and escape into the room. It happened that day, and to the astonishment of the visitor the professor suddenly collapsed unconscious, overcome by carbon monoxide. They rushed him to hospital where he lay in a coma for eight hours.

Eldest daughter Kazuko, happily and prosperously married, worried about her parents, who were not getting any younger. She wanted them to live close to her so she could help more. After her father was on his feet again she came with a proposal: "Sell this Suginami house—it is too big now—and build on the vacant plot beside us at Asakusa." That is how Satoko and her parents came to live in a new two-story house behind the Matsuya Department Store in Asakusa, about two tenths of a mile southeast of the famous Kannon Temple. The Sumida River was only a few minutes away to the west.

In the early 1600s the new Tokugawa Shogunate set up headquarters in a little village called Edo. During the 250-year Tokugawa reign Edo grew in size and importance and by the time of the Meiji Restoration in 1868 Edo was the nerve center of Japan. Emperor Meiji moved from Kyoto to Edo, changing the name Edo to Tokyo, or East Capital. He made the Tokugawa castle his palace and emperors have resided there ever since.

Running east of the palace to empty into Tokyo Bay is a small river called the Sumida, which had assumed a vital role in the commercial life of the city and came to be called the Thames of the Orient. It assumed importance in literature, too, many Japanese writers making it the scenario of their stories. The great playwright Zeami wrote a Noh drama called *Sumida River*. The man who is recognized as the greatest haiku poet in Japanese history, Basho, settled in his small thatched hut on its banks and celebrated it in verse. Osamu Dazai, the novelist many critics say might have won a Nobel Prize had he not terminated his young life by suicide, made the Sumida River the setting for several of his books.

Chushingura, the story of *The 47 Ronin*, is Japan's all-time popular saga, presented more often on Japanese stage and screen than any other single drama. The story reaches its climax on the banks of the Sumida. Japanese are very sensitive to "mood", and *The 47 Ronin* is a classical mood story. Japanese of all classes regard *Chushingura* as one of the nation's most seminal stories, a perfect example of Makoto and Bushido. The saga commenced 290-odd years ago with young Lord Asano, a country *daimyo* possessed of more raw courage than court sophistication. Tricked into a grave breach of palace etiquette by a scheming and insulting court official, Kira, whom he had refused to bribe, Lord Asano drew his sword and wounded Kira. As punishment for this grave breach of court behavior he was ordered to commit *seppuku* (*hara-kiri*). Tragic Lord Asano carried out the terrible ritual immediately. His domains were confiscated and his family publicly disgraced. Forty-seven of his samurai took a vow to restore the honor of the young lord and his family by striking down Kira. The latter, realizing their code of Bushido might prompt them to this, surrounded himself with bodyguards, and heavily fortified his large residence by the Sumida. For a year the forty-seven ronin prepared, sacrificing personal comfort, even neglecting their wives and families. As a heavy snowfall muffled the streets of Edo in the small hours of December 14, 1702, the forty-seven breached the walls of Kira's residence, cut down his heavy personal guard, and beheaded Kira. They marched in orderly ranks to their lord's grave, left Kira's head there, and gave themselves up to the Shogun. As they had so clearly foreseen, he sentenced them to *seppuku*. They carried this out with such "courage, nobility and serenity" that they became instant heroes to every class of Japanese society, then and to this day. No matter when you visit their graves in Tokyo's Sengakuji Temple you will find people praying there, lighting incense sticks to honor them as martyrs to absolute faithfulness, to Makoto.

A definite mood hangs over the Sumida—as a definite mood hangs over the Thames and the Tower of London. The Sumida and the Thames have been silent witnesses to events that have alternately thrilled and saddened the whole nation. Monuments along the Sumida testify to this. In 1657 a huge conflagration roared through the houses on both banks and into surrounding suburbs; 108,000 Edo citizens perished. The authorities gathered up the ashes of the dead and interred them in a Buddhist Temple beside the river. Subdued Buddhist pilgrims were a common sight for years, travelling down the river by all manner of crafts, to pray for the dead in Ekoin Temple on the east bank.

Their pilgrim boats had to jostle for position with very different boats heading for Asakusa, opposite Ekoin Temple, on the west bank. Travellers on these other craft were men in search of carnal pleasures in the "nightless city". They could swagger along a walk in Asakusa and peer through small windows to decide which of the indentured women they would have that night.

As previously described, on September 1, 1923, a horrendous earthquake struck Tokyo. Over 366,000 houses were destroyed, mostly by fires. Sixty thousand people perished and forty thousand were injured. The place of greatest carnage was on an open ground on the east bank of the Sumida, not far from Ekoin Temple. An estimated forty thousand people fled from the flames and packed shoulder to shoulder on the vacant ground. Most came with what clothing, bedding and so forth they could carry or stuff into handcarts. Flying sparks ignited this baggage and thirty-five thousand were burned to death or asphyxiated. A three-story temple was built over their ashes. To this day incense, burning to console their spirits, is never allowed to go out. It went out once, the time in early March 1945, when LeMay's B-29s destroyed the docks and suburbs on both sides of the Sumida, requiring another monument.

In September 1950, Professor Kitahara and his family moved to their new two-story house built beside eldest daughter Kazuko's home and wholesale shop. It was on the western side of the Sumida, near the Matsuya Department Store. Had Satoko crossed the main road running parallel to the river and gone down the bank she would have come across a weird assortment of huts and shanties, the like of which she had never seen. Within several months an extraordinary Polish Franciscan, Brother Zeno Zebrowski, would take Satoko there, and ignite a fire very different from the fires that had destroyed the place three times in the past. Brother Zeno plays so prominent a place in the Satoko story that he must be introduced at some length.

Chapter 14

The Polish Friar Tuck

1772 was a disastrous year for Poles. Germany, Russia and Austria solved "the Polish problem" by dismembering the nation and absorbing the parts. The very name Poland disappeared from world maps and vast areas of eastern Poland became part of Russia. Poles who resisted Russianization were rounded up and driven to inhospitable scrubland or tundra. It was presumed they would find it impossible to make a living there and leave the country—or, just as good, die of starvation and disease. Zeno Zebrowski's great-great-grandparents were among these patriot exiles sent to scrubland. With not much more than bare hands they cleared the trees and coaxed crops from soil that was frozen for half the year.

They banded together, formed villages and built churches. The Russian authorities moved in to tax and control them and eventually built municipal offices and rough schoolhouses where Russian was the only language that could be used. Inspectors made surprise visits and if Polish was being spoken in classrooms heavy fines had to be paid. The biography of Marie Sklodowska, who as Madame Curie was to win Nobel Prizes for chemistry and physics, gives graphic details of how patriots continually outwitted the officials and taught Poland's language and traditions to Marie and her classmates.

Zeno was born on December 27, 1891. Almost as soon as he could stand he was in the harsh fields beside his brothers. When he was older and stronger he accompanied his father on timber-gathering forays and learned the lore of surviving in forests. As they lived close to Russia proper it became impossible to get away with teaching Polish in the schools. Zeno's parents and neighbors simply kept their children from school rather than have them learn in Russian. In the long months when much snow covered the ground, patriots would travel about teaching Polish children in cattle sheds and hay barns. Risks curtailed effectiveness, however, and, frustrated at the poor education his children were getting, Zeno's father scraped some money together and sailed to the United States. He hoped to earn enough to bring his family across the Atlantic one day.

World War I ended his dreams. He returned to protect his impoverished family when Field Marshal Hindenburg's German Army smashed across the borders of Russian Poland in 1914. German field guns made no distinction between Russian and Polish buildings and left a trail of destruction through Zeno's village. When the invaders began rounding up all livestock Zeno fled to the safety of the treacherous forests he knew well, taking as many farm animals as possible. He lived there by his wits for a year. The harsh life toughened him and taught him more arts of survival.

When the Armistice came the Poles took weapons from retreating Germans and formed the first Polish Army in more than one and a half centuries. Their jubilation in raising the Red and White flag was short-lived! Having defeated the White Russians, the Bolsheviks marched into Poland determined to destroy this upstart Polish Army and its newly emerged nationalism. Zeno promptly enlisted in a machine-gun unit but being experienced with horses he was sent to a Warsaw cavalry unit. As Russian field guns sounded just outside the capital and Polish wounded poured in, Zeno was transferred to hospital duties. The broken bodies and sometimes deranged minds changed his romantic notions about war. When the Russians were driven back, the army pressed the resourceful, tough Zeno to stay on permanently—but he had seen enough killing and maiming.

Despite messages from his mother, Anna, pleading with him to come home now the war was over, Zeno decided that farm life was not for him. Footloose, fancy-free Zeno would cut, he imagined, a swathe across Poland. He needed money for a start and tried his hand first as a shoemaker, then as a tailor, but discovered he could make much more money smuggling goods across international borders. He contacted his father who still had money he saved in the United States, borrowed some and bought a "sure thing" mine near Danzig (Gdansk). Alas, all the money went down the mine, and with it Zeno's grand illusions. He was now destitute but too embarrassed to go home to face his father. However Christmas came and evoked a nostalgia that was stronger than his shame. He set out with nothing to take for his parents except a chastened heart.

Nearing his home town he faltered and decided to bolster his courage by calling on his favorite, warm-hearted sister-in-law. When Rozario came to the door she quickly wiped off his sheepish smile: "The worry and suffering you caused your mother she didn't deserve! And now you turn up, when we're just back home from burying her!"

A stunned Zeno ran wildly along a road half-covered in ice until he reached the cemetery. In the gathering darkness he made out a mound of fresh clay and stood before it sobbing like a forlorn child. He begged her forgiveness for not answering her messages and ceasing his religious practices. He knelt to pray for the first time in a long while. He remembered how she had once spread her rough red hands and told them: "These helped bake the bricks to build our village church. If you remember nothing else I've taught you, remember it is the Mass that counts." Zeno made a solemn promise there before her fresh grave to recommence his Christian life and go back to Sunday Mass.

He found employment as apprentice to a local Jewish blacksmith. There were some nasty remarks from village anti-Semites but Zeno liked his boss and defended him. The relationship was mutual and here began Zeno's life-long practical ecumenism. He was eyeing several girls from houses with "a special flower garden in front"—an indication that a marriageable girl lived inside. But he was attending daily Mass, too, and he began wondering about religious life. To his father's chagrin he left home again, determined to try an order where he could "meditate about God in a peaceful garden". Alas again for Zeno! He tried the Conventual Franciscans and was taken in tow by indefatigable Father Maximilian Kolbe. Instead of his romanticized monastery garden, Zeno found himself living under atrocious conditions in harsh Grodno, a struggling half-frozen settlement in the far northeast of Poland. Maximilian Kolbe's dynamic personality and grand vision was the only reason Zeno stayed.

As a youth Kolbe had dreamed of military exploits to free Poland from foreign domination. Instead he joined the Franciscans, gained a doctorate in philosophy at the prestigious Gregorian University in Rome, followed by a doctorate in theology, and was now putting out a popular monthly called *Knights of the Immaculate*. Impoverished, war-scarred Poland had little but the heady wine of nationalism to live on. From the spartan monastery in Grodno, Kolbe was writing articles encouraging starving, confused and demoralized Poles to believe in the future. His message was both Marian and simple: Mary was Christ's best disciple. He gave her to us from the Cross to help us live his Gospels. True devotion to her leads us to the heart of Scripture and to a deep prayer life. This very Marian spirituality was presented by Kolbe in down-to-earth Polish, for he wrote mainly for peasants and factory workers, which is what most Poles were in this land that had been colonized for generations. But intellectuals also began reading this magazine from the hands of an extraordinary man with two doctorates.

Zeno, ill-fed and ill-clothed like Kolbe and the rest of the small band, was put in charge of an ancient, hand-cranked printing press that evoked old army cursing—of necessity under his breath! As orders multiplied he got less and less sleep. Rushed off his feet he decided the place was a madhouse and he would leave. He went to tell Kolbe but the latter prayed him out of it! That was 1922. By 1926 Zeno and Kolbe were turning out a sixty-page magazine having a monthly circulation of forty-five thousand, and a widening circle of supporters from all over Poland. When young men began turning up asking to join them, Kolbe sent a very reluctant Zeno out begging money, like the Franciscans of old, to buy the site and materials for "a big monastery and modern plant we will dedicate to the Immaculate". Kolbe's advice about begging: "If people give, that's for Our Lady. If they rebuff you, that's for Zeno. It won't do him any harm!" The begging was successful and Zeno became clerk of works in building a series of barrack-like huts that became a huge monastery. It was situated a little west of Warsaw. Kolbe called it Niepokalanow, The City of the Immaculate.

Eight years later Kolbe left this dynamic monastery housing hundreds of Franciscans who were putting out a national daily newspaper and several flourishing monthlies, to begin a Conventual Franciscan foundation in Japan. Zeno, Kolbe's committed jack-of-all-trades, readily agreed to join the little pioneer group. They landed in Nagasaki on April 24, 1930, possessing one suitcase each and no Japanese connections. Their only language preparation was via a rough Polish-Japanese dictionary composed by a Pole in the Czar's army during the Russo-Japanese War of 1904–1905. Kolbe always left much to Providence! Biographers still are amazed by it, but within a month the first Japanese language edition of *Seibo no Kishi*, (*Knights of the Immaculate*) was on the streets. It was soon to become, and remains, Japan's most popular Catholic magazine.

Kolbe put Zeno in charge of practical matters—finding things like lodging, a secondhand printing press and eventually land for a monastery. Zeno was out begging again. He had overcome his initial loathing for it in Poland by murmuring Kolbe's words like a mantra: "Gifts for Our Lady, rebuffs for Zeno." To his delight he discovered that Japan had a living tradition of religious begging. Huge Buddhist monasteries that have stood for a thousand years as architectural masterpieces had been built by begging. Ever curious Zeno discovered that part of a Zen priest's training was to go out with a begging bowl. These Zen beggars are called *unsui*, meaning cloud/water, an abbreviation of the dictum that a true Zen follower travels "as freely as a cloud in the sky and as spontaneously as water running down a mountainside". Zeno became a Christian *unsui* and again money steadily came in. They ate and lived poorly, increased the magazine circulation and began attracting Japanese recruits.

There was a Protestant minister in Nagasaki, the Reverend Hachimaki, who was also a professor of history. He had a special interest in Saint Francis of Assisi and regarded his reform in thirteenth-century Italy as a kind of Golden Age when Christians lived like the first, post-Pentecost disciples. He went out of curiosity to visit the newly arrived Franciscans and was excited by their gospel lifestyle. He began telling his Protestant friends that Kolbe's group lived exactly like the first Franciscans and the first Christians. Reverend Hachimaki, taking a great liking to big, smiling, red-bearded Zeno, helped him get the land in Hongo cho where they built a monastery. Kolbe accepted the site because it backed into mountains where he could build a natural Lourdes grotto.

In 1936 Kolbe, recalled to Poland for a general meeting for his order, was elected superior of the huge monastery he had built in the 1920s. It now housed 432 friars. The monthly, *Knights of the Immaculate*, now had a circulation of a million. They also put out a one hundred thirty thousand circulation daily newspaper and ran a radio station. Kolbe missed Japan sorely but threw himself into his new job like "a cheerful volcano of a man with plans to change the world"—to quote Anglican journalist Diana Dewar, one of many who have written a biography of Kolbe.

The Nazis invaded Poland on September 1, 1939. They planned to turn the nation into a huge grain producer for Germany, wiping Poland off the map when German farmers were ready to take over the vast wheat fields. As soon as Poland surrendered the Nazis began rounding up Polish intellectuals and leaders in a careful plan to wipe out Polish nationalism. On the day Danzig (Gdansk) fell, just sixteen days after war was declared, Kolbe was imprisoned by the Gestapo. In May of 1941 he became No. 16670 in Barrack 17, Auschwitz. On August 14, 1941, he died in a notorious starvation bunker, taking the place of a married man with children. This episode was to have a profound effect on Satoko and will be discussed in detail later.

The day the Nazis invaded Poland, Zeno and the Polish Franciscans in Nagasaki became enemy aliens as Japan was one of the Axis powers. That same day the dreaded *kenpeitai* police arrived at the monastery, gave Father Mirochan, the Guardian, a very hard time and placed everyone under house arrest. No one could leave without permission of the *kenpeitai* until a strange request came from Nagasaki police: Zeno could be trusted completely—he would never betray Japan. Let him come and go to buy provisions. Zeno had been always careful to follow Kolbe's instructions: "We have come to Japan to teach a gospel of love, not to condemn the Japanese people." Practical Zeno had gone out of his way to befriend everyone he met and do them a good turn. When war rationing became rigorous from 1937 he noticed that police on the beat wore shoes in need of repair, as leather and shoes were in short supply. Zeno began repairing police-men's shoes, refusing any payment. "You walk all time to keep all citizens safely." The policemen came to have real affection for the Pole who spoke very broken Japanese but was kind to everyone.

Zeno continued to move freely around the city carrying milk from monastery cows to Saint Francis' Hospital, calling to pray with families who had just lost a son at the front, encouraging people who were becoming dispirited. On August 1, 1945, the *kenpeitai* took Zeno's confreres off to Tochinoki, near Mount Aso in Kumamoto Prefecture, with orders to kill them as possible collaborators when the US troops landed. Zeno was left behind, still free to move about.

Then came August 9, and the A-bomb. The monastery was more than three miles southeast from the epicenter and pro-tected by mountains. Zeno was unharmed. On August 15 the war ended and everyone reassembled at the monastery. Several days later a strange-looking man appeared—a Buddhist hermit who lived an ascetic life in the mountains. He led four small, frightened children. Their parents died in the atomic blast, he told the Franciscans. "Will you take care of them?" That's how the monastery became a temporary orphanage and Zeno was put in charge of the orphans. He soon discovered many other orphans in Nagasaki railway stations, beneath bridges and in air-raid shelters. The sights troubled him deeply, espe-cially when winter was near. The monastery was poor and food was scarce, yet Zeno kept bringing back all the orphans he could persuade to come with him. The community shared what they had with the waifs, and Zeno's old friends in the city began bringing food. Several male school teachers whose families had been wiped out by the A-bomb, men whom Dr. Takashi Nagai had previously brought out to the monastery for Saint Vincent de Paul retreats, moved into the monastery as permanent volunteers with the orphans. Reporters came and published articles. Zeno asked them for copies. These articles became his train tickets!

Zeno would march importantly onto a station without a ticket and sit on a bench until a US Occupation serviceman came along. Zeno always wore his Franciscan habit and most soldiers would look, see his big smile and begin a conversation. Zeno would produce his newspaper clippings, some in English. Soldiers would usually ask if they could help. "Yes" would reply Zeno, in broken scraps of English. "I no ticket." In this way Zeno travelled as far as burned-out Hiroshima, Osaka, Nagoya and Tokyo. He brought home orphans and disturbing stories of homeless, destitute adults in every big city. Government figures calculated that at least 509,469 people died in the air raids on Japan. Millions of homes had been destroyed and thousands of orphans were wandering around aimlessly. Zeno's beard was red when the war started. A year after the war ended it was white.

Zeno made sure the children from the makeshift orphanage went to local schools. One day a volunteer teacher who lost his whole family in the A-bomb attack and now helped Zeno, found some of their children missing school and scolded them severely. They began crying, saying they hated school because everyone there picked on them for their patched, hand-me-down clothing. The teacher ended up crying, too. He went to see Zeno who decided to appeal to the US Army base where an old Japanese Army barracks stood unoccupied. He asked Catholic historian, Professor Kataoka to go along as interpreter. As they approached the armed guard outside the

US gates the professor asked whom they were going to see. "Dunno now but...." Holding up his rosary he said: "She know and will fix." The professor confesses he was sweating freely a few yards from the burly, unsmiling guard when an army truck screeched to a halt behind them. "Can I give you a lift, Padre?" drawled the American driver. He took the pair inside where Zeno found a sergeant born in Poland who made the necessary contacts. Zeno obtained the use of the empty barracks for classrooms and the promise of food leftovers in the US mess. Zeno called his school The Garden of the Holy Mother.

After some time, however, city authorities told Zeno he must move as they needed the land where the old barracks stood. A man with a property in mountains two hours northeast of Nagasaki heard of the problem and offered it as an orphanage site. Zeno obtained permission to dismantle the old barracks and use the timber to build an orphanage and school there.

In May 1949, Zeno took a party of fifty young people to the new site in the mountains. They de-trained, loaded themselves up with roof tiles, beams, floorboards and so forth and set out exuberantly to pioneer their new home. Along the mountain road, younger orphans began to run and whoop excitedly in reply to the welcoming, liquid notes of the *uguisu*, the Japanese bush warbler. Someone picked sprigs of *yamabuki*, the thornless mountain rose with yellow flowers bright as European buttercups, to place before the statue of the Virgin and Child that one of them carried.

Alas, Zeno was not always the most practical of planners. On reaching Saienji temple he discovered the unpaved road disappeared—with a mile and a quarter still to travel. The sun had already declined behind western peaks. Zeno, who never believed in getting flustered, marched up to a Buddhist temple entrance and called out confidently: "*Gomen kudasai.*" The *Jodo Shinshu* priest who soon appeared was startled by Zeno's wild beard, his outsize rosary hanging from the cord that belted his battered habit—and above all by fifty suspicious-looking boys wearing an odd collection of clothing. He was shocked by Zeno's request, in the worst Japanese he'd ever heard, for lodging for the lot! With an unamused glance at the alien rosary and large crucifix he said coldly: "Don't you think it audacious that someone aggressively propagating a western religion in a Buddhist land should ask a temple to put you all up?"

Zeno had long regarded rebuffs as mere opening remarks. He bowed deeply and with a big grin creasing his leathery face replied: "Us don't look goodly, heh, but gold, real gold." Allowing his eyes to sweep over his urchins he continued: "Not looks what counts. All of us, precious gold from one same Maker. You too true gold, I know?" Suddenly the Buddhist returned Zeno's smile and said: "Anyone who has achieved that *satori* (enlightenment) is welcome here. Come on in." Then and there a friendship was born.

The boys were settled in tatami-mat rooms used for temple pilgrims, and allowed to cook their rice on the kitchen range. He invited Zeno to share the *o-furo* bath with him, a high-water mark of hospitality in Japan. Before the two went to sleep side by side the Franciscan knelt saying: "Zeno, deep thanks. Say Ave Maria for you and temple folks." The Buddhist bowed low, listened to Zeno's prayer in badly accented Japanese and replied: "And I shall say the nembutsu prayer to the Merciful Amida for you and your orphans." Zeno was perfectly at home with all of this. He noticed, he once said, that homes where a Buddhist or Shinto altar was displayed, usually gave him something when he went begging for the poor. Zeno thought Jesus had made it very simple when he said in Matthew 25 that those who love and help the needy will certainly enter heaven.

Zeno went out on to the roads for months, again begging. A one-and-a-quarter-mile long road linking the orphanage to the village, and the cables and stanchions to bring electricity to the orphanage were spun from his beggar bowl. Much of the money came from Buddhists and Shintoists.

Zeno, like Robin Hood's Friar Tuck, could be dismissive of finer points of law to help the destitute. One cold day in early December 1949, he called on Father Tagawa in his rectory at Sasebo. "OK to enter great priest's home? Zeno have no lice, no bed bugs, this time. Make promise." The priest ushered him in but had a visitor. "No worry. Zeno wait your chapel." When the visitor left Father Tagawa found Zeno asleep, half-sprawled, over a kneeler. Zeno had missed sleep lately, busy trying to get help for Sasebo's many homeless. He wasn't getting very far. Could Father Tagawa give him money for timber to build sheds on a nearby park? "But that's government land. Have you permission?" Zeno replied: "Now December. Cold, cold. By time law argument finish, men dead bodies. People of Japan own Japan parks. God says OK."

Chapter 15

The Boss of the Ragpickers and a Law Man

An *unsui* monk moves freely. Zeno travelled freely, too, when the Japanese government, recognizing the remarkable work he was doing, gave him a complimentary pass on any government train or bus—from Sapporo in Hokkaido to Nagasaki in Kyushu. Japanese and Poles had cooperated on welfare projects before. After the cataclysm of World War I and the Bolshevik Revolution, over a thousand Polish orphans were left behind in Russian occupied areas. A Polish woman wrote letters to many nations asking help to get the orphans back to Poland. Japan was one of the few nations that responded. The Japanese Red Cross put up thirteen thousand posters to solicit funds across the nation and, with energetic help from Empress Sadako, raised enough money to ship 840 Polish orphans to Japan in 1921 from a port in Siberia. The waifs were feted, given nourishing food, medical attention, new clothing and schooling. They were kept for almost a year until a ship was found to take them on the long-way-round trip to western Poland. The Poles were deeply moved. When the earthquake devastated Tokyo and Yokohama in 1923, impoverished Poland was among the first nations to send material assistance. About thirty years later Emperor Hirohito visited Nagasaki in May 1949 and called on Zeno's orphanage. An onlooker saw Zeno wave a Japanese flag vigorously when the emperor's car appeared. Tears were streaming down the tough Pole's face. He was proud that he could repay Japan's kindness to Polish orphans.

In the freezing December of 1950, Zeno visited Tokyo. He alighted at Ueno Railway Station, distributed a sack of food and clothing to shivering station dwellers and walked several miles east to the west bank of the Sumida. He was on a fact-finding tour of Tokyo's most destitute areas. He stopped near the Kannon Temple in Asakusa where his troubled eyes focused sharply on a now familiar sight. A group of disabled ex-soldiers, wearing the white cotton uniform their amputations entitled them to, stood on a corner singing old Japanese songs. A sad-looking man missing one leg leaned on his crutch as he led them with a beat-up accordion. At their feet on the footpath was a comrade missing both legs who performed the remarkable feat of bowing low before passers-by. The rusty jam tin in front of him held very few coins. Zeno had no money but, responding with a deep bow, lowered his big frame to the man's ear and muttered above the music: "You pray Maria-sama. She Mother of Jesus and you. She understand and help." Zeno had imbibed Kolbe's extraordinary trust in the intercessory power of the Mother of Christ.

He walked on down the street passing several beggars huddled by a wall. One was an amputee—probably an air-raid victim. With a respectful bow Zeno bent down again and took out some bread rolls he was carrying in a paper bag, murmuring words of encouragement.

In his heavy black satchel he always carried newspaper clippings about his work, which served as his *meishi*, his visiting card. He also had back editions of the Japanese monthly *Knights of the Immaculate* and some copies of a small pamphlet on Kolbe and his death in Auschwitz. Several young women were walking toward him, well-dressed and exuding vitality. The contrast was too great. Zeno stepped up to them and said to one of them: "Please, missy, see poor beggars. Mother Mary very sad for many poor family, 'ere 'er card for missy. She pleased if you 'elp 'er children." He handed her a cheap picture card of the Madonna and Child. Blushing, the woman snatched the card from Zeno's leathery hand, set off with her friends and promptly tossed the card away, leaving Zeno with only the hard sounds of their fashionable shoes echoing on the pavement.

A little later he was passing the Takagi Footwear Wholesalers. A shop assistant standing just inside the door greeted him: "*Shinpu san, Konban wa.*" (Father, good evening.) Zeno, encouraged by a smile for a change, stepped inside. The assistant told him the sister of the owner was a Catholic and invited him to sit down. While another of the staff fixed up some green tea, the assistant went upstairs where Satoko was playing the piano and told her she had a visitor "who looks like Santa Claus". Satoko takes up the story in a letter she wrote six weeks later to a university classmate who had recently received baptism.

"I walked into the shop and saw a big foreigner, wearing a black Franciscan habit and with a luxuriant white beard. He stopped his animated conversation in midstream as he saw the rosary in my obi. 'You Christian, heh!' I replied that I'd been baptized recently in the Mercedarian Convent. 'Good, good. Maybe you become nun?' I was startled by his question but even more so by his extraordinarily penetrating yet gentle eyes. I had the sensation that here was someone who could see into the depths of my heart. I stammered a reply, and he smiled warmly. 'Good, good,' he repeated: ''oly Mother, she pray for good graces to you. But I beg you. Pray for poor, pitiful poor on cold streets.' He opened a heavy briefcase and gave me a pamphlet. Then: 'I busy, busy. Must sayonara. But come more again.' He stood up and disappeared like the wind, leaving me totally nonplussed. I asked the staff where he came from but no one knew." Back in her room she read the small, cheaply printed booklet on how Father Kolbe once worked in Nagasaki and later gave his life to save a fellow inmate in Auschwitz. It was all news to her.

Some ten minutes later Zeno came across a settlement of dustbin sifters. The Japanese press called them *bataya*, ragpickers. This group was living on the bank of the Sumida. Zeno soon attracted the attention of some ill-clad ragamuffins who gathered around him studying his beard, his "round eyes" and his garb. "You all good kids. Come." He reached into his voluminous pockets for sweets and repeated: "You all good kids, good, good. Pray to Maria-sama. She become big 'elp."

The children's smiles disappeared as a small but stocky man with a round face tapped Zeno on the shoulder. "Heh, you. You're not Japanese I see. We don't regard it as polite to burst in on people." He said it icily. "You Boss around 'ere?" asked Zeno, putting up his thumb the way Japanese men do to indicate the top dog. Zeno laughed and, despite himself, so did the other man. Around here everyone called him *Oyaji* which means the Boss.

"I see by your gear that you belong to the Amen religion. You look a decent kind of individual but we don't encourage begging around here." He looked disapprovingly at Zeno's bag of sweets.

Zeno bowed humbly. "Sorry. Sorry. But the kids, they don't need nuffing?"

"No, definitely not", countered the boss with an edge on his voice. "Not things, anyhow."

"What you want then?"

"We want people with a conscience who will give us a fair go!" He tapped Zeno's chest and added: "People with a heart."

"Hah", responded Zeno. "You wonerful! God love such man." Holding up the crucifix on his rosary he added: "God on your side. Give you fair go."

The Boss, Ozawa-san, had worked in a construction firm in Manchuria before the defeat. Returning to Tokyo after the surrender he was staggered by the almost total destruction caused by B-29 napalm raids and by the number of people without homes or the prospect of a job. From the Sumida's banks, he began collecting bottles and newspapers, tin and other scrap which could be sold. A shrewd businessman, he began employing drifters on a daily basis. He had had his eyes on an almost wrecked building in the public park beside the Sumida River. It had been a small lumberyard, one of the enterprises set up during the war by a volunteer group helping the widows and dependants of soldiers killed in action. Municipal authorities had allowed them to use part of Sumida Park but the enterprise was abandoned when a cyclone wrecked the buildings. Boss Ozawa found the volunteer group who had run the lumberyard and outlined his plan to set up a scrap-collecting business here, repairing the main buildings as his office. He would invite homeless people to work for a share of the profits. Ozawa would help them put up lean-tos that would at least give shelter. The association leaders had no further use for the wrecked lumberyard sot they told Ozawa he was welcome to the site—"though really it is municipal property".

Ozawa and his young wife, Katsumi, set up an "office" on the site with scales to weigh what the ragpickers brought in. Each dustbin sifter was paid according to the weight and quality of scrap. Women were paid to sort and stack the scrap. However a number of problems arose and Ozawa knew he needed legal advice. This is how an enigmatic man, Tooru Matsui, appeared on the scene. He was soon to become a central figure in the Satoko story.

The last year of the Pacific war saw Tooru Matsui in Taiwan writing scenarios for musicals performed by a professional group of singers called Kikyo (the name of a flower celebrated in ancient Chinese verse). There was a large contingent of Japanese on Taiwan, many of them military personnel. Tokyo viewed Kikyo as a worthwhile morale booster.

When thirty-five-year-old Matsui returned to Tokyo after the surrender in 1945 he was shocked by the utter devastation caused by the B-29 firebombing. Japan's future looked unbelievably bleak and so did his own. In an effort to make some sense out of it all he retired to a Buddhist monastery on Mount Hiei, the massive mountain range dominating the northeast skyline of Kyoto. Hiei had been a holy mountain since A.D. 788 when a great religious reformer, Saicho, built his first monastery on its heights. As an eager young monk, Saicho had been disillusioned by the heavy formalism that had settled on the Nara monasteries. He decided to make the dangerous crossing to China, seeking the pure wellsprings of Buddhism. His search ended when he discovered Tendai-shu, a profoundly metaphysical form of Chinese Buddhism. Having mastered its main tenets and spirituality, he returned to Japan to teach it on a mountain above Kyoto. Disciples gathered around him until, a few generations later, flourishing Tendai monasteries covered the mountain. Francis Xavier, writing from Kyoto in 1549, describes "the great Buddhist university on Mount Hiei".

Matsui, like the young Saicho, was searching. He threw himself into the study of Tendai-shu, rising at dawn to pray and read the sutras. During the day he had time for solitary thought as he wandered along mountain paths shaded by centuries-old *hinoki* (Japanese cypress trees). For awhile he believed he had found the peace he longed for, but the old restlessness and a new cynicism began to emerge. He had been a passenger in the roller-coaster ride of Japanese ultranationalism and militarism through the 1930s and 1940s ... only to be hurtled into the seemingly bottomless, hopeless abyss of total defeat. His anger at the generals who had been beaten turned to a cynicism toward all authority figures—including the new shogun, MacArthur, and his gum-chewing, super-cocky soldiers who patrolled the cities in jeeps.

Now his cynicism turned on Japan's spiritual leaders. Saicho and the first generations of monks possessed genuine spirituality that brought them peace of heart, a peace that reached out to help the poor and afflicted in the land. The present breed of monks, however, were phoney! They were doing nothing to help the destitute masses in Japan's gutted cities. They had long abandoned the celibate and ascetic life that Saicho taught as essentials of monastic spirituality.

Matsui left Mount Hiei disillusioned and bitter. Somewhere along the line he tried Christianity but that failed the test, too. He admired Christ and Saint Paul, as he admired Saicho and early Buddhist monks. However the Christian churches he saw in Osaka and Tokyo were "whited sepulchers". Unlike the poor Christ who went among the destitute, priests and ministers lived comfortably and doled out cheap grace to bourgeois congregations—among whom Christ of the Gospels would feel a stranger!

Matsui abandoned the dreams he had cherished, as a student at Waseda University, of becoming a great playwright like his famous father. He now felt too bitter and antisocial to write anything that would appeal to anybody. He would give his confidence to no one, and that included his wife. It is hard to get precise details on his wife as his marriage was a taboo subject! But a few facts about her emerge. She had graduated from a university of music in Tokyo, was older than Matsui and had been a member of the Kikyo Music Group in Taiwan. Matsui stated that before marriage she agreed to certain conditions: the marriage would not be consummated and he would be free to live separately, celibate and poor. This would allow him to dedicate himself to help the destitute masses of postwar Japan. One has the suspicion he married to have someone to look after his widowed mother. This meant his wife would at least have a good home. Matsui owned a valuable house in fashionable Sengokubara, Hakone, in the highlands just east of Mount Fuji.

But Matsui had to make a living and 1950 found him working in Tokyo for the Fujita Law Firm. Law, he thought, could be a sharp weapon to help the oppressed. When Ozawa, the Boss of the ragpicker settlement on Sumida Park began having problems with *Yakuza* (Mafia-like gangsters) demanding protection money, he decided to consult the Fujita Law Firm. He also knew his group of dustbin sifters would have a better chance against municipal officials if he established them as a legal body. City authorities had already burned down a number of shantytowns like the one on the Sumida. There was also the problem of their tenuous permission from the volunteer group who had built the original lumberyard to help the dependants of soldiers killed in action. Was it possible to establish a legal argument from the actual occupancy of homeless citizens on a city park? When the Boss called on the law firm, Matsui was put in charge of the matter. Possibly Mr. Fujita did that because Matsui had already proved troublesome, and Boss Ozawa's appearance indicated he might prove a difficult client, too.

At the beginning Matsui suspected Boss Ozawa of a scheme to defraud defenceless day workers. However to Matsui's surprise he came to see the ragpicker commune was helping a considerable number of homeless people, including children and dependent old folk. Matsui suggested Ants Town as a name for the new legal body, because "ants work hard, anywhere at all, and gain strength from community." Matsui became so interested in the possibilities of the Ants Town commune that he told the Boss he was willing to move in with them and help defend them against municipal expulsion. The Boss was delighted. So was Matsui because he had found a cause that he

could fight for that might stop him going insane—or taking
his own life. There were times when suicide seemed a more
courageous option than compromising his principles by living
in a society that was so unjust. So the Boss found living space
for Matsui who promptly left the law firm.

Matsui decided that if he could get some hard-hitting newspaper articles published on Ants Town, public opinion would
support them and maybe stop the authorities from driving the
ragpickers off Sumida Park. He had once worked as a script-
writer for the big movie company, Shochiku, and contacted old
friends there to help him get articles into newspapers. However,
whether because of Matsui's abrasive manner or because every
Japanese city had thousands of destitute people, no newspaper
was interested in Ants Town. Matsui was angry and morose. At
precisely this moment someone told him the Boss was arguing
with a bearded foreigner dressed in "Amen" garb.

One look at Brother Zeno and the large rosary hanging
from his belt and Matsui detested him. He detested that whole
breed of professional religious, Buddhist, Christian or whatever. Matsui had a particular dislike for western missionaries
who had poured into Japan since the defeat. Matsui angrily
repeated what the Boss said: "No, we don't need your help!"

"No nuffing?" asked Zeno, looking at the dirty children and
the ugly huts built on a field of mud.

"No material things anyhow", Matsui said coldly. "We
could do with some public awareness of what municipal
authorities do when they burn down places like this. You get
our story into the newspapers if you want to do something!"

Zeno's eyes lit up. He produced a batch of newspaper articles from his heavy briefcase, unembarrassed that they carried
photos of himself at work among the homeless.

Matsui got on to a phone and told a number of newspapers,
"The famous Father Zeno is here." Matsui thought Father
would be more convincing than Brother. But no one was

interested—they were about to go to press for the evening editions and had already run Zeno stories. One newspaper remained. Matsui, without consulting Zeno, dialed the *Asahi* and said brusquely: "Hello. This is Ants Town. We are going to build a church here, thanks to Father Zeno. He's here now and I can hold him for another twenty minutes if you're interested.... Yes, that's what I said. A Christian church among the ragpickers' huts." A reporter was there in no time and the evening edition carried a big photo of Zeno, Matsui and Ozawa discussing the forthcoming church, and the plight of homeless ragpickers who lived in bare huts because there was nowhere else. Matsui's bold-as-brass lie had worked marvelously.

Chapter 16

A Different Christmas Eve

The shop assistant raced up the stairs to Satoko's room waving a newspaper. "Look, your Father Christmas is in the newspaper!" Satoko jumped up excitedly. She hadn't forgotten the bearded Franciscan with the remarkable eyes who came and went like the wind. A church in a slum called Ants Town? She had only seen churches in spacious, clean surroundings. This slum church and the name, Ants Town, intrigued her no end. With growing interest she read of "Father Zeno" and the ragpicker commune of "Ants".

Some days later Satoko was upstairs in her married sister's house, about to pull the wooden shutters across the windows as the light of the winter's day was fading into darkness. Her eyes casually swept the wet street below. She started. Zeno was right below her, rushing through the light rain, innocent of an umbrella. He gripped his black briefcase to his side while the chill north wind tugged at his habit and his beard. She flew down the stairs, through her sister's shop, slipped into wooden clogs and ran out after him without taking time to find an umbrella. He was nowhere to be seen! She hurried under the Tobu Railway bridge and ran several blocks with eyes darting left and right. Stepping up to a small kiosk she asked where "Ants Town" was. "Somewhere nearby", was all she learned. Ah, the address was in the newspaper article she'd put aside! She rushed back home, out of breath and wet. She jotted down the address, found an umbrella and set out for "Sumida Park near the Kototoi Bridge". She'd never before ventured into the unsavory-looking park running down to the river. She came across a rickety fence with a big board proclaiming: *Ants Town Boundary.* Inside she asked a grimy man if a foreigner had just come in. "'e's over there with the Boss". She continued her journey in the direction he indicated and stumbled several times as her wooden *geta* caught on the uneven ground. It was now quite dark and heavy rain splattered off her umbrella.

There was no door on "the Boss's place" and "for the first time in my life I went into someone's home uninvited." There was only a dirt floor and furniture seemed out of fashion. Weak light came from a room to the left where three people squatted on tatami mats. She approached them, suddenly embarrassed and hesitant. Two of the occupants looked up sharply at the young woman in the expensive kimono. Zeno came to her rescue: "Ah, ah, yes. Young missy from *geta* shop. Come come." The Japanese accent was harsh but the voice unmistakably welcoming. Removing her *geta* she sat *seiza* style on the dirty tatami mat. Zeno quickly resumed the conversation about some people living in cold subway stations. She was amazed at how well he could communicate with such rough and unsyntaxed Japanese. The Boss, too, seemed to be fascinated by the strange Japanese. After a short time Zeno's hand dived into his voluminous habit, pulled out a huge and ancient timepiece and said: "Oops! Must be go", and sprang to his feet. "Come, missy. We be go."

They moved out into the cold pelting rain, Zeno insisting that his battered felt hat and short Franciscan cape were protection enough. Satoko would not listen and moved close to him, sharing her umbrella. She immediately noticed the bad smell, like the smell in "the Boss's" place. She struggled against the impulse to move away or hold her breath. He took her about three-tenths of a mile south along the river where the Tobu Railway crossed the Sumida to show her how people had dug holes into the river bank, living there with only cardboard and newspapers spread on the damp earth. By the city light reflected from the river she could just make out squatting human forms. They moved on and she saw others in huts hardly bigger than the kennel she used to have for their dog, Bank. She had once read a depressing story about brutal conditions in coal mines somewhere or other, and she thought this forlorn place was like those mines. The rain drummed louder and water rushing down the river bank found its way into some of the huts and holes. Could this be Tokyo, the capital of Japan? Could this forlorn and horrible place be less than a mile from her two-story home with its fragrant tatami matting and thick carpets, and a gas stove in each room?

Satoko lost track of time. When they finally returned to her home they were both wet through. She stood Zeno in front of a blazing gas stove and went up to her room to change and wring out her sodden kimono. When she returned Zeno had opened his black leather satchel and spread out selected newspaper clippings and photographs on the low table. In his homespun Japanese, which sometimes required concentration, he took her on a tour of the seediest places in Tokyo. Around Imado and Asakusa Honganji, for instance, people lived permanently in subways; some even in public toilets. There were homeless in Ueno living in huts erected on top of a graveyard dug for anonymous people killed in air raids. Tokyo's homeless numbered thousands and some of them wouldn't get one decent meal in three or four days. Yet in Nagasaki, Hiroshima and especially Nishinomiya, Zeno assured her, people were even worse off! Authorities often drove them from subways and burned down their squatter huts. Then they would dig holes in river banks and wrap themselves up in cardboard and newspapers, as they had just witnessed. Similar conditions existed in Osaka, Nagoya and Yokohama.

He handed her a letter from a man in Yokohama. "Missy, read please." Zeno apologized that although he'd been in Japan twenty years he could neither speak the language well nor read it. As a matter of fact, he added, he had never been to school anywhere! Satoko took the letter. The writer, expressing himself in classical Japanese honorifics, said he was the man Zeno found shivering and hungry outside Sakuraki Cho Station in Yokohama. He thought he was dreaming when Zeno took him off to buy him a warm shirt, trousers and buns with a bean filling. He had come to believe that there was no one left in the world who cared for the down-and-out. "You warmed my body but above all my heart, and made me want to go on living, giving me a sense that God did care after all." Zeno had addressed him as "my friend", he wrote, and shown such concern that he was emboldened to write and ask another favor. He was quite unwell and knew he was getting worse. He felt he would die if he did not get medical help. He had no money, however, to pay for it. Could his friend Zeno help? Before Satoko had read the polite traditional conclusion she had already decided she would go down to Yokohama and pay for the medication he needed. Zeno produced his ancient timepiece, gasped at the hour and despite his bulk was off like the wind—but with the promise of calling again.

Satoko continues the story: "I lay down in bed but could not get to sleep. Brother Zeno, a man without formal education, unable to read Japanese, had bridged a chasm separating two nations and two cultures. He had discovered a part of Japan I did not know existed, where thousands lived in unbelievable destitution. Many of them lived less than a mile from my home! I had lived in the pampered, educated ignorance of an over-sophisticated world while this unlettered foreigner worked without thought of self in the world of painful reality.... I lived surrounded by carpets and gas stoves while he went without even an umbrella into the terrible twilight world of destitution."

As she lay sleepless she began reflecting on the yearning for the Pure that began in childhood when she saw *miko* serving at a Shinto altar. She remembered how upset she felt during the war at the lewd conversation and behavior in the Naka-jima Airplane Factory. When she attended university her disappointment increased as fellow women students com-promised their integrity with young men from prestigious universities like Todai and Keio. The despair expressed in the novels of Osamu Dazai, as in the "pan pan", the women who became prostitutes in exchange for P.X. goods from US soldiers, increased her yearning for an authentic and uncom-promising ideal. The statue of Mary in the Yokohama church and the nuns teaching at her little sister's school had led her to the very different world of the Gospels. She had been try-ing hard to live them but chapters like Matthew 25, where Christ identified with the imprisoned, the destitute and the homeless, disturbed her! She had joined a group who visited orphanages but this was little more than a painless hobby! For months she had been vaguely uneasy and had prayed for guidance. Were tonight's hours in the rain with Brother Zeno God's answer?

Satoko's nickname at university had been "The Princess"— she tried to do everything with class! She always dressed taste-fully in a kimono, loved symbolism, and almost worshipped the theater. She could never become very interested in the "mere ordinary", so much so that some regarded her as aloof. Emotionally she was intuitive, quickly sensing someone's mood and responding sympathetically—sometimes too much so, and overdramatically, some thought. Others thought her a little too fragile—she could be hurt when people failed to respond to her, above all if they rebuffed her, and yet could be too demanding of others. She expected them to share her idealistic vision that life must always be "beautiful". She could be intolerant of people who did not work hard to make everything successful. Because of this temperament Satoko both upset some and exercised a powerful attraction on others. The nickname Princess was well chosen.

Since baptism she had been praying to find where she could serve people and the Lord with all her heart and soul. She became elated at the certainty of Zeno being "the angel of the Lord", sent specially to her—though his fellow friars would laugh at anyone thinking of tough, hefty Zeno as an angel!

Several days after her night foray with Angel Zeno, a shop assistant came upstairs to tell her "your Santa Claus is here again". Satoko's eyes brightened and she rushed downstairs where Zeno waited with a middle-aged man with an intelligent but sharp, off-putting face. Affable Zeno spoke. "Kitahara-san, this one Sensei of Ants Town, Matsui-Sensei." *Sensei* is a term given to doctors and teachers. Matsui Sensei responded to her deep bow with a slight, stiff nod. "We wanna Christmas show for Ants kids. You 'elp do?" Christmas was only days away. Satoko did not like doing anything without preparation, and hesitated. Ex-playwright Matsui Sensei maybe suspected the reason for her hesitation. He said with urgency: "I realize there's little time and our request may seem unreasonable. But it's very important to Ants Town. Won't you give it a try?" Matsui had no feeling whatsoever for a Christian celebration but this could be useful in attracting more newspaper articles to generate public sympathy.

Satoko agreed to give it a try. Yes, she could go and start practice today. Her grandmother came into the room and looked intently at Matsui-Sensei. She was a Kabuki buff and remembered seeing him and his famous father at plays before the war. Zeno and Matsui seemed in a great hurry and excused themselves almost immediately. Satoko's mother, encouraged by the Kabuki-loving grandmother, thought it was a worthwhile request.

"I left home at 1:00 P.M.," Satoko writes, "going by Kototoi Bridge. A cold wind whipped off the river and stung my face. My emotions wavered between excitement and fear as I neared the rickety wooden gate that gave entry to a completely strange world.

"I entered the park and saw Ants Town in the light of day. The storm had turned the place into an obscure blur on my first visit at night. Now I carefully observed the higgledy-piggledy dwellings. I could see that the 'office' was actually a triangle of roof. I later heard that it was blown off the main building when Typhoon Kitty demolished the original lumberyard."

She stood there for some time, both repelled and attracted by this ugly place that was home for one hundred people. The dingy huts were built from odds and ends, the bare earth was a festering mess of mud, puddles and rubbish. Some roughly dressed men and women had emptied a big cart full of rubbish collected from city bins and were now sorting it, indifferent to her presence. Suddenly she found herself doing something so typically Japanese. She lifted her eyes from the squalor, focussing them on the serenely flowing Sumida, and then on across the river to Mukojima, where cherry trees flung up bare limbs in silent prayer for spring to come quickly. Silhouettes of rooftops and chimneys stood out sharply against the opaque winter sky. "It was like a Sesshu *sumie* painting", she writes. "I was moved by the beauty of the setting." Poets like Basho praise souls who can discover beauty, howsoever wretched be the landscape. This is called *wabi* taste, something very important in Japanese aesthetics that will be taken up in detail later in this story.

Several knots of children had been standing behind the Boss's place, sheltering from the northeasterly, trying to squeeze a little warmth from the struggling winter sunlight. One of the Boss's assistants had told them to wait for Satoko but as soon as she appeared they dashed off and hid! Later Satoko reproached herself for going there thoughtlessly dressed in a warm red kimono—which cost more than their fathers could earn in a year of dustbin sifting. It branded her as one of the "strangers", the outsiders whom the children instinctively feared.

A man noticed her and called out: "Hey you kids, she's 'ere. She'll teach ya songs. Learn 'em good. Come on." Takagi-san had anticipated the problems and held aloft a bag of watery-looking sweets to coax the children out of hiding. An old, senile lady saw the candies and she came out, too. Takagi-san laughed and gave her a sweet: "But ya gotta practice proper." The singing class started there and then on the yard, the only place available. Satoko began with the Christmas carol that she loved, "Angels We Have Heard on High". Their first attempt to repeat it after her was like a gramophone run down. Music lover Satoko wondered if the children weren't being deliberately bad. But no, they just had no idea of music, nor did the old lady. She was nicknamed "The Bonze" because she had shaved off her hair to combat lice.

Satoko persevered and older children appeared and joined in. They were now fascinated by her voice and they desperately tried to sing like her. "Look, children, let's go up to my place. The piano will help you get the idea."

"You gotta piano? Wow!"

Satoko was amazed at their transformation inside her spacious home. An hour ago they would not say "boo" and looked down to avoid the eyes of the scary alien in the red kimono. Once inside the carpeted parlor they were like birds let out of a cage! "They couldn't believe their good fortune at being allowed into a fabulous house like this. They jumped around and yelped excitedly, as stray dogs will do if you call them and pat them." She queried them about going to school. There was a chorus of replies: school was no good. Everyone hated them and tormented them about their clothes, and if parents gave them a new pencil-case or something, they were accused of stealing it. If anything was stolen at school they'd say: search the ragpickers. Even teachers. No, they didn't go anymore.

"Suddenly I felt an urge to hug these pitiful little children", she writes. "They were beautiful, beautiful! Hot anger surged through me as I listened to the unadorned tales of injustice and segregation. Somehow someone must find a way out of this ugly maze to give them hope for the future. I became absolutely determined at least to make their Christmas Eve a really good one."

She arrived with her young sister Choko late in the afternoon of December 24, 1950, and saw that Zeno and the men had made a cardboard Santa Claus and erected a crib. This primitive crib struck Satoko as touchingly authentic in the wretchedness it shared with the ragpickers' huts. Zeno had made a straw roof above the crib and while he was trying to fix a star on top, his support collapsed and down went the big Pole with limbs, habit and straw flying in all directions. Zeno thought it was a wonderful joke, and so did the whole settlement. Zeno had dressed a dirty, snotty-nosed urchin in an angel's outfit, adding a halo made out of marbles. The Boss's wife, Katsumi, was wrapped in a piece of blue cloth as Mary, and Zeno told her to kneel down in the crib. She was handed a child born some weeks before in Ants Town. Zeno signalled the adults to put their ragpicking baskets on their shoulders and gather around the Mother and Child. Ants Town's inquisitive goat came with them. Zeno was almost in tears of joy, so much was it like the very first Christmas crib that Francis of Assisi, his beloved founder, built in Greccio.

Matsui found the whole thing distasteful but he pretended enthusiasm in the hope of getting newspaper coverage. He wanted Tokyoites to know about the hordes of homeless, and about this successful commune that the city authorities were threatening to burn down. Satoko's clear voice pierced the dark stillness with the first line of "Angels We Have Heard on High". Suddenly a newsreel crew's light came on and a reporter's flash bulb exploded. The goat reared up, terrified. It was calmed down by a ragpicker nicknamed Cliff Face.

The singing finished and Zeno began talking excitedly. "Wonerful, wonerful! This place just like place Jesus came two thousand years before. Just like. This true Christmas— most true Christmas in Japan, maybe most true Christmas in world!" Zeno was never fainthearted in praise and a reporter wrote it all down. But suddenly the big Pole was kneeling on the moist ground. Bowing low he then took his giant rosary in his hand. The ragpickers followed him to their knees and, despite himself, so did Matsui Sensei. As he would write later, he could accept the honoring of an impoverished Holy Family surrounded by the likes of Cliff Face. It was just religionists he could not stand.

Zeno searched in the mysterious folds of his none-too-clean habit, pulled out his ancient watch and said he would have to rush to be in time for a meeting in Akabane. The rising north wind was getting bitterly cold so Satoko ushered the children into a shelter of sorts. As she took out a bundle of *kami-shibai*, cardboard cutouts, to explain about Christmas, the naked electric bulb went out. It was a power failure and the whole suburb was in darkness. "The children all squealed and a sad-faced little lad, Hisa-chan, who was worked unmercifully at ragpicking by his father, grabbed me with his tiny hands and clung tight, calling 'Sensei, Sensei' (Teacher, Teacher). No one had called me anything until then but now they all were calling Sensei and trying to snuggle in next to me. I was deeply touched by this changed attitude. I had prepared a Christmas talk for them with some conclusions about goodness and badness. But now as they nuzzled in close, wanting to be held, I somehow felt my theoretical 'lecture' would be inappropriate."

"What shall I talk to you about?"

"Tell us a story."

"What kind of story?"

"A ghost story", someone yelled. They all took up the call.

Satoko had a fund of Japanese ghost stories like *The One-Eyed Temple Acolyte* and *The Ogre of Rashomon*. Each time she lowered her voice presaging the appearance of a ghost the children squealed and burrowed in closer to her. By the time she had finished she no longer noticed the smell or their sleeves dirtied from wiping runny noses.

Her mother was not as large-minded. She had waited anxiously for her daughter's return and when Satoko appeared ushered her into the living room and brought her hot green tea and senbei biscuits. When etiquette-observant Satoko began rubbing her hair the mother jumped up, looked closely and gasped. Lice! She rushed Satoko to the bathroom, stripped her and washed her all over with warm water and lysol.

Chapter 17

A Family Suicide Contemplated

You can see a change taking place in Satoko in letters she wrote her friends. Not too long after this first Christmas she wrote to a close acquaintance Shizue, who was expecting her first child. Having promised Shizue her prayers for a safe delivery, she wrote of "her own children". "It has become a real joy spending time with these little disadvantaged ones. My heart swells with special joy for your child because I too have come to know the joys of motherhood—thanks to my children in Ants Town."

A letter she wrote to a university classmate Mayumi Ohta gives details of her life since early December when Brother Zeno appeared. This classmate had also received baptism and lived in Ashiya, a suburb of Nishinomiya City, thirty minutes west of Osaka. Ohta-san had no need to take a job but was putting her pharmaceutical degree to good use, regularly driving nuns around the slums in her car and dispensing medicine to the sick. "But I return home, bathe and change into evening dress to attend a Kabuki play or Noh. I sense a painful contradiction in my life, and a gulf, ever-widening, between us and the poor. How, Satoko, are you able to bridge the gap in Ants Town? Is there some medicine to heal this morbid situation? Maybe you can send me the prescription!"

Satoko replied by describing how Brother Zeno responded to what they found not a mile from her home: vagrants sleeping in cardboard boxes on winter nights, children with a tiny square of thin mat in subways, women who have to hire out their bodies to get a meal. "Ants Town is in Sumida Park, which is not a park at all now. After the air raids they used it to dump charred timber and rubble. In places the piled-up rubbish is as high as the railway. People have built huts, some barely 7 feet by 7 feet out of scorched beams, rusted tin and whatever. Brother Zeno's practical concern for the poor is touching. They take advantage of him sometimes and lie to him. He is sharp-witted and knows it, but he never lets on."

She continued: "On one occasion Brother Zeno tried to cheer up a depressed vagrant with a word about Jesus and his Mother. 'Don't give us that garbage. There ain't no Buddha, there ain't no God. Would anyone be in a bloody mess like this if there was?' He shouted this and disappeared into his hut. Brother Zeno went to the entrance and began a patient explanation about God and heaven where our true homeland is. The man's mood gradually changed and I heard him mutter: 'Maybe ya right. If ya say there's a God, well ... I believe ya. So I s'pose I believe God's real.' Then I actually saw big tears, washing the anger from the vagrant's tired eyes."

Tokyo was still in the grip of winter when Satoko went with Zeno to a wartime cemetery near Imado Primary School. The cemetery had been opened to bury the ashes of air-raid victims whom nobody claimed—because they were burned beyond recognition or because the whole family had been wiped out. New victims of postwar poverty had moved into the graveyard and pulled up the thick funeral posts covered with inscriptions from Buddhist sutras and used them as supports for huts they built right on top of the graves! It made Satoko's flesh creep. The Japanese show great respect for the dead but the cold had driven these people to desperation.

Satoko, at Zeno's request, was busily jotting down all she saw and heard. She was surprised when he questioned the dwellers in this ghoulish village built on top of the dead, about what they needed most. She expected them to be odd people, maybe even demented, but they answered politely, just like normal people. Their homes had been destroyed in air raids. They had no relatives who could help them and could find no employment. They told Zeno of the problem of getting water. At first they went with tins to the fishmonger but their number increased to such a degree that the fishmonger, decent though he was, had to refuse them. Now they went to a public bathroom and filled their tins from the washbasin tap. They felt very bad about that.

They told him about the intense cold. Their children were coming down with influenza, and the worst of winter was yet to come. They wondered if Zeno could get them some building material to keep wind and rain out of their huts. A brazier and some charcoal would mean a lot, too. Adequate nourishment was the biggest problem, especially for the children, another added. Satoko noticed some of the children suffered from trachoma. A number of the shanty dwellers were obviously alcoholics and too inebriated to say anything sensible.

Some people turned their backs on Zeno, but Satoko was amazed at the number of people who knew him. In every area, she wrote, one or two would smile broadly and greet him: "You helped me four years ago in Osaka. Thank you." "Thanks for those meals in Kobe." She even noticed tears in some of their eyes. "In this strange new world", she wrote to her friend Mayumi, "I am like a small and helpless child. Brother Zeno leads me all the way."

Long after darkness had settled over the shanty towns one winter night Zeno pulled out his watch, sighed and said he must return to the monastery for evening prayers. He asked Satoko to draw up a report on what they had seen and heard. If they took it to Honganji Temple or the Water Board, or found some official with a specially kind heart, something might be done. He took out a large brown envelope filled with reports that people from the Ueno area had done for him and asked her to incorporate them.

She said farewell to him and went home, tired and cold. The piping hot *o-furo* bath her mother readied for her (after pouring a warm lysol solution over her) followed by a good meal before a glowing gas stove, had taken the chill from her bones. Refreshed and relaxed, she began reading Zeno's wad of reports, beginning with a statement made by a man named Kimura.

Kimura had been a POW in Siberia until 1948 and he was delirious with joy when repatriated to Japan. He hadn't had a word from his family for three years. When he rushed to where his home used to be in Fukugawa near the Sumida, he was stunned. There was nothing—his home and family had perished in the air raids! For months he roamed the streets looking for work. Occasionally he got a part-time job in street stalls. He slept in parks in mild weather and in subways when the rain and cold came. Memories of family life before his military call-up were the one thing that saved him from despair. They had lived in a none-too-elegant industrial sub-urb but how beautiful that home was to him now! He had suffered much during the war, especially in Siberia, but there was no pain as intense as homelessness!

She turned to other reports, growing more disturbed. She suddenly stopped, put everything back in the envelope and told her parents she had to go out again to finish a census in nearby Ants Town. Zeno had told her that many ragpickers returned well after dark. Her parents were quite apprehensive about this. Her father warned her about the dangers of her new way of life but never tried to force his wishes on her. Satoko put on a thick *haori*, the coat-like top that women wear over a kimono in bad weather, and set out for Ants Town.

She passed by the Matsuya department store and walked along Asakusa Doori. Tramps were sleeping in sheltered places on the pavement, covered in matting, cardboard or newspapers. She shuddered at the harsh, broken English of two prostitutes calling after American GIs, with voices as strident as their make-up. Anger surged through her until she remembered the extraordinarily gentle look Zeno had given some prostitutes who tried to chat with him earlier in the evening. Zeno had just whispered to Satoko: "Pray Maria-sama for them", and she did just that as she hastened to Ants Town.

Leaving the main street she went down the slope of the park and was immediately in darkness, walking gingerly over the uneven ground. Passing around great heaps of air-raid debris she walked toward the glow of tiny candles from inside a cluster of low huts. Only the "office" and several huts had electric light. Heads poked out suspiciously. "I was conscious of cold, mistrusting eyes studying me. I felt very unwelcome and ill at ease but pressed on trying to find one particular hut. Its occupant had answered Zeno's question very courteously when they met out in the streets that day. His language indicated education and good upbringing." A possible contact man.

She found the hut. As it had no door she could see inside. Around a single candle squatted a husband, wife and three small children. It was the man all right, and Satoko marvelled at how beautiful his wife was. "*Go-men kudasai mase*", she called out with a bow. "Excuse me please." They stopped talking and looked up at her intently. She explained how she was doing a census for Brother Zeno with a view to finding out how many lived in the area and what they needed most. The father immediately made everyone squeeze closer together in the already crowded hut and insisted that Satoko join them. When he saw her features in the candlelight he said: "I saw you with Zeno-sama and if I'm not mistaken you are the young lady living next to Takagi Wholesalers."

Satoko introduced herself as Kazuko Takagi's sister and asked the man how he knew the Takagis.

He explained how he had a good job in a firm that went bankrupt, and he found himself out of work. The little money put aside in that difficult postwar period soon ran out. No relatives who were in a position to help them had survived the war. Unable to get another job or pay the rent for their lodgings, he and his wife decided that the only course was family suicide. With their last money they would give the three children the best day they could, and die with them that night. They hired a rowing boat on the Sumida and the children had a wonderful time. As the day drew to a close the mother began losing her resolve. The unsuspecting children had never looked so beautiful, happy and precious! When the boat neared the bank she noticed the little huts built on Sumida Park. It was Ants Town. Pointing to the tiny dwellings she said to her husband: "Couldn't we build a hut like those? We have nothing to lose trying just once more!"

The husband agreed, returned the boat to its moorings up the river and led his family in the direction of Ants Town. Along the road he noticed a two-story house, newly built, with leftover lumber in the yard. Their desperate situation overcame his repugnance for begging and he went up to the house. A middle-aged woman opened the front door, listened very kindly and told them to take all the leftover wood they needed. While making a number of trips with the lumber he noticed Satoko and heard her call the woman *O-ka-san*, mother.

He insisted on Satoko having a cup of hot green tea. It was very thin tea but the night was freezing and she appreciated it. He gave her very precise details of the families squatting in the park and of their needs. Satoko returned home very excited. She had prayed hard to the Lord to be shown what to do with her life. She now felt sure Zeno's appearance was the Lord's doing. He had led her to this world of good but destitute people. The husband impressed her as being a man of character, and his wife, despite their poverty-ridden surroundings, had not lost her unmistakable refinement; nor had threadbare clothing affected the children's manners. Meeting them was too much to be a coincidence. It was God himself who had led her to meet them! How many other families were there, driven to the very edge of suicide?

Chapter 18

Storm Warning over The Sumida

Satoko learned a lot from Zeno about helping the poor without demeaning them. When he ran out of food and clothing, he gave them a holy card of the Madonna and Child or at least a warm smile and a kind word. He took her to unimagined backwaters of misery that mainstream citizens knew nothing about. Coming home tired one evening after a day with him, she ran into a crowd of well-heeled people pouring out of the Kokusai Theater. She stopped and watched them chatting away unconcerned. Anger surged through her and weariness vanished. "Don't these people know what terrible things are happening to thousands of poor all around Tokyo?" she wrote indignantly into her notebook that night.

The problem of the poor of Tokyo became a consuming matter for her. She would go down to Ants Town in the morning to help the smaller children, and in the late afternoon gather the older ones in her home. Most had stopped going to school because they were treated as "dirty ragpickers". The few who attended when they weren't made to help at collecting and sorting were terribly behind in everything. She decided that her first priority was to get every child to school. First she would coach them individually until they were advanced enough to face a classroom. She gathered them in her home as there was not a suitable place in Ants Town. Her parents were bewildered but accepted it, though the mother insisted on Satoko's daily delousing in the bathroom and fumigating the piano room used by the children.

Neighbors were far less understanding. They began visiting the *geta* shop to complain to the assistants. "She's letting a vicious little gang of thieves into our neighborhood. Things will begin disappearing any time. They live like pigs, with parents too lazy to clean their hovels or move out of them. We'll be catching their diseases next." Some of the children had trachoma. All had lice. Satoko would hear the complaints secondhand, and her temper would flare up in defence of the Ants. Her mother changed and began to defend Satoko. She remarked caustically how Tokyoites, who helped one another in the grim days of the war, had quickly become so unfeeling toward people still down on their luck, above all toward children.

Many in Ants Town had been living hand-to-mouth for five years now and had despaired of ever again living in a real home or having a decent job. *Shochu*, the strong spirits distilled cheaply from rice, millet, barley, potatoes or even barnyard grass, became one way to drown betrayed hopes. But it was not the answer to their troubles; it caused more problems. Shochu drinking led to fights, sometimes with knives or blunt instruments, destroying friendships and even families. The first fights Satoko saw shook her badly.

Soon after going to Ants Town she noticed Hisa-chan. He was the oldest of the teenagers and a loner. Because his father was very hard on him he suspected all adults, including Satoko. Having learned the sad details of his home life she decided "to become his big sister". Finding him moping in the settlement one day she coaxed him to talk about himself, probably the first adult to do so. When he had finished pouring out years of pent-up loneliness she asked him was there a sport he liked. His dull eyes lit up. "Karate and judo", he replied. "I like judo", she said. "I went to the Kodokan when I was in high school." He was overawed. The Kodokan was the holy city of judo. In the last year of the war Satoko and her classmates were given training in how to throw any US soldier intent on killing or raping them. She had learned one good judo throw. With the nonchalance of a black belt she adopted a judo stance in front of the boy. "May I take you on?" asked Hisa-chan, eyes shining. She replied with mock coolness: "Certainly, but you're asking for a fall!" When he came at her she grasped his hand and threw him neatly. He scrambled to his feet, lunged again and twice more ended up on the ground. "Wow," he conceded, "you are a real judo sensei!"

That evening he came to her home for the first time, but not to study with the others. "Sensei, ready for another bout?" Satoko was rather pleased with her earlier success and putting out her hands gave the judo cry *hajime*, it's on! He shouted, imitating Benkei in the famous battle with the young noble Yoshitsune on Gojo Bridge. The other children squealed in delight. Hisa-chan launched himself in a flying tackle, hitting her in the chest and sending her crashing to the floor. She was dazed and immediately knew she had hurt her back badly.

Her pride was hurt, too. She was furious at being beaten in front of her class! Painfully reaching up she snapped out the light and levering herself on her arms she hoisted herself up the stairs backward! She asked her mother to tell the dumbfounded children to go home as she had wrenched her back. She would contact them when they could come again—which turned out to be over a week later.

The slum children, staggered the first day she invited them to her home, were equally staggered by being dismissed after her exit in pitch-darkness! Hisa-chan, when he realized he had hurt her, was devastated. For once his attention was not fixed on the miseries of his own life. Late each evening when he came in from searching garbage cans, he would park his big two-wheeled cart outside Satoko's house and go around to the kitchen to enquire soulfully how Sensei was doing. Satoko's mother was both touched and amused. Satoko began to see the funny side, too.

A week later Satoko still could not walk properly but she asked her mother to bring the lad up to her room. He came in and sat in formal *seiza* style by her side looking utterly crestfallen. He was trying to say something but was too confused to get anything out. So she spoke: "Hisa-chan, I'm almost better again so stop worrying. I had mother bring you up here because there's something I need to discuss with you. The nuns at Koenji have invited us all to a party in their convent on Easter Sunday. I'm banking on you going, Hisa-chan."

The dumb boy found his tongue immediately: "I'll go for sure."

"Good boy! I'm grateful. I have another request. I think we should contribute something to the party. I want your opinion. Do you have any ideas?" She knew the lad had leadership qualities if only she could get him to begin using them.

Hisa-chan brightened, forgetting his grief because, for the first time ever, an adult had asked his opinion! Still, years of being scolded and silenced by his father with whom he lived in Ants Town, warned him to keep his guard up. "Well...."

"Yes, Hisa-chan, do you have a suggestion?"

He hesitated again and then came out with it. "A play. Let's put on a play!"

"A play, a play? That would be splendid. Could you help put it on?"

The lad could barely control his excitement. His father had once written plays, he explained, and he himself had written children's plays and had acted in plays, on real stages, before his father went bankrupt "and had to leave in a hurry". Hisa-chan became animated, words and gestures flying about as if the cage of his emotions had suddenly been opened.

He assured her he would write a play just for the occasion!
Satoko was dumbfounded: Hisa-chan's surly, bitter father
once wrote plays! Once owned a business!

Two days later the undernourished ragpicker lad came to
Satoko's home wreathed in smiles. On salvaged stationery he
had written his play *Chocho* (Butterflies). It opened in heaven
with God telling "an angel butterfly to go down to earth
and visit larvae who had lain helpless since dark, cold winter
spread gloom over the land". The angel butterfly woke the
larvae to tell them that spring had come. They were now
real butterflies, with wings that would lift them high into
the skies. One by one they blinked, threw off their casing,
"danced about and flew high into the heavens where they
sang in unison: 'Almighty God, thank you, thank you.'"
There were some other bits to it and it was plain to Satoko
that the diminutive playwright was writing about himself
and his "long dark winter" in Ants Town. The word he used
for God was Ten-shu-sama, a Christian word. Hisa-chan
had never before shown the slightest interest in Satoko's
religion.

Eventually the day for the Easter party came: "I rose early
on Easter Sunday morning, March 25, went to Mass and
assembled sixty children from Ants Town and the slums in
Imado and Honganji. The children were excited and went
bouncing along the streets leading to the convent." Mother
Angeles met them at the gates of the school yard, inviting
them to use the swings, parallel bars and volleyballs until
the meal was served. When they were called to the dining
room the children couldn't believe their eyes. A very large
table was heaped with plates of o-sushi, doughnuts, eggs in
brightly colored shells and big glass jugs brimming with milk.
Satoko writes: "The happiness on those little faces brought
an overwhelming rush of emotion. I was just so happy for
them."

Then, like the storm that scattered the harvest merry-makers in Beethoven's *Pastoral Symphony*, disaster struck! An unsmiling foreign priest came in, called Satoko aside, and asked her to point out the Ants children. She did so very proudly but her smile vanished as he said: "Watch them closely and don't give them a chance to go into any rooms by themselves. Kitahara-san, Ants Town is a nest of thieves."

Satoko opened her mouth but nothing came out. She looked up at the priest's angry eyes, shaking her head in wordless plea. "No," he continued harshly, "it's in the papers. I read it very carefully in the English *Mainichi*. Surely you read the newspapers." She had been so absorbed these last three months that she had rarely read the papers—above all the English *Mainichi*! She continues: "I just stood there, hanging my head and biting my lip, not knowing how to reply, terrified that my children would hear what he was saying. Suddenly darkness enveloped everything that was happening here." A grim-faced nun now stood beside the priest and supported his attack on Ants Town. She had seen the newspaper article, too.

At this juncture Mother Angeles came back into the room and began tousling the children's hair, to their delight. She did not appear to regard them as little thieves. The priest delivered a parting blow, telling Satoko to keep a close watch on the children. "Ants Town is in very serious trouble with the police." He said he was prepared to see the governor of Tokyo to intercede for the ones who were going to be picked up by the police. Telling her to inform Matsui of his offer to intercede with the Governor he ordered her to report back to him on Matsui's reaction.

Satoko writes of how the unsympathetic attack on Ants Town by two authority figures "plunged into darkness the whole landscape that had just begun to appear so beautiful and promising.... I had been knocked flat to the ground and

left there, utterly dejected." Only two hours earlier her ela-
tion had matched that of the slum children as they skipped
along the streets for the Koenji convent. Now, without her
saying a word, the little playwright Hisa-chan and his cast
sensed her sudden change of mood. They grew silent and
then came and told her they didn't feel like doing the play!
She numbly nodded. The other slum children became quiet,
too. Without a word being spoken they felt unwelcome and
even threatened. "We want to go home", they said. She did,
too, and led them off.

Satoko still had high hopes of becoming a nun in the Mercedarian Order she admired so much. Once when she asked
a sister what she must do to be accepted she was told one of
the hallmark qualities was obedience to one's superiors. So
now, though it went right against her judgment, she decided
to give Matsui Sensei the priest's message. She felt sure Matsui Sensei disliked her and despised her religion. Confronting
him with the priest's message would surely anger him and
worsen their relationship. Still, it had to be done, decided
naïve Satoko.

It was now dark and a cold wind blew across the Sumida.
The Sensei wasn't in his room but his light was on so she
decided to wait. "I felt quite drained", she wrote, "while I
waited there a long time. I became conscious of a chill, like
ice water along my spine. My head began to spin. I tried to
steady the giddy sensation by crouching down by his door,
pulling my shawl tight against the dampness. He won't be
long now, I thought, determined to get it over and done
with tonight. But things worsened until I knew I would pass
out if I stayed there like that. Regretfully I stood up and
walked home shakily."

Satoko as a schoolgirl

The bronze of Hachiko,
Shibuya, Tokyo

The Mainichi photo of Kamikaze departure, Chiran Airfield, April 1945

Youthful Kamikaze drink a last toast immediately before take-off
for Okinawa, April 1945. (Mainichi photo)

Re-enactment of the times of the Kitahara ancestor priest, 1,000 years ago

The statue of Our Lady of Lourdes, Yokohama (Photo by Hiroshi Fukawa)

Gracia Hosokawa and daughter, Lourdes Altar, Sacred Heart Church, Yokohama

The Moonlight Bodhisattva, Nara

Miroku, the Buddhist "Saviour-to-come"

Miko, shrine maiden,
Kasuga Shinto Shrine

Kannon, a male Bodhisattva, but
characterized by motherly compassion
(Drawn by Rev. Fumon Sagawa,
Priest of Todaiji Temple, Nara)

On the day of Satoko's baptism, 10-20-1949.
With her is Mother Angeles Aguirre.

Polish war orphans, cared for by the Japanese Red Cross, Japan 1921

Post-war Tokyo. A family of three in their hut. (Mainichi photo)

Brother Zeno and a war orphan, off to the Garden of the Holy Mother (Mainichi photo)

Zeno and children of Ants Town

Ragpickers carts and baskets, Ants Town

Satoko checking the Ants Town scales

Satoko and Summertime Ants

Vallade the ragpicker

Satoko and her Ants

われは主のつかいめなり
仰世のめくわれになれかし
エリザベト聡子

Winter photo of Ants Town on which Satoko has written: Behold the handmaid of the Lord

Satoko and Zeno in front of the Lourdes grotto

Painting of Maximilian Kolbe, Auschwitz 1941

マリア・ヴィノフスカ著 岳野慶作訳

Photos of Satoko taken not long before her death

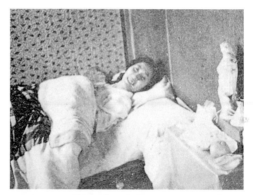

Ragpicker mourners at Satoko's funeral Mass

Tooru Matsui, December, 1988

Satoko's mother and sister (Kazuko) meeting John Paul II

Two old friends, New Ants Town, Tokyo

Satoko memorial card. On reverse side is a prayer for her beatification.

Chapter 19

Duel of a Ragpicker Thief

Her mother took one look at Satoko's ashen face and put her straight to bed. Her temperature was over 102.2°F and stayed that high for days. The young priest, in the meantime, grew impatient of waiting for Satoko to report back to him. He marched off to the settlement and demanded to see Matsui Sensei. It was not the first time the young priest had been there—after the report in the newspaper about building a church there, the Boss allowed him to begin catechism classes for adults. The straightforward, no-nonsense Boss made sure people attended his classes, despite some grumbling. Matsui hated it but went along with the charade in his hopes of more media coverage.

The foreign missionary and Matsui shared almost nothing in common except a mutual dislike. Matsui saw the priest as a camp follower of the US Army that had come to force its will, and if possible its religion, on people it had conquered by sheer material might. The missionary, on the other hand, regarded Matsui as a sham intellectual, a proud and bitter opponent of the Christian faith "that alone could lift Japan up to the level of civilized nations". It was his opinion that Matsui's concern for the poor was an artifice calculated to get himself known.

The priest was now in Matsui's room and opened with a harsh accusation, omitting the title Sensei that everyone else used: "Matsui-san, criminals are being harbored here. Real criminals who by rights should be behind bars! Don't waste any breath trying to deny it. I've read all the evidence."

The foreigner's Japanese was good but Matsui wasn't sure if he understood written Japanese. "What Japanese paper did you read it in?" he asked.

The priest flustered momentarily. "I read it in the English *Mainichi* newspaper. The proof is there, chapter and verse. Modern newspapers, English or Japanese, can't afford to print libel. Don't try to worm out of it. I've come to try to help you people out of the mess you have gotten yourselves in. I will go personally to the governor and try to improve your chances of a more lenient deal. But I'm warning you, I'm a busy man and will leave you to your own foolish selves if you don't give me your word that this place will reform its ways!"

Six months previously, in the latter quarter of 1950, a movie was released called *Ketto no Kawa* (River of Duels), about a ragpicker living on the Sumida who had carried out thefts totalling millions of yen. An article had recently appeared in a Tokyo newspaper claiming that this was a real story, identifying the daring ragpicker thief as Saigyo, a resident of Ants Town. This article was reprinted in the English language *Mainichi*, the daily read by most foreigners. The man who fed the story to an unsuspecting journalist was a crooked scrap dealer who saw the Ants ragpickers' cooperative as a threat to his profits. The remittance he paid the workers he hired on a daily basis contrasted badly with what Ants ragpickers earned. He secured the help of a politician who saw that political points might be gained by having Ants Town burned down and Sumida Park restored.

Matsui immediately confronted Saigyo and discovered he had once been the willing victim of a petty police frame-up. Police officers sometimes improved their statistics and "solved" crimes like minor thefts by arresting vagrants at random and keeping them in cheerless cells until they "confessed". The vagrants had no money to pay in restitution so no one pressed the matter further when police released them. Saigyo had once been picked up in this way by police and cheerfully confessed to a theft when he saw it would get him out of prison without further charges. The streets offered better opportunities than cold cells and awful food. This was his "record" which the reporter thought he verified. The crooked scrap dealer had also bribed a vagrant convicted of real crimes before the war, to name Saigyo as his accomplice.

Matsui Sensei went for twenty-four hours without sleep to ferret out the evidence when Saigyo was named in newspaper articles that followed the movie. He then stormed into the offices of the newspaper concerned and presented the facts. He had no intention of mounting a libel case, he added, if they were prepared to come and see all that was being accomplished in Ants Town and write it up. It was precisely at this juncture that the foreign priest burst in on him with his demeaning offer to help square things with the police.

Matsui's face was flushed. The missionary correctly surmised he had been drinking and despised him for it. If Matsui-san really cared about the poor in this slum, he would not indulge in the extravagance of drinking to excess. Matsui, however, was a lonely man with no intellectual friends in Ants Town. Sake had become a silent friend that helped when the journey was particularly rough. Right now Sensei's eyes were bloodshot from lack of sleep.

Matsui, who had been struggling for some time to compose a formal letter to the newspapers, cursing the rickety fruit box that served as his desk, now looked up fiercely at the foreign priest, despising the pressed black suit and polished shoes. "Do you know much about Buddhism?" he demanded. "Of course I do", replied the priest. He was a very good person, Satoko would say later, sincere, hardworking, clever, kind, and he meant the very best. He had studied Buddhism in his

Western seminary, however, merely to demolish arguments against his own Catholic faith. His professors knew Buddhism from the outside, regarding it as an alien and dangerous doctrine leading to nihilism, fundamentally flawed in not accepting the basis of Western philosophy, Aristotle's principle of contradiction. How could anyone argue seriously with Buddhists who said the first and ultimate principle was *Mu*, which means Nothingness!

These were the days before Vatican II effectively told Catholic seminaries to train foreign missionaries along the lines of the Jesuit pioneer Matteo Ricci. Ricci made sure he understood the language and its nuances before making decisions about Chinese religious beliefs.

Matsui, warming to his favorite hate, organized religion, made uncomplimentary remarks about Christian hypocrites that the priest, not unnaturally, took personally. He responded in kind with unflattering comments about Japanese Buddhists.

Suddenly Matsui's pent-up anger, frustration and resentment toward "glib and Japan-ignorant foreign missionaries" poured out violently like a burst logjam. Fuelled by the dangerous mix of sake and animosity, he peppered his tirade against Christianity with abstruse Buddhist words and phrases that would be incomprehensible to many Japanese! The priest decided he was being made fun of. He interrupted angrily, got up and stomped out. Walking at a furious rate to Satoko's house, he threw the sliding door open with a clatter and called roughly: "*Gomen Kudasai.*"

There was anger in his voice which carried up the stairs to Satoko's room. She recognized the voice, and the anger, with apprehension. Her mother went to the *genkan* and explained that Satoko was in bed with a high temperature. The ideograph for anger is made up of the ideographs for heart and enslaved! The priest was a case in point! Rendered insensitive by what he regarded as just anger he failed to notice the grave concern on the mother's face. He launched into an attack on Matsui, dismissing him as dishonest like the other thieves in Ants Town, and worse than them because of his education and position of leadership. The amount of money involved in Saigyo's robbery made it a very serious criminal affair. The police were bound to come and there would be big trouble. Matsui had met his honest offer of help with a Buddhist tirade. There were too many genuine people about for him to waste any more of his time with that dishonest lot! Satoko was in grave danger of wasting her time and talents, too!

Satoko heard it all. Later she ruefully wrote: "Why, oh, why did I not wait at Ants Town on Easter Sunday night until Matsui Sensei returned? What a mess my softness has now got us all into." She slept badly that night, awakening many times, trying to think of ways to defuse Matsui Sensei's animosity for the foreign priest who was essential if Ants Town and Sensei were to become Christian. Her selfish weakness in not waiting had further jaundiced Sensei's attitude to Christians and probably hardened her mother's prejudice, too.

In Japan people who cannot control their tempers are regarded as deficient in the peace of heart that is a sure sign of genuine spirituality. A religious leader just cannot afford to display tantrums. Satoko knew her mother would be unimpressed by the priest's outburst, and discuss it with her husband. That would be another mark against the Christian faith she prayed they would embrace.

It can be a dangerous thing to be a perfectionist and that is what Satoko was. It made her feel more depressed and guilty as she surveyed all the trouble caused by her softness in not waiting for Matsui Sensei. She decided the only thing to do was to go down to Ants Town first thing next morning and try to clean up the mess she had left behind.

Chapter 20

Night More Lovely Than the Dawn?

At the end of the fitful night she rose and dressed. Despite her mother's protests—it was obvious she still had a temperature—she set out for Ants Town. She writes: "People were returning from a night of ragpicking with cartloads of paper, cardboard and scrap. I went straight to Matsui Sensei's cramped room. He was just finishing a document he had worked on all night, by the look of things. His quarters were submerged in sheets of paper he had started writing on but had crumpled up and thrown aside in disgust. There was hardly anywhere for me to stand. I had to be directly under the roof beam or my head touched the sloping ceiling. Little natural light came in, leaving the corners of the small room depressingly dim. Cracks in the wall were pasted over with brown paper."

He looked up from the mess of documents and Satoko noticed the crimson in the corners of his eyes. He said sharply: "What do you want?" It was not the time for a talk!

"Sensei, I'm sorry to have burst in on you. It's obviously not a good time, and I will come back...."

He cut her short: "Stay. I've something to say to you."

He motioned her to step up from the ground onto the floorboards of his room. She did and they creaked unsteadily under her. He sat on some frayed straw matting beside his box "desk". She gathered her kimono skirts under her insteps and sat on the uneven mat, *seiza* style. At last she was in his den. The foreign priest, who had been coming here to teach catechism until recently had urged her to win Matsui Sensei over. She had looked for opportunities but Matsui had always avoided her. If she cornered him he would ask the time, slap his forehead, say he was late and charge away like an express train. Now she could talk with him—but she was lost for words. Her headache throbbed and the naked electric bulb hurt her eyes.

He began icily: "Kitahara-san, I'll be blunt. I have a great dislike of Catholicism and especially of missionaries. I have found that people who peddle organized religion can be remarkably lacking in honest concern for others. Your priest is just a cheap hypocrite. He came here ostensibly to help people but in reality only to increase his number of scalps. That is why he walked out on us at the first whiff of bad publicity about Saigyo's supposed thefts. He's not genuine. He actually despises the people here...."

Satoko cut in: "There's been a misunderstanding. Father does really care about the people here. I know he cares from his heart."

"Well, he can stop caring! There's nothing we need from him."

"But Sensei, he knows of the eviction threat and intends to go to the governor of Tokyo about it. It is just that the newspaper reports made things look bad to outsiders. He is concerned about that article in the English language press."

"Ah, yes, the English paper report! Of course he, the superior Westerner would no doubt accept a newspaper produced for foreigners but disbelieve us Japanese to our faces!" There was venom in his voice.

"But Sensei, he just said he was ready to make things easier with the law if the report proved to be true. He didn't say he doesn't believe you."

"Look, Miss. If a real crime was committed I'd go straight off and get a lawyer. I've no recollection of asking him to put his nose into our personal affairs. You Christians are full of superior talk about your 'Almighty God', who has given you all the answers in the Bible. Well, why don't you follow your Bible and stop mistrusting people?"

"But surely, Sensei, you can't ask Father to trust everyone here blindly. If, for instance, the charges against Saigyo-san...."

Matsui cut in very sharply with a quotation from an old folk story about Hakuryo that all Japanese read at school. "Doubting others is an earthly vice that is not experienced in heaven where there is no deception." Hakuryo the fisherman rowed back to the beach one day and found a priceless robe hanging on a pine tree. As he grabbed it, calculating the fortune he could make, a supernatural being cried out from the surf, begging him not to steal it. Without it she could not return to heaven. Bewitched by her beauty, he ordered her to dance for him. She said: Willingly, but I need my robe for that. Oh, no, he replied. You'll take your robe and just disappear. She replied sadly, hurt by his accusation doubting her honesty, that people from heaven cannot even contemplate deception. Ashamed of himself, Hakuryo handed the robe back and was rewarded by a dance of ethereal beauty.

Matsui drove home his point: "This is our heritage, Japanese morality and wisdom that has stood the test of time. Your foreign missionary knows none of this. He has neither love nor understanding of us and our ways. He despises us because we were beaten in a mad war and because our economy has been destroyed. I have come to see he has no love for the ragpickers; he actually despises them. Yet he arrogantly claims he has a superior morality with which he has come to save us!"

"Sensei, how can you say he is arrogant, just because he is prepared to go to the authorities to help the ragpickers?"

"Look, get this straight, Kitahara-san. We in Ants Town don't like people who look down on us from on high and offer 'help' condescendingly. We are only interested in people who will come and share our problems and our pain—and drop any 'helping' pose just because they own more material things!"

"So, Sensei, it's wrong to give material things to people in need?" Satoko was dizzy with fever, and her throbbing head was making her say things that didn't help.

He narrowed his eyes and said deliberately and brutally: "Thousands of years of what your religion calls charity have made no difference to the poverty of the world. Yes, rich young ladies like you and nuns in fine robes get bored and take a stroll through the slums, scattering a few leftovers. That's the extent of Christian charity! Were you not sensitive enough to notice the sullen mood your priest and nuns created when they brought that pile of leftover clothing to Ants Town recently? There wasn't a spot of grime or sweat on their expensive 'religious' habits! Do you expect the people of Ants Town to go into rhapsodies when well-heeled professionals give them a few old leftovers that they cadged from some agency? No, the whole thing is a sad charade. Were they genuine followers of Christ they would be poor and share the painful life of the poor. I'll be blunt about you, too. That Easter spread of yours, in a convent school built for children of the rich and costing millions of yen, was equally offensive. You Christians seem to have forgotten Christ's warning about the camel going through the eye of a needle. Surely you don't imagine you are followers of Christ just because you give the poor what you don't need at Christmas and Easter. You people *use* Christ's beautiful life. You cover up your rotten consciences with extravagant vestments and sentimental hymns twice a year—and take credit for solving the poverty of the poor! You in your fine two-story house, you wouldn't have a clue about the misery of people who have to live in destitution 365 days a year!"

"I had been determined", Satoko wrote later, "to take him on point by point to defend the Catholic faith, until that last accusation. It left me speechless. It seemed that Jesus had just spoken to Elizabeth Satoko through this man who was an unbeliever, exposing my pharisaic pride. It was all I could do to get out a hoarse word of apology. The same dizziness that came over me as I waited here in the chill air four nights ago now overwhelmed me again."

Crushed and confused, she prepared to go. He gave her a parting word, and she wasn't sure if it was sarcastic or genuine. "As you know there has been that talk of putting up a church in Ants Town. If you people still want to do that there is a condition. You'll find that condition in 2 Corinthians 8:9!"

She struggled home, too ill to worry about churches or 2 Corinthians. Her mother was alarmed when she took her temperature and immediately telephoned Dr. Tajima as their family doctor was away. The doctor shook his head when he took her blood pressure and ordered her to an x-ray clinic. A hiatus hernia and the beginning of shadows over both lungs showed clearly. Like many wealthy people who could afford maids, the Kitaharas decided to keep their daughter at home when the doctor ordered plenty of rest, nourishing meals and isolation. Her mother said she would nurse her, herself.

In the days before streptomycin reduced the numbers dramatically, tuberculosis was widespread in Japan. Doctors had noted the high incidence of the disease among gifted writers and creative people. Why was this? It had long been recognized that psychological factors influenced TB. Anxiety, depression, fear, etc. could dispose some people to succumb to the invasion of the tuberculosis bacillus. That explained, a number of Japanese doctors held, the high incidence of

TB among writers and poets. They were usually more highly sensitive and so vulnerable to depression in the face of the harsh realities of life. As a price for being able to capture in words the emotions of people and the moods of nature, they tended to suffer more from of the injustices, inequalities and contradictions that abound in human society.

Whether this explanation is correct or not, Satoko went through a period of inner suffering as she lay day after day with nothing to look at but walls and ceiling. Visitors were kept away—the doctor insisted both on the danger of TB infection and on her need of absolute rest. Any heavy reading was forbidden, and Satoko had lost her taste for superficial literature during her journey through the world of the destitute. Suddenly made conscious of the vast need in the slums of Tokyo and Ants Town, she felt terribly frustrated by the doctor's orders to do nothing.

Tending to introspection from childhood, she reviewed her life and felt as though it was a series of unfulfilled and defeated dreams. She remembered her tremendous enthusiasm to work for her beloved Japan, and to fight and die if necessary. Then the disillusionment of the total surrender. She remembered the bitter words of her brother after the surrender: "Life is meaningless. Worse, it betrays you. Those who died in the war were the lucky ones!" In her utter weariness of body and spirit she could empathize with his dejection. And despair? Had she given up on trust in God? The terrible possibility assailed her. No, she was not going to despair, but her faith and love seemed so shallow. Matsui's bitter words echoed in her memory. He had accused her of hypocrisy, of using Christ. Was he right? A dark guilt invaded her mind and robbed her of any peace and comfort.

Though in her dejection she wondered if she really loved God or had just "used" him as Matsui suggested, she was quite sure she felt love for her parents and sisters. Yet she had brought them little but worry. Why had she not been more tactful, more convincing, in explaining her baptism? It had only upset them. Why had she been so hasty and clumsy in explaining why she wanted to enter the convent? Again, she had only hurt them, this time more deeply. "Hasty, shallow, thoughtless Satoko", she upbraided herself. Her family was further from the Christian faith than ever. What a poor disciple of Christ she was.

Then the debacle at the Easter party. Total failure! Over-exuberant when she took the children to Mother Angeles' school, totally deflated when the missionary attacked her. Just no constancy, plain unreliability in crisis. The children were robbed of a chance to put on their play because of that. Far worse in its consequences for the children and Ants Town, her failure with Matsui Sensei. Now he and the priest were sworn enemies! She tasted the bitterness of personal failure and apparent abandonment by God. It seemed to be a purification by what spiritual writers call "the dark night of the soul".

The expression, "dark night of the soul" was first used by Saint John of the Cross, the sixteenth-century Spanish mystic and poet, co-worker with Saint Teresa of Avila in the Carmelite Reform. Called "a Luther determined to wreck Spanish Catholicism" by his former confreres, he so disturbed them that they locked him up in a tiny dungeon in a monastery for nine months. They harangued him continually for his pride and heresy, refused to allow him Mass or Communion and gave him just enough food to stay alive. Physically and emotionally deprived of all comfort, he began to fear he was going to pieces. But he held on to the convictions of his conscience, and clung to his desolate prayer. By a single ray of light coming through an opening high in his cell, he wrote his spiritual autobiography in the form of poetry so true that it continues to stir great souls—like Protestant Dag

Hammarskjöld for instance—to risk all for God. In that near darkness, John of the Cross received from God, experts in mysticism tell us, "the infused light of contemplation". This is a grace given directly by God to souls stripped of reliance on merely rational thinking and human safety, souls totally open to God's will. Before his imprisonment was over, consoled to the depths of his being and overwhelmed by a sense of God's great love for him, John saluted the enforced darkness as his friend and guide: "O guiding night! O night more lovely than the dawn, Uniting the Lover with his Beloved."

The single ray of light that came into Satoko's darkness as she lay almost totally alone for weeks, was the text hurled at her by the cynical Matsui, 2 Corinthians 8:9: "For you know the grace of our Lord Jesus Christ, that though he was rich, yet for your sake he became poor, so that by his poverty you might become rich." Here was an apparent contradiction, an unbeliever challenging her with Scripture. There was a strong antithesis in the Scripture words, too. What was Matsui saying to her? Was he a cynic, or a God-given guide? She struggled with these questions as a Zen novice does with a *koan*. The latter is a seeming contradiction or impossibility, given by the Zen master so that the novice "tastes" the limitation of the rationalizing mind. A *koan* might be: "Picture your face before you were born." The novice is led to see the inadequacy of the human mind and the need of the Absolute—which can only be experienced by the "heart", not grasped by the mind. The ideograph for Zen *satori* (enlightenment) is made up of the ideograph for "self" and "heart".

Satoko simply stopped trying to understand her sickness, her failures, the problems of Ants Town, the way to lead her parents and Matsui to belief. She accepted it all as a mystery beyond her. With blind trust she put everything in God's hands. The peace that came with her acceptance of reality gave her a first deep inkling of Christ's mysterious words:

"Blessed are the poor in spirit, the Kingdom of heaven is theirs", and, "Unless you become like little children you cannot enter the Kingdom of heaven." One of the great modern Zen leaders, Japan's Abbot Yamada Mumon, stated that the essence of Zen *satori*, enlightenment, is contained in those words of Jesus about becoming little children. But arriving at this heart of a child is no childish business. Satoko came closer to this Gospel ideal only after enduring a crucible of suffering. She went through that process of purification of which the Bible speaks in several places as fire cleansing gold of dross.

PART THREE

First Fruits

And God saw everything that he had made
and behold, it was very good.
And there was evening and there was morning.

Genesis 1:31

Chapter 21

The Green, Green Willows of May

"After about a month my temperature dropped back to normal, and the doctor allowed me to get up and walk about the house. Then one cloudless day I went outside and strolled down to the Sumida River with my New Testament as companion. The cherry blossom trees were barely in bud when I took to my bed. For a whole month my eyes had been denied the sight of anything save the drab walls and ceiling of a sickroom. Now, set free again, they drank in the beauty of young green leaves on the weeping willows by the bridge. Forgetting my manners I sat down on the stone steps and marvelled at the lively river scene. A clattering sound interrupted my reverie. A ragpicker who was at least in his sixties had dropped the lid of a trash can and was rummaging inside. He fished out some saleable items and deposited them in the wicker basket on his back. He had found some partly eaten bread and now sat down and contentedly ate it. That sight would have sickened me just a few months ago. I could not have continued looking! But now I found myself fascinated by his honest face—and by my feelings of solidarity with him! He finished the bread and took out a cigarette butt no doubt picked up from the street, and lit up. Light blue smoke curled around his face, softening his pinched features and creating a picture of contentment. Finishing the smoke he rose leisurely and moved off to another trash can."

She felt so happy that her black depression had lifted. There was something else. "Until that day I had thought the ragpickers were to be pitied. Now as I watched this man move away I realized I felt at home with ragpickers and even kinship with them. I was physically well again, and, no doubt that and the cloudless blue sky of early summer contributed to my sense of well-being. I wanted to reach out in love to the dwellers of Ants Town, take their hands and dance. The faces of the children of Ants Town came to me one by one.

"But the sad succession of events came back, too—the Easter that turned sour with the priest's accusations, and the fight with Matsui Sensei. I turned for comfort to my New Testament, opening it again at Saint Paul's words to the Corinthians: 'For you know the grace of our Lord Jesus Christ, that though he was rich, yet for your sake he became poor, so that by his poverty you might become rich.' With a start of realization I stood up. In my pride and insensitivity I had not seen what God was trying to show me. I had thought I was a great Christian because I condescended to dole out some free time, helping Ants children with their homework! To save us, God sent his only Son to be one of us.... He really became one of us! It hit me now. There was only one way to help those ragpicker children: become a ragpicker like them! At precisely the moment that truth took possession of me a child's voice shouted 'Kitahara Sensei!' It was Hisa-chan, returning with his ragpicker cart. 'Sensei, are you better?' 'Yes, today I could get up and go out. And thank you for calling on my mother every day to see how I was doing.... Now I can go more judo rounds with you.' We both laughed.

"A frown came over his face as he told me he and his father were leaving Ants Town. This was his last day's ragpicking. He hoped to make it a bumper load but gestured to the meager pickings. 'Right,' I said, 'let's try to make it a bumper load for your dad. Come with me.' I led him to my sister's wholesale store and explained the problem. Big Sister dropped everything and went through the place, collecting cardboard boxes, straw rope and anything that could be spared. With my mother helping we loaded the cart almost beyond capacity."

Hisa-chan thanked her effusively. She told him she had a farewell present for him and gave him a small Bible. But, she added, she wanted something from him. She wanted to pull his cart. He was amazed but let her into the shafts. When she took hold of them and lifted, they flew high in the air and the back of the cart hit the ground. Pull as she would she couldn't get the shafts down. Two ragpicker children happened to pass by and helped get the cart going. As they moved closer to Ants Town one of them struck up the Christmas carol she had taught them: "Angels We Have Heard on High," and the other two joined in. As they neared Ants Town children heard them and came running out, joining in the singing and cart pushing. Several mothers looked up and called out greetings to Satoko.

As she helped Hisa-chan sort the scrap, Matsui Sensei passed by. "That's not Kitahara Sensei I see, surely!" She bobbed her head in reply and continued sorting. He came up and mystified Hisa-chan by asking her abruptly: "Did you read 2 Corinthians?" She straightened up, looked steadily into his eyes and said yes. His sharp features softened visibly. Bowing graciously he said *arigato gozaimasu*, and disappeared.

The Boss appeared next, wide-eyed to see her with Hisa-chan sorting the scrap. "Ah," he said warmly, "our wonderful young lady is back!"

"Please don't call me that", she replied firmly. "I'm now one of the ragpickers."

He gaped: "You, a ragpicker!"

She nodded, emptied a box of scrap onto the ground and bent down to sort it. When they finished the lad said she could have his wicker basket and cart.

Satoko's father saw her at the back of their home the next day, oiling the cart wheels. Apprehensively he asked: "What are you doing?"

"*O-to-sama*, I'm a ragpicker and this is my cart. I took for my baptism name Elizabeth. She started off doing things for the poor but finally realized she had to become one of the poor to truly help them. *O-to-sama*, I've suddenly realized I was doing things but neglecting people."

Her father never forgot the pain his own father caused him by trying to make him abandon the university, and he had no intention of forcing Satoko to do anything. However he did point out her plan to become a ragpicker seemed impractical and imprudent, given her health. He knew what the doctor would say!

Pentecost Sunday came some days later. Satoko had returned from a sung Mass in Asakusa parish church and just begun breakfast. Two ragpicker children, Yaksuko-chan and Morio-chan, came running to the house calling out for her.

"What is it?" she asked.

"Matsui Sensei wants to see you immediately."

"Why, what's up?"

"It doesn't matter, just hurry up and come."

She finished breakfast quickly and followed them. She had no chance of keeping up. Pausing for breath below Kototoi bridge, she looked down on Ants Town and marvelled at its beauty. Framed by the bridge like a beautiful painting, it reminded her again of a Sesshu landscape.

Suddenly she started. There was a large new building in Ants Town, and on its roof a cross was silhouetted against the clear summer sky. A church in the middle of Ants Town! She remembered Matsui Sensei's words about a church and a cross. This must surely be the work of the Holy Spirit. And today, Pentecost Sunday. She began murmuring the words of the hymn that had been sung at Mass: "Come Holy Spirit,

Lord of light, from thy clear celestial height, thy pure radi-
ance give."

The Boss and Matsui had decided to put up the church all
of a sudden. When talk again filtered through from municipal authorities that they were definitely planning to burn
Ants Town down and reclaim the park, some of the men
began muttering: Over our dead bodies! There were well
over one hundred living in Ants Town now. It was their
only home. If the authorities tried tossing them on to the
streets a number of them would certainly fight. People would
get seriously hurt and the Ants Town experiment would be
doomed forever.

The Boss and Matsui reckoned that even government officials would have to think hard before destroying a place of
worship. For Matsui the church would be a ploy but for the
Boss it would be a spiritual focal point, above all for the children. They contacted Zeno and he was delighted. He had
already put up a number of much bigger buildings. Furthermore he had contacts with lumber merchants who would sell
them building materials cheaply.

They assembled the materials at night and, with all hands
helping, put the building up over the weekend. By the time
angry city officials heard of it, a narrow, eleven-yard-long,
two-story building was up, crowned by a wooden cross. The
top story was a chapel. Zeno put in a simple altar with a
decent-sized crucifix and a plaster statue of Mary. The floor
was of tatami mats with wooden fruit cases to serve as desks
where the children could study and do homework. The
ground floor was mainly a refectory where the ragpickers
could eat together and strengthen community bonds.

Satoko immediately took over the chapel-study room and
fixed times when the children would come along and do
their homework together. She began classes there, too, aimed
at giving them confidence and satisfaction in their study. She

went after school hours to meet their teachers, explaining the unique circumstances and why these children deserved special understanding and help. The Boss made sure every child attended the local school each day.

The Boss had the children assemble each morning for the ten minutes calisthenics program on NHK, the government radio station. Then the children would go up to the chapel for morning prayers Satoko organized. The Boss began joining in and some parents, too.

Satoko next turned her attention to the communal refectory. She told the Boss of deficiencies in the children's diet and how this dangerous situation could be remedied. Many of the children had only one parent, who would often spend the day collecting scrap or sorting it. This left little time or energy for preparing proper meals for their children. The refectory made it easier to improve the diet. Satoko suggested better hygiene, too—not just in the refectory, but with drains, etc. in Ants Town. She didn't rush these changes and made sure it was always the Boss who announced them—and saw to their implementation. Finally she brought up the matter of a bath-house, at least for the children.

Lewis Bush wrote his famous book *Japanalia* to give Westerners a concise, authentic explanation of Japanese ways. There is a section in *Japanalia* entitled "Baths and Bathhouses". It begins: "Probably no other people are so particular about bodily cleanliness as the Japanese, and few of them will go without a daily o-furo (bath) unless they are too poor." He explains the *o-furo*. Japanese strip in an anteroom, enter the spacious bathroom and, sitting on a wooden stool beside the bath, dip piping hot water from the tub, soaping and washing themselves thoroughly. With all the grime and soapsuds washed off they get into the deep bath and soak like the ancient Romans. It is a very leisurely and relaxing affair—and so important that the famous Japanologist, Edwin O.

Reischauer is reported as saying the *o-furo* has had a profound beneficial effect on Japanese history! There has always been tension in Japan, with so many living on the small habitable area. Japanese cities and houses are unbelievably crowded by Western standards and people have traditionally worked long hours. But each night almost everyone, without any class distinction, can have a totally relaxing hour in an *o-furo*, coming out feeling as expansive as a Roman senator. In recent years public *o-furos* have been disappearing as people have been installing o-furos in their own homes.

An *o-furo* seemed an impossible luxury when people first built their shanties in Ants Town. So the adults and their children got used to being dirty all the time. Lice proliferated. These factors widened the divisions between them and ordinary citizens. The children were teased at school and left. Satoko persuaded the Boss to build a small bathhouse. A large gasoline drum, cut from top to bottom, made two baths when laid sideways and heated on a wood fire.

Satoko organized bath times for all the children, bathing the littler ones herself if their mothers were out ragpicking or sick. Quite a few children had trachoma or skin infections and she would wash them separately, using disinfectant and ointment. When older children misbehaved in the bathhouse she was known to establish order with well-aimed buckets of cold water.

There was much sickness in Ants Town. The hard years during the war had impaired people's health. Unsanitary huts and lifestyle worsened the situation. Satoko spent much time helping the sick and visiting the ageing. Gradually the resentment many had felt toward the wealthy stranger disappeared. One mother told of how her own resentment dissipated. She was looking out her window at some of the children trying unsuccessfully to move a very heavy cartload. Satoko happened along and they asked her help. She put her shoulder to the cart until it was out of the rut. She said good-bye to the children with a bright smile but, when they had gone, leaned dizzily against a fence, close to the unobserved mother. Satoko's sickly color and the pain on her face told the secret onlooker that this was no rich girl dabbling in Ants Town because she was bored. She was here because she loved their children. From that day the woman became Satoko's staunch ally.

Chapter 22

The Reluctant Ragpicker

It was good to have a study room but the only desks were fruit cases they had salvaged. She threw out some hints about real desks and prayed. One evening Morio-chan, annoyed by the way his box wobbled, said something she'd been waiting to hear. "Why don't we go out and collect enough scrap to buy desks?"

Satoko writes: "I had come to change my fastidious ideas about collecting scrap from trash cans. It not only provided a living for people with no work but actually helped the national recovery, saving preciously scarce materials. Something I once saw as dirty took on noble qualities! I responded to Morio-chan with enthusiasm: 'That's a great idea. Yes, let's do that. I shall go out with you.' Morio-chan's eyes lit up. 'Right, let's go and start now!' The other children chorused approval."

The children collected shoulder baskets and carts not in use. Satoko told them to "go on ahead. I'll follow". At this stage of her life she still dressed in a tasteful kimono and now she rationalized that it would be ostentatious if she went along like that with the ragtag ragamuffins and their grubby carts. She would collect scrap alone. She hadn't gone very far when she saw in the gutter a piece of rice-straw rope. That kind of rope was commonly used in those frugal days. She wanted to pick it up but a thousand years of genteel breeding bound her hands! After stealing a glance left and right she bent down, snatched the rope and shoved it into her *tamoto*, the ample sleeve-pocket of her kimono. She writes: "I didn't have the courage to pull a cart. Even with the rope hidden in my sleeve I ran home in embarrassment! I forced myself to venture out for several more forays until I found a length of straw rope that would not fit into my sleeve! I bent and grasped it, straightening up to find the eyes of a next-door neighbor looking straight into mine! I felt cheap and embarrassed, and knew my face was crimson. I retreated into prayer, silently calling out Maria-sama! In that instant of prayer I was freed of false human respect. I went straight back for a cart to pull on the streets. As I went, Maria-sama's words of response to the angel came to me, bringing deep peace: 'Behold, I am the handmaid of the Lord, let it be to me according to your word.'

"I worked with my cart from the Shoten area down to Hanakawado where I knew footwear wholesalers would be cleaning up at sundown, maybe throwing out straw rope and packing. From there I went along the river bank and doubled back on the other side of the street behind the Matsuya Department Store. I found myself lifting the lids of rubbish boxes and getting excited like the children when there was saleable scrap. I joined up with the children's carts and together we collected three cartloads, worth over 100 yen." The basic wage of a laborer in 1951 was 240 yen a day.

That night she set out again with the bigger children, crossed the Kototoi bridge and did the round of garbage boxes on Mukojima. All they found was thrown-out food. Adult ragpickers would sometimes eat such food but the children had been strictly forbidden to do so. With their weaker constitutions they might get sick. Disappointed, she led the children further afield until they were passing along strangely narrow streets. Gaudily dressed women with heavy make-up stood outside narrow doors calling out to passersby. Some intoxicated men walked uncertainly down the street from the opposite direction and blocked Satoko and the children. They spoke to her roughly and one reached out to maul her. The children screamed and Satoko led them away as fast as their legs and cartwheels would go. Matsui Sensei later heard them telling their breathless tale and for a change roared with genuine laughter, teasing Satoko good-naturedly for visiting Hato no Machi, a red-light area.

Satoko continues: "When I've made a mess of something I have no peace until I've corrected the thing. Several days later I set out in the early evening, crossed Kototoi Bridge and went along the eastern bank of the river. Nothing doing. I tried rubbish boxes in the factory area. Again I drew a blank. It was now 11:00 P.M. I decided on one more run and came across a rubbish box full of cotton strips that had been used as oil rags, and filled my cart. I pulled the cart back to Ants Town and was thrilled to discover the cotton brought a worthwhile price."

In her university student days, says Kazuko her elder sister, Satoko became a spendthrift if there were good plays or movies around. When she had used up her own allowance she would brazenly ask Kazuko, married to a successful footwear dealer, for a "loan". The sister never refused and never expected to get the money back from this prodigal of whom she was very fond. When Satoko made the decision to throw in her lot with the ragpickers, however, she resisted any temptation to ask for financial help from her family. The only way to help the children was teaching them self-reliance.

A friend of her father's had a factory that produced *wagashi* confectionery, exquisitely fashioned to look like maple leaves, chrysanthemum flowers, etc. and used at *cha no yu*, the traditional tea ceremony. The *wagashi* maker was intrigued that the professor's daughter was on the streets with ragpicker children collecting scrap to buy desks. He heard donations were not acceptable but telephoned Satoko to say he had good clean scrap paper. As it meant several hours walk each way, she was offered their train fares. She refused and led her small friends to the factory on foot.

Chapter 23

Stars Shining in Muddy Pools

"I knew from my own childhood", wrote Satoko, "that if you hand in homework that has been well done you win praise from your teachers and respect from your fellow pupils. You feel good and enjoy school." This was the problem with the Ants children. She had most of them attending school now but they were so behind the others that teachers treated them with sarcasm and classmates followed suit. Satoko intended to use the summer vacation to remedy this situation.

The children brought home their summer assignments. Satoko groaned. They had to do essays and projects about the mountains and the sea. The Ants children had never been as far as mountains or the sea! There was only one thing to do: take the children to the mountains and the sea. She called on the travel section in the Matsuya Department Store.

Japanese railways and travel agencies always display beautifully executed posters highlighting the beauties of nature at the various resorts. Satoko was captivated by a poster of Lake Ashi-no-ko, a lake in Hakone, with a reflection of majestic Mount Fuji setting off its serene beauty. That's it! Take the children there for several days and swing east to Odawara and the seaside. The clerk took an abacus and calculated bus and train fares at six thousand yen, well over five hundred dollars in today's Australian currency.

She told the children her plan and they became wildly excited. "But we'll have to collect six thousand yen's worth of scrap to pay the fares."

"We can do that", they shouted back.

Satoko the romanticist went blithely off to see Matsui the cynic. He was sitting glumly under a willow tree on the river bank. She outlined the plan without drawing breath.

"And if you can collect enough scrap to pay the fares—which I doubt—where will you stay in the mountains?"

"Why, we'll sleep under trees. It's summer—no ragpickers worth his salt would mind that!"

"You'd better improve on that", he muttered sarcastically. "Don't you realize they are only children!"

The bourgeois girl's face went red. She was stung by his undisguised scorn for her naïveté. His attitude softened, however, as he reflected on what it could mean to the children. "I have a friend with a summer house in Sengokuhara that is often empty. He may put everyone up ... if the children can raise six thousand yen for fares!"

She walked home sombrely reflecting on raising six thousand yen. Some adult ragpickers made little more than one hundred yen a day! She went straight to her room and knelt before the statue of Mary. "Dearest Mother, forgive me if my pride and hastiness has gotten the children excited about an impossible plan. Let me suffer whatever I should over this but please, Mother, get the children to the mountains and the seaside."

She went early the next day by steam-train to the Hakone tablelands and alighted at Sengokuhara where the air was clear and cool after muggy Tokyo! Matsui's friend was charmed by Satoko. Yes, she and the children could have the house for several days from August 11. That gave them three days—tomorrow was August 8!

A telephone message waited for her at home from another friend of her father, also intrigued that the professor's daughter was helping slum children collect scrap. He had a big pile of empty tins at his dairy foods factory. She could have them after the factory shut down at 10:00 P.M.

The Boss readily gave her three big carts and, despite the late hour they would return, she and the children found willing adult helpers. One was a diminutive adult ragpicker who was a hunchback. When he stepped between the shafts of a big cart Satoko's mother, who had accompanied her, was moved and said she was going too.

The factory was some two miles to the south. They arrived back late that night sweating from pulling three loaded carts, but excited. There were at least eight more cart loads of empty tins. They collected six more loads the next night and went early the third day before the factory opened and collected the remainder. The top quality tin was weighed and was sold for precisely six thousand yen! The children were jubilant.... Satoko believed it was the intervention of God. Her mother and the Boss, who did not share Satoko's Christian faith, were nevertheless impressed.

By 5:00 A.M. on August 11, 1951, ten excited children assembled in the faint light outside the Kitahara home. Accompanying the children and protesting at the ungodly hour was a ragpicker whom the Boss decided to send along. He was a year younger than twenty-two-year-old Satoko, and a little eccentric, but she welcomed the addition of his strong arms and back. As they set out he burst into popular songs from the Takarazuka Ladies' Revue. People stopped to gape at him and the motley band, but Satoko was no longer troubled by people's stares.

Their train was rushing along the Hakone tableland by late morning. The children squeezed past each other at the windows, letting the cool air tousle their hair, marvelling aloud at the great stretches of land with wild flowers, instead of the greasy slum streets they knew. Before noon the children stood before a house that seemed more like a palace. Slum-dulled eyes drank in the cool moss garden with its finely trimmed trees, carefully positioned rocks and winding path of sunken stones. One thousand years of practice have taught the Japanese how to create gardens that are truly microcosms, with tiny replicas of seas, mountains, rivers, forests and plains. This was the first such garden these disadvantaged children had seen.

They stood there, spellbound, until one of them broke the silence with a hushed: "It's like a castle from a fairy tale." Satoko led them through the gate and up to a ponderous front door made of dark oak. "Maybe a wizard lives here," said daydreamer Gen-chan, "and we can only get in if we know the magic word." Yoshi-chan stood on tiptoe to look through the glass window in the door and shrieked: "There's a wizard's cave inside!" Satoko looked over her head and saw it was a big open fireplace. The children had never seen one. Gen-chan spotted the stove. "Look, the oven that the wicked lady from the woods stoked to cook Hansel and Gretel in!" Yoshi-chan squealed: "*Hora!* This is the house made of bread, thatched with cake and barley sugar for windows!" Their emotionally starved imaginations had fed ravenously on the fairy tales she had told them.

They went in and Satoko switched on the light. It was a chandelier suspended from a chain and startled the children. "Aladdin's lamp!" cried Gen-chan. "Aladdin's lamp, Aladdin's lamp I'm hungry. Make me food by your magic." Children began opening the food knapsacks.

"Wait", said Satoko, "we must put the magic castle in order first." She slid back the heavy storm doors on the wide verandahs and sunlight came flooding in. She unpacked "Japanese flag" lunches, flat rectangular containers of white rice with a bright red pickled plum in the center. It all soon disappeared as they used their chopsticks.

Japan is a geologically young country, emerging from the sea about sixty million years ago. Nature has not had time to settle down. Earth tremors are frequent, but one happy result of this ongoing geological activity is the number of hot spas.

These provide relaxation and natural healing for the millions of Japanese who patronize them the year round. Sengoku-hara where Satoko and the children now were, was famous for its hot sulphur spas. She handed everyone a *te-nugui*, the small cotton towel that Japanese use to dry their glowing bodies after sitting almost submerged in a piping hot *o-furo*, and set off down the hill to a public spa bathhouse.

They went into separate baths for males and females, with a nine foot high wall in between. The children stripped, soaped themselves thoroughly outside the bath and threw bucketfuls of hot water over themselves until they were clean. Then they stepped into the huge baths that were two feet deep and large enough to swim in. No one else was there. The running hot spa water filled the place with steam and the sensation of being part of an exotic fairy story subdued the girls. The boys, however, began to swim and soon started a water fight, shrieking and whooping until Satoko's voice sounded: "Right, that's enough. Calm down, get out and dry yourselves or I won't take you up Mount Kintoki."

They left the bathhouse and moved across the wooded northern slopes of Mount Daigatake, with majestic Mount Fuji in the distance. Satoko marvelled at how the leisurely soaking had changed the children's looks. Little fingers "glowed like the tips of maple leaves in autumn". Tall, straight cedar and cypress trees along the track thrust themselves up against the high summer sky and cast cool shadows at their feet. Small legs scampered faster and faster as the top of Mount Kintoki came closer, leaving Satoko puffing in the rear. They reached the summit, about two miles above sea level. The usually garrulous Ants were constrained to silence by the wonder of the scene below them. To the west was the vast Sengokuhara Plain covered in waving susuki, the Oriental cousin of pampas grass. To the south Lake Ashi shimmered in the strong sunlight. Way below them were tiny knots of buildings, faint wisps of steam rising from ubiquitous spa bathhouses.

Time stopped as slum-dusted lungs inhaled mountain air and dulled eyes were washed bright by undreamed of beauty on every side. The children lay on their backs and looked up at the bright sky and the smaller ones fell asleep. But nature never dozes. Suddenly the mountains echoed with distant thunder and heavy clouds came scudding across the sky, darkening by the minute. *Hora*! A *yuu-dachi*, a summer storm! "Quickly, back to the house before the rain", Satoko cried. A closer rumble of thunder sent tiny Katt-chan's arms around Satoko's legs. The singer turned into a samurai who must lead the survivors back to the castle through enemy lines. Satoko smiled to see how the deprived children loved this make-believe and tore off after him, imitating his Bushido calls.

The rain came before they reached their destination. Being caught in a summer shower was nothing new for the ragpicker children. "Shout the magic formula 'ninja jinja' and these enemy arrows cannot harm you", cried the "samurai". The children repeated the words and stood mocking the rain with wild laughter and gesticulations, enjoying the sensation of rain on hot bodies. The magic words, however, did nothing to protect the firewood left in the backyard where they planned to do the cooking. The song singer-samurai could coax little but smoke from the wet wood, and he sent the children searching for dry pine cones. It was a very long time before he had a fire going.

Satoko, like other young ladies in wealthy homes with maids, had rarely lifted a finger in the kitchen. She did not know you put noodles into the pot after the water was boiling. She put the noodles in a pot of cold water and set it on the fire. When she poured off the boiling water, the children peered into a mess of glue-like stuff. She tried to redeem it with sardines and lashings of soya sauce, but she didn't fool the children. Suddenly it dawned on them that this rich girl, whom they regarded as a princess, couldn't cook! They laughed and made outrageous jokes about what the mess might be.

Long after bedtime ten drowsy children slipped between light futons and thin mattresses on the tatami floor. Within minutes they were sound asleep. She tiptoed in to look at them and wrote: "There they were, each so different. Megumi, who never listens, Morio, the stubborn one, Yak-suko who loves mischief, Shizuo who is spoilt, Katt-chan the crybaby. Children who have seen trouble and could end up in much more trouble. Yet now, with their little hands open in sleep, and tiny Akira snuggled into his sister's arms, they are truly beautiful and even holy." She knelt and asked God to guide these children and their mothers and fathers in the difficult times ahead, and one day home to himself in heaven. She asked him to guide her, too, and open a way to the convent.

She fell asleep but jumped up when Yoshi-chan called out in his sleep, *O-ka-chan*, Mother! His mother died last year. As Satoko lay awake she remembered a scene from her own childhood. It was late afternoon and her big sister Kazuko had scolded her for something. She ran out of the house crying, running to the end of the gravel path, where there was a bed of portulaca. They were so beautiful in the golden light at the end of the summer's day that she forgot her tears and the scolding. Who taught her to turn to nature for reassurance? She did not remember, but she must teach the little Ants to do so—to look beyond the trash that surrounded them in Ants Town and discover the hidden beauty everywhere—even in the sky and stars reflected in dirty pools of rainwater at their feet. Neither the squalor of the slums nor the death of a mother would turn them to despair if they learned to find that beauty and its source.

Chapter 24

When the Dam Broke and Poor Zen Laughed

Several weeks later the Boss ordered all parents to come and inspect the children's display. There were crayon drawings of Mount Fuji, Odawara seascapes, a startling black and white sketch of lakeside reeds, and neatly written essays about the mountain climb. The parents had come grumbling but were now visibly impressed.

The Boss harangued them: "I had to drag you here tonight. I heard some of you admiring the exhibits and wondering aloud why your children hadn't told you about these things before. They wanted to tell you but you were too busy to listen, too busy drinking sake or gossiping about other people! Satoko Sensei came here nine months ago and has done nothing but good for our children. The trip to Hakone and Odawara beach has worked wonders for them. Under her leadership they paid their way on a wonderful excursion that has helped their schoolwork. We adults have to learn from her and them. If we plan and work together we can make Ants Town a heaven on earth!" He looked fixedly at each one of them. Many of the faces were red from imbibing cheap sake after a day of ragpicking.

He continued: "We have to give a lot more thought to the kids and their future. Satoko Sensei is leading the way by example. We have to give her a lot more cooperation." Suddenly tears began flowing down the Boss's cheeks, which startled the ragpickers! Matsui was surprised, too: the Boss, who was tough enough to stand up to Yakuza, had fallen under her spell! He was sure he would not let that happen to him. He tolerated her here because of the media coverage she was attracting. A number of newspapers and weekly magazines had done articles on her—which made it harder for the authorities to destroy Ants Town.

In September Satoko and the children announced they were hosting an outdoor party for everyone whose birthday occurred that month. The Boss ordered everyone to attend it, and most did. It began with a little play performed by the children. Satoko announced the next item as a *nodo jiman*, a solo song contest, and before they realized it, a number of adults had been talked into performing. Children applauded their parents loyally and urged more to join, some of whom were well-fuelled with *shochu* spirits. Satoko had a word of praise after each song, and a joke. Genuine laughter was being restored to Ants Town.

October is the month when Japanese schools and companies hold an *undokai*, a fun sports day. Satoko dropped the seed of this idea and before the day was out the children were begging the Boss to help hold one for them. Caught up in their enthusiasm, the uncomplicated man agreed. The cantankerous Rocky heard about it and went off to Matsui Sensei's room, complaining and hoping for a free drink. Matsui was in a bad mood and expressed irritation at the influence the rich girl was having. "Anyhow", said Rocky, "there won't be any adults there. They have better things to do."

Satoko and her little helpers set to and with help from the Boss pegged out a circular course on vacant ground. The Boss bought them balloons and paint for the markers. Rocky was at work, too, cajoling parents into drinking bouts and extracting some tipsy promises of a boycott.

Sunday dawned into what the Japanese call *aki-biyori*, a cloudless autumn day. Long before anyone had time to begin drinking cheap sake or moonshine, Satoko and a band of well-scrubbed children appeared before each hut. They bowed deeply, announced all was ready, begged everyone to attend, and bowed deeply again. Rare is the Japanese who can remain unmoved by a genuine *o-jigi*, the slow deep bow! Promises to Rocky dissolved and they all turned out—including Rocky when he saw the numbers were against him.

The children marched in to the arena to scratchy popular tunes from a beat-up gramophone someone had found. Their races began and the parents cheered. Then it was time for the fun races. Adults and children had to start together and run to a point where they received a sealed envelope with instructions. Even Matsui laughed when a red-faced housewife opened her envelope and came galloping up to Rocky. Grabbing his hand she shouted: "Quick, we have to pull a cart backwards up to the tape." In the next event Zen's wife, built for endurance rather than speed, found herself hustled on to her feet and struggling to pull a cart loaded with shrieking children. People did not know what terrible things had happened to Zen during the war, but he never laughed or even looked happy. However as he watched his wife's flushed cheeks pumping in and out like bellows, the dam inside him suddenly broke and laughter came cascading from his mouth. He was still laughing at the end of the day. Rocky, mellowed by generous servings of other people's moonshine, declared it was the best day they had ever had in Ants Town.

Chapter 25

Ari no Machi no Maria—Mary of Ants Town

The parents agreed with the Boss: they could do nothing better than entrust their children to Satoko Sensei. The Boss asked her to draw up a definite program for the children that would include daily prayer and church on Sunday. The rules decided on were as follows: (1) All children will attend daily morning prayers with Satoko in the little chapel. (2) All will attend school daily. (3) All will go to Mass with her at nearby Asakusa church every Sunday. As it was still summer, morning prayers would begin at 6:00 A.M. except on Sundays.

In the middle of September Satoko was absent for several days on family business and in her absence a fight erupted during a sake bout. A woman burst into Matsui's room: "Quick, Sensei. They're at it again. Naoki has a kitchen knife. Come and stop him before he kills my husband." When Matsui got there, a drunken Naoki was maneuvering the other toward a corner. Matsui roared an order, stepped in between them and demanded the knife. The blade flashed and cut him twice before he could disarm Naoki. The small crowd that had gathered was shocked to see that Matsui, who had left his home and job to become their adviser, was bleeding. Naoki, seeing their menacing looks, dashed out of the hut and dived into the murky Sumida. Naoki's wife stood there, white and shaking, with their children, Kii-chan and Katt-chan, who were crying hysterically.

Matsui's cuts weren't bad and he felt more disappointment than anger. The Boss was adamant: the Naokis had to go. But where? That was their business. Naoki's wife was given until tomorrow morning to be out with her children and their belongings. Satoko arrived at that moment and pleaded their cause, but to no avail.

At morning prayers the next day she and the other children offered their prayers for the outcasts. When they finished praying she called the two miserable children to the front and all sang *Hotaru no Hikari* (*The Light of Fireflies*), the Japanese equivalent of *Auld Lang Syne*. She handed the two holy cards of the Madonna and Child. "Keep these with you always, no matter where you go or what you do. If you are ever in trouble come back here and talk it over with us your friends." Just then a fierce September rainstorm burst over them with a deafening noise on the tin roofs. Satoko studied the two little faces gazing out at the storm with utter melancholy. She felt melancholic, too. How could the drunkenness and fighting be stopped?

It was Sunday Mass in Asakusa church some weeks later, and Father Chiba was preaching on the government-sponsored Red Feather Community Drive for the needy. All over the country every autumn groups of collectors would stand on busy streets with Red Feather boxes slung around their necks soliciting donations. As they walked back after Mass, Satoko said to the children: "Wouldn't it be wonderful to join in the Red Feather Drive!"

"What", responded Toshi-chan, "and go around the streets with a box around our necks! Cut it out!"

"No", she replied. "Pulling our carts. Collecting scrap to make money for the drive. It could be great fun. Think of all the sick children and old folk we could help! We made six thousand yen for our fares on the summer excursion. What if we try to double that and raise twelve thousand yen for the sick and the feeble. I'm sure we can do it over a month!"

"We can, we can", several replied. Even cautious Toshi-chan was caught up in the excitement.

Satoko asked the Boss's permission. He agreed and later said to Matsui: "She's a born teacher and everything she does is so simple! She's teaching the children how to be happy by forgetting themselves and working for people worse off. We must help them!" He found Satoko and the children scrubbing their scrap carts clean and said: "I'll be back in a little while with paint so you can make your carts really beautiful." The children cheered. By nightfall each team had painted its cart in gaudy colors. Immensely proud pullers and pushers were on the streets the next day, Monday, after school.

Adult scrap collectors made one hundred yen a day without killing themselves but it would be a real feat if these small ragpickers could make twelve thousand yen over a month. Being children they grew bored and sick of it some days, especially when they worked till after 9:00 P.M. without collecting much. Satoko talked one adult into going with each team. She herself kept switching to the worst teams and their enthusiasm would revive as she hurried ahead and dug up to her elbows in garbage cans.

Matsui made sure the media knew about it and photos and articles duly appeared in the newspapers. One reader who was impressed was the Governor of Tokyo. When Governor Yasui learned they had raised the twelve thousand yen by the end of the month, he invited Satoko and the children to hand the sum over to him in his prefectural office. He informed the media, and reporters crowded his office to take photos and write articles.

One reporter who was quite captivated by Satoko saw her as a princess who had become a Cinderella. To get more information on her he went to Ants Town and asked different ones about her. He discovered that devotion to Mary was very special in her life and in the prayers she taught the children. There were always fresh flowers before Mary's statue in the chapel-study. Whenever there was some special need she took the children up there to say the Rosary. When his article came out it carried the headline: *Ari no Machi no Maria—Mary of Ants Town.*

The name caught on. From then on whenever reporters wrote about her work they always called Satoko Ari no Machi no Maria. By the time she died not many years later, there was hardly an adult in Tokyo who did not know of Ari no Machi no Maria. Within a year of her death Japan's premier cinema company would make a movie about her life, making Ari no Machi no Maria known across the nation.

In Japanese Buddhism probably the most popular bodhisattva is Kannon. A bodhisattva is like a saint in Catholicism for whose intercession people pray. According to orthodox Buddhist teaching all bodhisattvas are male. However, over the centuries, the images of Kannon, and they can be seen in every town and village, have taken on female features. The common people find in Kannon a bodhisattva of motherly compassion. The old legends tell of Kannon coming down to assume the identity of suffering devotees in order to lead them to salvation. Kannon has even become a member of a robber band in order to lead the robbers to eternal salvation. The reporter who called Satoko the Mary of Ants Town appealed to something deep in the Japanese religious psychology. Though only 1 percent of Japanese are Christians, Satoko began to take on the rare status of a religious cult figure—especially after her early death among the ragpickers.

Satoko gained great satisfaction in watching the children as they handed the twelve thousand yen to the Governor. They had grown so much in confidence and unselfishness. However the month collecting had cost her much. Sometimes she would arrive before 5:00 A.M. to finish sorting and weighing scrap collected the night before, and organize that day's teams. She would lead the children in radio calisthenics and morning prayers. After breakfast with the children she would help with their homework and see that they were all ready for school. Then she would go around visiting the sick and the feeble in Ants Town. When the children arrived home from school she would go out collecting with them, often until late. There would be the sorting, weighing and tallying and she might not get home until after midnight. Her meals were often skimpy and sometimes missed. Toward the end of the Red Feather campaign, Matsui heard a story from one of the parents that worried him. Children had been sworn to secrecy by Satoko but ended up telling him.

Late one afternoon when she was pulling the heavy cart while the children filled it with scrap, she stumbled and fell on the ground. The frightened children asked her what was the matter but it was some time before she could speak, her face terribly white. When she finally managed to say she was all right, they said she should go home and lie down. She replied: "We are doing something special for Jesus and his poor. Everyone has worked so hard that there is no need to worry. Mary our Mother will certainly keep me going. Just one thing: promise me you won't talk about this to anyone. They will only worry and we shouldn't make people worry! Come on, off we go. We'll get that twelve thousand yen yet." She smiled beautifully, the child said, but looked very sick.

Her family offered to make up the shortfall of the twelve thousand yen but she politely refused, saying it was essential that the children be allowed to collect it all. In November she looked so unwell her mother brought the doctor along. He was alarmed, ordered her to bed immediately and said she should go where there was clean mountain air for total rest. When Matsui heard the news he felt guilty at the way he had used Satoko and set out to see her.

Chapter 26

Death Row, Manila

Satoko's mother met Matsui at the *genkan*, showing no sign of the resentment he expected to meet, and took him up to Satoko's room. Despite her sallow color her eyes were bright as she handed him a letter. It was from a Hiroichi Horiike in the Philippines, who explained how he had been a member of the Japanese Imperial Navy during the war. After the surrender he was falsely accused of atrocities, tried as a war criminal and sentenced to death with sixty-nine other Japanese. He now awaited execution at Muntinlupa Prison, on the outskirts of Manila.

He had studied the Christian Faith while in prison and received baptism. Like her, he now believed in a God who knows everything, and he had put himself in his hands. Knowing he had committed no crimes he was not afraid of death and was at peace. But one thing had been disturbing him greatly. Reading Japanese newspapers they received, he was shocked by the increasing murder, robbery and chaos in postwar Japan. Then he came across an article in *The Sunday Mainichi* about Satoko's work in Ants Town. "Reading about you dispelled my gloom and brought peace back to my heart. You are in my grateful prayers every single day. You make it worthwhile for me to die for Japan."

Matsui finished the letter and remained silent. Satoko said: "Sensei, I was feeling sorry for myself, preoccupied with my own sickness, when this letter came. Sensei, we must do something to help that young navy man and try to save him from execution. I feel sure he is not lying about his innocence in the war. Will you help me?"

Matsui's initial reaction was negative. Satoko saw this. "I've wanted to tell you this for some time," she said, "and now it's the right time. Will you hear me out?" He nodded.

"The Mercedarian Sisters where I studied for baptism told me the origin of their name. Mercedarian means Mercy. Seven hundred years ago a Spanish nobleman, Saint Peter Nolasco, began the Order of Our Lady of Mercy to ransom Christian slaves from the Muslims. They took a vow to do everything possible, even becoming Muslim slaves themselves, to ransom captives. Many ended up as galley slaves on Muslim ships.

"The Mercedarian Sisters are a modern order who take a vow to spend their lives helping others save their souls. I think it must have been very hard for the Spanish and American sisters at Koenji to leave their own land and family and come to Japan to help us save our souls. That's why I respect them so much. I wanted to join them but they told me I am not healthy enough. But I am trying to live their spirit. I intend to write to the President of the Philippines, pleading for the life of Horiike-san. I will tell him I am prepared to go and work for the war orphans and war widows in the Philippines if there is a place for me there."

In a book he wrote about her after her death Matsui said this conversation was a great turning point in his life. Until then he had regarded her Christian faith as something shallow, based on the passing attraction of pretty ceremonies, organ music and sentimental hymns. Now he understood that her faith was strong enough to take her to the poor of a foreign country. Then and there he apologized for misjudging her and her faith, and promised to give her full cooperation in getting Horiike freed.

With Matsui's assistance she wrote a letter in English to the President of the Philippines and to several other influential

people who might help. Matsui telephoned a reporter working for *The Tokyo Shimbun* and the newspaper carried an article on Satoko's crusade of prayer to save the former navy
man from execution. Horiike had been a farmer in Shimizu,
which is just southwest of Mount Fuji. The newspaper contacted his wife, Toya. She came to see Satoko, bringing her
little daughter and father-in-law. The parish priest of Asakusa,
Father Chiba, offered a Mass of petition and they all attended
it—including Satoko's ragpicker children, who were praying
very earnestly for the condemned man.

The distraught wife later spoke of how deeply she was
moved by Satoko's gentleness, and her concern for the little
daughter. Satoko told them of the great power of prayer
and, though Toyo did not share her Christian faith, it gave
her heart. Satoko continued to correspond with the family, and with others who might help by their influence or
their prayer. In mid-1953, Horiike was freed. Late in July
he came to Tokyo to thank Satoko. He was very upset to
discover she was very ill in bed. He felt tense because he
believed he was meeting a real saint. His tension, he said
later, was relieved by her marvelous sense of humor. But
this is jumping ahead.

To return to Satoko's story, two years before Horiike was
freed, the Christmas of 1951 was approaching. Satoko's doctor told her to remain at home resting in bed if she wanted
to regain her health.

In early December Matsui came to see her, excited about
his plans for Christmas! Father Chiba was coming to show
slides and Matsui himself was making a crib. Blunt Matsui
meant to cheer her up but his offhand way of explaining it
gave the oversensitive Satoko, miserable at still being in bed,
the impression that her Christmas the previous year was a
poor job and that Ants Town was doing quite well without her.

That night she wrote: "I was angry today because I'm proud and must work alone to get all the credit! I still have to compete with others and do things better than them! I felt anger and, yes, ugly jealousy today when I heard what Father Chiba and Sensei have planned for Christmas. Father Evangelista, the Jesuit, has asked me to send him newspaper and magazine clippings about my work. I intended to do so but this would only increase my vanity. I shall have to refuse. How sad that I cannot master my pride!"

Heavily wrapped up on Christmas Eve she went with her mother for a short visit to Ants Town. The chill north wind coming off the dark Sumida matched her mood. Telling her mother she wanted to watch just for ten minutes alone in Ants Town, she stood in the shadows while her mother went home. She longed to be able to bound up the stairs and hug the children noisily practicing a play, but a terrible sense of fatigue and failure weighed her down. She was tormented by guilt for being soft. Unlike the real people in Ants Town, she had for years used her parents' money and prestige to indulge her own selfish whims and fancies. She felt she had used the innocent children as her playthings. She half-desired that outrageous title "Mary of Ants Town", she who was totally unlike Mary. That she experienced little joy this Christmas, because others were running things, proved she had failed as a follower of Christ.

God, it seems, was allowing her to taste the misery of human selfishness and impotence so that he could purify her more in a further "dark night of the soul". The Scriptures put it: "As gold is purified by fire. . . ." As with Thérèse of Lisieux, part of this darkness that God used came from the shadow of tuberculosis in her lungs!

A Christmas carol broke sweetly on the chill air, leaving her "overwhelmed with a sense that I have proven unworthy of these good children". She took the rosary hanging from her obi but, instead of her favorite Joyful Mysteries, she began the Sorrowful, asking the beaten and broken Jesus to forgive her and help her.

"Ah! Soo 'tis. Missy Satoko. How you be?" It was Zeno.

"I looked up at the beautiful kind face and white beard and a warmth swept over me. I felt like a child that has been taken into her mother's arms! I replied: 'Well, I'm half sick and half well.'"

"Don' do too much yet, Missy Satoko. An' don' forget: heaven be time of wunerful peace."

She said she was on her way home, so Zeno said he'd accompany her. Seeing she was a little unsteady on the uneven ground he took her arm. "Moved by his kindness as we walked beside the dark river I blurted it all out. He listened very patiently before replying: 'Ole Zeno know just how Missy feel.' He told me, in his quaint Japanese, of all his troubles before he decided to enter the monastery. From Father Kolbe he had learned to place great trust in Mary, the Mother Christ gave to John and all Christians, as his last gift before dying on the Cross. When he learned to do that, Brother Zeno averred, he discovered true inner peace in the midst of turmoil. I looked at the serene face of this man who had spent twenty years in poverty-ridden places throughout Japan. I felt as though I were walking beside a great, tall church! Would I ever achieve the deep wisdom of this great soul?

"He took me to the front gate and, saying good night, lifted up the rosary hanging from his belt and said: 'Missy, in suffering time, just this!' Then he added with great gentleness: 'Jesus' Mother, Maria-sama, no matter what trouble, she help.'" Satoko bowed deeply and stood some time looking into the darkness that had engulfed him. She lifted her head and was startled by the beauty of Orion and Sirius blazing serenely in the eastern sky. Just a walk with the holy man Zeno was restoring clarity and perspective.

In January Matsui, much humbler and kinder than this time one year before, came to see her. He gave her encouraging news of the children: "After Christmas they gave the presents the Asakusa Catholics had sent them to an orphanage. On December 29 they were invited by the nuns at Koenji Convent and given presents, which they brought home and divided up for children worse off than themselves. They used the mochi rice cakes to make New Year *zoni* soup for some homeless men living close by. They collected scrap for Governor Yasui's appeal for the leper hospital to the tune of five thousand yen."

Matsui concluded: "Satoko, see what you have achieved. You have taught them to find happiness by thinking of others. We are all very grateful and very proud of you. Thank you! Now I have a request to make of you. Your parents told me what the doctor said. It is absolutely necessary for you to go for a complete rest where the air is better. My mother is living in her villa in Hakone, an ideal place with clean mountain air. She wants you to go up and stay with her until your health is restored. I have heard you tell the children that we must use God's gifts well. Your life and your health are gifts he wants you to look after. I beg you, we all beg you. Go up and stay with my mother."

Chapter 27

Strange Homecoming for Miss Urashima

Her parents were relieved to see her packing for Hakone, a tableland famous for its good air and hot spa baths. She left Tokyo physically very unwell, very disappointed that her sickness had forced her to leave the children and Ants Town, still under threat from the municipal authorities. She wrote: "Going to Hakone is a cross I must accept. I shall wait there as Horiike is waiting in the Philippines prison. All I can do is pray with Christ in the garden: 'If it be possible, let this chalice pass from me; nevertheless, not as I will but as you will.'"

That half year in Hakone was a desert experience for her—even though letters came to her via Ants Town from unknown people all over Japan, thanking her for doing so much for the ragpicker children and alerting the nation to the plight of the poor. Many gifts came, too. She told her mother to distribute them all to people in need. In early June, 1952, she wrote to her father saying she felt well enough to return to Ants Town.

He immediately went up to Hakone hoping to persuade her to stay there another six months. He said: "Satoko you have done so much for Ants Town. Just the other day at a conference I was introduced not as Professor Kitahara but as the father of Mary of Ants Town! But Satoko right now you need more rest to recuperate fully."

"*O-to-sama*, I've had a letter about new threats to destroy the Ants community. How can I just sit up here luxuriating and doing nothing when they are in danger? But...." She hesitated and began again. "I have only one worry. Tetsu-hiko our brother is dead and Big Sister is married. I feel that maybe I should stay at home and look after you and mother in your old age."

"Nonsense", the father replied. "I didn't bring you up to look after me when I'm old, but to live your own life! I would refuse to have you staying on at home to look after us."

"*O-to-sama*, thank you. Now I can speak with an easy conscience. When I return to Tokyo I want to go to live in Ants Town, as one of the ragpickers. I've prayed a lot about this and I believe this is what God wants me to do." It was a big shock to the father. However he was a man of his word— he had promised his children complete freedom in choosing how to live.

Developments that Satoko had not heard about had taken place in Ants Town during her half-year in Hakone. A young woman, Keiko Sano who had read of Satoko's work, had volunteered her services to the Boss and Matsui. She was young, healthy and intelligent so they put her in charge of the children in place of Satoko. About the same time Tsuka-mato, a strong and mature young man from Asakusa parish, had come to offer himself, too. He was a natural leader, was soon given some important responsibilities, and was asked to assist Keiko Sano. As they were not sure how the recuperat-ing Satoko would feel, no one informed her of this.

She returned from Hakone in high spirits. Her father and mother had agreed to her living in Ants Town. Now Satoko would be a real ragpicker, and the children would see she was truly their elder sister. If the ragpickers were burned out of Ants Town, she would share their homelessness. She had long been attracted by the Gospel words: "Sell what you have, give all to the poor and come follow me." Now at last she felt she could follow them as Brother Zeno and Saint

Francis had, and a great sense of freedom and lightheartedness possessed her.

She reduced what she would take with her to one bundle that she tied up in a large *furoshiki*, the square piece of cloth Japanese use to carry things. This included her Bible, Mass book and a small statue of Mary. Saying good-bye to her mother, Satoko assured her she would love and help her parents and family even more now by her prayers for them.

She had not informed anyone in Ants Town! She was sure the Boss would be very happy to find her a corner to live in. The very first person she met was Keiko Sano who promptly introduced herself as the one who had taken over care of the children! Several children appeared who were newcomers. Ignoring Satoko completely they asked Keiko Sensei to come quickly as the children were waiting for her in the chapel. The new Sensei excused herself abruptly and left Satoko standing there dumbfounded. "I felt like Urashima Taro", she later wrote. Urashima was the poor fisherman in the popular Japanese folk tale who spared the life of a tortoise he caught in his crab trap. As a reward for his kindness he was taken by a royal princess to the realm of the Sea King at the bottom of the ocean. He married the princess and after what seemed a short time he decided to go home to visit his parents. When he asked an old man he met on the seashore how his parents were, he was informed they were dead three hundred years! Urashima found himself bereft of family ties in his native village where no one knew him, and he was unable to return to his princess-wife in the Sea Kingdom. Satoko felt just like Urashima.

Matsui Sensei had heard of Satoko's plan to leave Hakone and live in Ants Town. Her parents told him what two doctors had said about her lungs. Certain that living the rough life of Ants Town would kill her, he told the Boss he would block her plans at any cost. He found her now, standing there alone looking lost; tears welling in her eyes as the truth hit home: the young energetic Keiko Sano Sensei's presence made her redundant in Ari no Machi! With poor health limiting her ragpicking ability, she would be more of a burden than a help. Matsui, steeling himself to appear cold and indifferent to this woman he had come to admire, launched his attack.

"Satoko, the world is a stage. You once played a lead role here as Ari no Machi no Maria. But you became sick and left. Another young woman has taken over the role of Maria! An actress must follow the script, not vice versa. Your old script had been changed—the directors have rewritten it for the new player!"

Satoko was shocked by his bluntness. "So it was all just a play?" she asked, deep hurt in her voice.

"Yes, and now that you have suddenly realized it, you are in tears!"

She had often received rebuffs from the Sensei in the past but was now shocked to find him utterly merciless.

Sudden anger stanched her tears. "Knowing that you regard it merely as a play I shall not waste my tears. As you, the director, consider my acting too poor I shall leave your play!"

"No," he countered, "it is not my play. I, too, am simply playing a role."

"Who, then is the director?" she asked.

Matsui, suppressing his emotions, looked steadily at her and replied: "*Ten-shu-sama.*" The word, literally meaning The Honorable Lord of Heaven, was chosen deliberately. It was a word for God used rarely by any Japanese but Catholics. Catholics used this in preference to *Kami-sama*, the normal Japanese word for God, because *kami* can also mean the millions of "gods" in Shinto. Matsui was not baptized but by using *Tenshu-sama* he was showing her he now respected her faith. He could see the word had touched her, the anger leaving her eyes. He continued: "Didn't you once tell me that the will of *Tenshu-sama* was the one, all-important guide in life? If you once rejoiced to play the role of Maria that *Tenshu-sama* gave you, because it was his will, won't you accept his will when he gives this role to another?"

Satoko lowered her head and became completely silent and still, as she often did when she was struggling to understand something. Matsui respected that silence. She raised her eyes steadily to his and said with simplicity: "Thank you, Sensei, for pointing this out. Isn't it strange that I did not see it? I told *Ten-shu-sama* I was prepared to give up everything to help Ants Town, especially to help the children. But I was not prepared to give up the role of being like Maria-sama to them, even when a more suitable young woman came along! Now you have enabled me to see all this clearly."

Forcing a smile she bowed deeply in a gesture of sincerity that he could not doubt. He had to restrain himself from telling her why he was rejecting her offer to live in Ants Town. She walked home without glancing back, swallowed her pride and told her mother another young woman had come to look after the Ants children. Apologizing for the worry she caused her parents she went up to her old room, unpacked and placed the statue of Mary on its shelf again. Her mother came up some time later and found her deep in prayer before the statue. What Mary of Ants Town said to Mary of Nazareth no one knows. However something Satoko wrote gives some clues.

She was an inveterate writer. She always answered letters and sent greeting cards on special occasions like New Year's Day. She also kept a diary and wrote in it frequently. Furthermore she had a habit of writing lengthy letters that she never sent! Apparently it helped her think more clearly and come to decisions. Matsui discovered this when he saw her tear up many pages and put them in a garbage tin. By that time he had come to regard her as a saint. So, without feeling any guilt, he pieced the pages together and copied them. He also managed to sneak a glance and copy some pages from her diary. That is how he discovered what went on in her heart at the time he rejected her attempt to live in Ants Town.

It was not long before her twenty-third birthday, which was August 22, 1952. That day was also, before Post-Vatican II changes in the Catholic calendar of saints, the feast of the Immaculate Heart of Mary, and patronal feast of the Catholic Church in Japan. She decided to prepare for this August 22 by a novena, nine days of prayer. Here are some snatches from what Matsui copied:

"Most Holy Virgin, be our Mother!... It is still very hot.... My twenty-third year is about to begin.... What is the path I must now follow? It seems the Lord wishes me to walk a painful road. My only personal desire is to dwell for-ever in the Heart of my Heavenly Father. I do not yet see the way he has chosen for me to reach him in heaven.... Reli-gious life in a convent, which I desire so ardently? Working for him in the secular world? Or again, will he call me to carry the Cross of illness, which I am to carry with Jesus?

"... I am ready for whichever of these missions he calls me to. I shall accept whatever he sends without complaint.... Lord, not my will but thy will!... Entrusting myself to Mary, following her path of serene goodness....

"On August 14 and 15 as I prayed, attempting to conjure up my accustomed image of Mary, I was unable to, despite my best efforts. Instead I saw only the image of our Lady of Sorrows! It gave me a fright! Why? Daily I ask her to pray to God for me. Why can I not accept some of the suffering she went through as she stood alongside Jesus crucified?.... It would be a precious grace if God asked me to offer myself so that I could make our Mother, our Lady, smile.... I feel my path to heaven will be a long and painful one. I do not intend to work just for my own eternal salvation, closing my eyes to the people around me. No, I want to offer God many beautiful sacrifices so that I may help others avoid the pains of hell, and reach him in heaven. If my sufferings can help achieve that, what a joy! Then let me embrace suffering!.... May the saints in heaven help me discover joy in suffering.... It is easy to mouth these words.... What I must do is ask the Lord for the grace to abandon myself totally to his Divine Providence. Most sacred Heart of Jesus, I trust in You."

Satoko took a special red box down from its shelf. It contained many newspaper and magazine articles about Ants Town and her work there—Matsui's efforts with media people had been highly successful! Father Evangelista, the Jesuit teaching spirituality at the Theological Department of the Jesuit University in Tokyo, had asked her to send him all these articles. He intended to send translations to his native Spain. But now she knew that would be wrong. She slipped out of the house and carried the box down to the bank of the Sumida River where she burned the contents. As she watched the light breeze pick up charred pieces and drop them into the water she apologized to the Lord and his Mother for the ugly resentment and jealousy she had felt toward Keiko Sano. Satoko Kitahara, Mary of Ants Town? What a travesty!

She stood there gazing at the slowly moving waters as she had often done in the past. She found it steadying in times of stress, sadness or crisis to gaze on the unfolding miracle of nature. Within the fleeting seasons, the sudden storms, the autumn north winds that strip trees and gardens, there is an abiding reliability. Crops flattened by hailstorms soon raise their heads again. However muddied the Sumida might become, an ever constant sea receives its waters and purifies them. Its friends the sun and the wind lift up those waters and take them back to its mountain source to begin the life-giving process, again and again. It was all summed up in a phrase which Satoko had first heard from Mother Angeles. She had come to love it very much: "the Providence of the good Father". However her faith in that Providence was soon to be tested sorely!

Chapter 28

Yakuza and Christ's Sake-Wine

Satoko had never lost her desire to be a nun. Now with Keiko Sano there, looking after the children, Matsui assured her she was not needed in Ants Town. Perhaps this was God's way of telling her to apply to join the convent again. Mercedarian nuns, however, insisted on a medical checkup. When that showed her lungs were far from cured, she was given a firm no! The nuns could not consider her as a candidate.

Her parents quietly rejoiced, hoping she would forget all about religious life and Ants Town. They thought that with rest at home she would get well and marry. Satoko rejected this idea. She was determined to live a life of poverty and celibacy, because "that is how Christ lived". If Ants Town did not need her, she was sure that other destitute people did. She began to search around for a religious order that actually lived and worked with the poor. She asked the priests at Asakusa parish, but no one knew of any such order in Japan. She wondered if this did not demonstrate the urgent need of such a religious order. Maybe she might have, in God's providence, a role to play in beginning such an order. The idea excited her and she took it to the Lord and his Mother in prayer. The practical first step was to get herself healthy and strong again.

Her health, however, did not improve. It steadily grew worse. The family doctor was called in and, at his suggestion, a tuberculosis specialist. Beginning her on a course of para-aminosalicylic-acid, he insisted that she go off to a TB hospital where she would be in the care of doctors twenty-four hours a day—and enjoy complete rest. Satoko refused to accept the idea of hospitalization. Why? No one is quite sure. Dr. Omi suspected it was because of her resolution to work for the poor. She intensified her prayer life, sure that God had given her a vocation to help the destitute. He would get her well in his own good time—and guide her to the place where she could dedicate her energies to the needy, like Christ. The Lord and his Mother had led Brother Zeno along that path, despite extraordinary difficulties. They would surely guide her, too. It was only a matter of continuing in prayer and waiting patiently.

But none of this happened. She lost her appetite and grew weaker. Her confidence that God had called her to do great things for his Kingdom on earth among the poor began to weaken. Had she deluded herself these last four years? Going against the obvious wishes of her parents she had refused to consider several good employment opportunities—and several marriage possibilities. She was *so sure* she could solve the problems of Ants Town and then become a nun. But Ants Town had rejected her and the convent said she was not suitable!

She was so sure that through prayer and the witness of her life she could win over her parents and family—and even Matsui's wife, who was then living in Hakone—to the Christian faith. But none of this had happened! Her great plans and hopes were based on pride and illusion! Suddenly she felt overwhelmed by it all. She continued to pray but experienced no consolation, no sense that God was guiding her. She was in darkness. Was he deaf to her pleading because all along she had no real love for him or for others? She loved only herself and her own grand ambitions! She was one of that class that Christ castigated so severely, the religious hypocrites!

One morning she got up after a bad night, dressed wearily, went unsteadily down the stairs and suddenly fainted.

Her mother telephoned the doctor, who came immediately, expressed grave alarm and ordered her to bed. He told her mother, who said she would nurse her, to make her daughter wear a face mask and to use strong disinfectant in the sickroom.

About the same time in Ants Town, the Boss called on Matsui "for a serious talk". He began by admitting that he once had connections with the Yakuza, Japan's equivalent of the Mafia. This wasn't altogether a surprise to Matsui. He suspected that some of Ants Town's earlier problems with the Yakuza stemmed from the Boss's previous links.

"Among the Yakuza", continued the Boss, "the first rule is that every *kobun* (ordinary gang member) must show absolute loyalty to the *oyabun*, the chief. A *kobun* who dodges that duty will be hounded by other Yakuza until they kill him. I watched Satoko Sensei for awhile when she first came and then began to listen to her. I don't understand religion and philosophy like you, Matsui Sensei, but I began to learn about Christ through her. Christ was an *oyabun* who served the *kobun* and laid down his life for them. The very opposite of a Yakuza chief! He told his followers they must be ready to do the same. I did not think there could be a religion that really did that. But she has done it! She came to Ants Town from her wealthy home and spent herself looking after our children. I thought: this is a powerful religion. Maybe this is real religion. That's why I began to go to Mass with her and stay on for the catechism class.

"I asked Satoko Sensei's father about her the other day. He told me the doctor says her health is really bad. She just keeps on going downhill. He said she may never get better. She has sacrificed her health and maybe her life for Ants Town. I have made up my mind to ask the priest to drink Jesus Christ's Sake. Some of the others say they will join me." In speaking of drinking Christ's sake the Boss had used a Yakuza expression. A member joins a Yakuza gang when he is called in by the *oyabun* to drink sake with him. The Boss was saying he had decided to be baptized.

In a book he wrote some years later, Matsui confessed that the Boss's words about baptism threw him into confusion. In the past Matsui had stated that he loved Christ but hated Christians because they did not follow Christ. But then he observed Satoko at close quarters. She followed Christ, literally—maybe she was dying now because of it. He had swallowed enough pride to join the Boss and other parents and children from Ants Town when they began going to Asakusa parish church every Sunday for Mass. He stayed on with them for catechism, and he had to admit they were being taught what Christ taught in the Gospels. Yet he did not want to commit himself to a drastic step like baptism. Why? The shock he now received at hearing the Boss and others would receive baptism, brought him to a sudden realization: his reservations about becoming a Christian did not spring from intellectual objections. They sprang from intellectual pride! He suddenly wished he had a simple, honest heart like the Boss. Then Matsui surprised himself by a sudden decision: "Right", he said, "I'll go with you to drink Christ's Sake, too."

They called on Father Chiba and told him they wanted to be baptized. He questioned them and decided they were ready. When he asked the Boss what saint's name he wanted at baptism, the priest was startled by the reply: "Ari no Machi no Maria." Told he must take a man's name he said: "Well, Jesus Christ."

"No", laughed Matsui. "You can't take the name of the *oyabun*!"

So the Boss settled on Zeno for his baptismal name. Matsui chose Joseph, "because he cared for Mary. I told myself I would now try to care for Satoko in her illness."

They asked the priest could they be baptized on October 26, because that was the day when Satoko was baptized. Father Chiba agreed and the Boss and Matsui went off to cheer her up with their news.

PART FOUR

The New Jerusalem

If you have seen your native land from afar you can bear any hardship ... in finishing the journey.

Bishop John of Naples

Chapter 29

Verdict from Chief Justice Tanaka

The doctor had just seen Satoko in her upstairs room when the Boss and Matsui arrived. He was sipping green tea with the parents in the parlor, looking very worried. He had dealt with enough TB patients to know how important psychological factors can be to the sufferer. Someone with a wife, husband or children to live for, for instance, can rally ever so much better. Someone who has no home to return to, or someone who becomes depressed, can succumb to the disease much more quickly. He knew the Kitahara family well and the hopes that Satoko had cherished to spend her life as a nun working for the poor. He understood how disappointed she was when both roads were closed off to her.

Matsui describes how they joined the others in the parlor. The Boss, blunt as always, asked the doctor if she was getting any better. No, the latter replied, and he had tried everything he knew. Each time he visited her, she was a little worse. Big tears formed in the Boss's eyes. Matsui admired his uncomplicated sincerity. "She's done so much for us", the Boss said, his voice husky. He cleared his throat noisily and continued: "If only she could get better and join in the celebrations when we get our own place and build proper houses in a new Ants Town." There was no hope of this in sight, but the Boss earnestly believed it would happen, somehow. Tears were now flowing freely down his cheeks. The mother spoke up. "She would love to be with you when you find a place of your own. You know, she seemed to live for Ants Town.

That's all she thought about, day or night." Ei Kitahara was biting her bottom lip. The professor lowered his head and mumbled: "Yes, Ants Town was the most important thing in her life."

Dr. Nakajima spoke up. "Maybe there is something we haven't tried. Maybe there is a hospital where a miraculous cure might take place."

"Where?" the mother asked immediately.

"Ants Town", said the doctor. "Let her go and live there as she wanted. It may not work, but then it might."

The professor agreed: "Given her spirit, it just might work."

The mother looked anxiously at the Boss. "But Ozawa-san, she's sick now. She has a highly infectious disease. It would be too much trouble to ask of you."

"What, trouble?" he replied. "After all she's done for us. Matsui Sensei, if her good parents allow us, we could fix up a bedroom for her in the storehouse."

Usually dour-faced Matsui showed extraordinary animation. Bowing his head low to the Boss he said: "Thank you, thank you!"

The mother was trying to wipe her tears at the same time as bowing and thanking the Boss, too. She added: "Even if Satoko died in a car on the way, she'd die happy!"

Matsui jumped up and said to the Boss: "*Oyaji* (Boss) I'll go and tell her." He bounded up the stairs and into her room. He was shocked to see how bad she looked. She was lying in bed, saying the Rosary. When he appeared she put on her face mask to safeguard him from infection. The usually smooth-talking Matusi tripped over words in his excitement to tell her. Her eyes widened in disbelief. "I would be too much trouble to you all", she protested weakly.

"Trouble? You trouble? No, no, no. Please say you'll come, please."

By now the Boss was in the room, his big moon face wrinkled in smiles. Satoko bit her lip to hold back her emotions. "Kitahara Sensei," said the hoarse-voiced Boss, "you are Ari no Machi no Maria. Nothing's the same there without you. We don't want you to do a thing when you come. Just be with us, just be Ari no Machi no Maria, with your beautiful heart." Satoko could think of only one response. She kissed the crucifix on her rosary.

Dr. Nakajima thought she could well be dead in a week, "but at least she will die happy!" He was due to leave Tokyo that week to attend a distant medical congress. He contacted Dr. Tajima and asked him to look after her. The latter specialized in TB and was keen to try a new medication that had recently been used with good results in the West. He explained to Satoko that if she allowed him to try it on her and it was successful, thousands of Japanese patients could benefit. She agreed immediately.

They partitioned off the shed they had built for storing sorted newspapers, bottles, scrap-iron, etc. and made a room for her measuring about ten feet by ten feet. As she had highly infectious tuberculosis, she would live by herself, wearing a mask when anyone visited her and putting a strong disinfectant into her spittoon. Even so there was an obvious danger that others in Ants Town could catch her disease. No one raised this problem with the Boss or Matsui, and no one came down with TB.

The Boss's wife and family lived outside Ants Town and the Boss usually returned home at night. Matsui, however, still lived in a cramped space not far from the storage shed. He took it on himself to fetch Satoko her meals. One of the women made them up in the communal kitchen. Satoko had insisted that her meals be exactly the same as those everyone else had. She prevailed upon her mother not to bring special meals from home but the Boss's wife often

turned up in the kitchen with fresh fish and vegetables for
Satoko.

Dr. Nakajima's intuition proved correct. She responded
quickly to Dr. Tajima's new treatment, her temperature
gradually subsided and Tajima eventually announced the crisis was over. She began sitting up in bed, and then walking
around outside if the weather was good. However the doctor
warned the Boss against letting her do any heavy work.

When she protested she was not pulling her weight, quot-
ing Saint Paul's words about not feeding those who refused
to work, Matsui replied: "Your job is not to pull a cart or sort
scrap. Your work is to pray, to pray for us all, to pray that
they won't requisition our land." Matsui later testified how
remarkably faithful she was to the job of praying. The Rosary
became her main prayer. She missed the Mass, he added, but
would become very excited when Father Chiba or Father
Tokugawa brought her Communion. One of the priests gave
her a rosary blessed by Pope Pius XII. It became her constant
companion for the rest of her short life.

Toward the end of 1952 when she seemed much stronger,
Matsui came along with a request. "I want you to write a
small book on your experiences in Ants Town. Could you
do that for us?" Matsui, influenced by Satoko, and the wider
world of Christianity he was getting to hear and read about,
thought that a straightforward "book from the heart" might
bring the needs of the poor and destitute to the attention of
more people. Certainly he was still concerned about the precarious toehold Ants Town had on their site in Sumida Park.
However there were all the other Ants Towns, and homeless
people who did not even have an Ants Town. He knew she
had an ability to write. He had seen it in the Ants Town
"newspaper" she had helped the children start the previous
year. When she told them to choose a name they settled on
Seibo no Ari—Ants of the Holy Mother. She persuaded some of

the older children they could write good articles and, helped by her hints, they did. *Seibo no Ari* had come out regularly ever since.

The idea of writing a book about her own work did not appeal to her. Matsui kept asking her, so she took the matter up with one of the priests when he brought her the Eucharist. He said he thought it was a good idea. People had to be alerted to the problems of the poor, so often papered over by bureaucrats and given a blind eye by the affluent. A good book can open hearts and consciences to God's grace. Look how many people were touched by Saint Thérèse of Lisieux's *Story of a Soul*—a book she wrote only because her superiors told her to. Satoko was convinced and began writing the book.

She began with herself and her deep yearning to find an ideal worth living for, explaining briefly how this became a conscious quest as she watched the *miko* serving in the sanctuary of Meiji Shinto Shrine—and as she stood in front of the statue of the Blessed Virgin on Yokahama Bluff. The book shifted focus to the problems of Tokyo's poor, which she described through the compassionate eyes of Brother Zeno. The main section told the story of Ants Town through anecdotes about the people who lived there, especially the children. The final section of the book was made up of descriptions of life on the streets and in Ants Town, written by the most literate of the children. Matsui wrote a postscript. In all, the book ran to 227 pages.

An indication of the importance of the book and the power of attraction she exercised on all kinds of people, can be found in the preface. It was written by one of the most respected Japanese of the day, Judge Kotaro Tanaka, the Chief Justice of Japan and the second Japanese to sit on the International Court of Justice at The Hague. He had a personal reason for empathizing with Satoko's journey—he had travelled a similar road himself. As a university student, in the Law Department at Tokyo University, Japan's most prestigious school, he had struggled to find "an absolute norm for law and morality.... If law and morality are simply relative and arbitrary, even love becomes absurd." After much searching "for a humanism based on absolute values and love", he decided to be a "churchless Christian". But that did not satisfy him. He took the plunge and was received into the Catholic communion.

In his preface to Satoko's book he wrote of the great thirst in postwar Japan for true love and authentic humanism. Because of this thirst, he said, the books by Dr. Nagai of Nagasaki had become national best sellers. What is the secret of Nagai's success? Love and humanism, based on authentic religion. That is why, he concluded, this unpretentious book by Satoko Kitahara is very important. She has lived a life of true humanism and love by following Christ literally, herself becoming one of the destitute.

Chapter 30

A Satoko–Matsui Love Affair?

Satoko's tuberculosis was stabilized by the new medicine she was given but her health was never again robust. Forbidden by the doctor to do any heavy work, she began spending time visiting the old people in Ants Town. There were almost no diversions to break the monotony of their lives, and some of them became depressed, especially the bedridden. They had been suspicious and even hostile when she arrived in Ants Town. However they came to appreciate her very much.

She began spending more time working for Matsui. He was still writing letters to municipal officials, and articles to make money for Ants Town. She became his secretary, writing his articles and letters in her fine hand, making copies and filing information. There were letters to answer even from overseas Japanese who read or heard about Ants Town. She also helped Matsui collect and tabulate statistics about the homeless of Tokyo. Together they began working on approaches to solve this huge problem.

Matsui had long since seen that the homeless must band together if they were to accomplish anything. Community had been one of the secrets of the phenomenal spread of Buddhism throughout Asia. After Siddartha Gautama the first Buddha "entered nirvana" in the fifth century B.C., his disciples taught the famous three treasures: (1) The life-giving perfection of the first Buddha, the Indian Siddhartha Gautama. (2) The cosmic "law" he discovered, which is the eternal truth that can liberate mortals in this life and lead them to nirvana. (3) The brotherhood, the community of celibate monks. The latter provided the dynamism that took Buddhism to all of Asia, including Japan. Matsui knew this well. Through Satoko, he saw the possibility of a community that was not necessarily celibate but was bound together spiritually, by a shared faith and prayer.

Both Matsui and Satoko saw that the only way to help the destitute was through profitable work that restored their dignity, work that was close at hand and required no specialized training. Ragpicking met those requirements. The two set about writing a pamphlet to convince Tokyoites of the wisdom of selective garbage collecting. If paper and cardboard, bottles, tins and metals were put out in different garbage containers, and better still on different days, everyone would benefit by recycling. Thousands of copies of the pamphlet went out via the ragpickers.

About the time Ants Town began, Abbé Pierre, a Parisian and a member of the French parliament, met a man who had just failed in a suicide attempt. He was deeply troubled by the tale of woe and took the man into his home. The priest began to walk the slums and was appalled by the number of displaced persons and vagrants who lived on the streets in Paris. With the would-be suicide helping, he brought many back to the run-down mansion where he lived. But there were so many out on the streets. Thus, in 1949, he came to the same conclusion reached by Matsui and Satoko. (1) Collecting junk would earn money for several meals a day. (2) The ragpickers would survive only if they formed real communities. Each new community Abbé Pierre founded was told to save some money to buy or rent a cheap lodging house for a new community. The priest gave his movement the name Emmaus.

Abbé Pierre realized a third component was also required— awakening the conscience of the affluent to the miseries of the destitute in every city. He began inviting young students on holidays to volunteer for work with his junk collectors. The media became interested and his communities multiplied, spreading beyond France. These communities banded together to form Emmaus International, which Ants Town would join some years later.

But back to Ants Town, 1953. Because Satoko was the only one in Ants Town with whom Matsui could discuss intellectual ideas, he spent more and more time with her. His wife, staying in Hakone, had grown understandably disillusioned by the kind of marriage he demanded of her. She joined the Jehovah Witnesses and came to believe that Catholicism, and all the other Christian denominations, were instruments of the devil. She began to accuse her husband of illicit relations with Satoko. Some media people sensed a good story but their efforts, before and after Satoko's death, failed to produce more solid evidence than the accusations of an angry wife who had never set foot in Ants Town. From start to finish, people like the Boss and his wife, the priests who brought Satoko Communion, Satoko's family, and friends who sometimes came to help her work, hotly denied the slightest semblance of impropriety.

Matsui is on record as saying: "I loved Satoko, but in the chaste way Saint Francis loved Saint Clare—if you will excuse the exaggeration of comparing me with Saint Francis!" G. K. Chesterton makes some remarks about Francis and Clare that are pertinent here. In his small masterpiece *St. Francis of Assisi*, Chesterton writes: "Moderns are distressed that Francis helped the beautiful seventeen-year-old Clare elope to the cloister.... If it had been a romantic elopement to be a bride instead of a nun the modern world would have called her a heroine.... They sympathize totally with fourteen-year-old Juliet who disobeyed her parents for Romeo." Why this difference? G.K.C. replies: "(Moderns) know that romantic love is a reality but do not know that divine love is a reality.... There is a direct revelation more glorious than any romance; the story of Clare's elopement to the cloister is simply a romance with a happy ending."

Many people who lived close to Satoko testify to her possession of what Chesterton calls divine love. It became clear to them that prayer was a joy to her. Her mother and elder sister, at a time when they were not Christians and tended to see her pursuit of God and her concern for the poor as "fanatical", were struck by her obvious relish of prayer. Her elder sister said she would become absorbed in prayer in all sorts of situations, such as travelling in a train. If the mother peeped into her room when Satoko still lived with her parents, she often saw her rapt in deep prayer before her crucifix and statue of the Virgin. One of Satoko's diary entries that Matsui managed to copy was written when she was bedridden in Ants Town. It runs: "It is difficult to be still while others are out working. Rest, they tell me!.... There is nothing I can do except renounce my self-will. And love Jesus! ... I have offered the Lord all I possess, and I am with him. Not my will but his be done. If I never forget that his Providence watches over all things that happen, my heart will always be at peace. Anyhow, why should I complain about my humbling sickness and suffering?.... Didn't Jesus carry a cross? Elizabeth Maria, it is good for you to suffer, it is good for you to meditate alone in your bed. As long as it is for God's glory, accept pain, make it your gift to him. Then you can truly be the handmaid of the Lord. May his will be accomplished in me."

(A little later in the diary) "Because of my great joy tears splashed all over my prayer book. Luckily I had a big handkerchief with me!.... As soon as I wake in the freshness of morning, let me begin with the sign of the Cross as my first deed and recite with the Psalmist: I shall awake and serve you, Lord. Praised be Jesus Christ. Jesus, Mary, Joseph, I entrust this new day to you, this day and all the days of my life."

Chapter 31

The Ragpicker Abbé of Nishinomiya

Robert Vallade was born in Cognac the year Kaiser Wilhelm's army got to within twenty-five miles of Paris, 1914. In 1939, just before German armies set out for the French capital again, Vallade was ordained a priest of the Paris Foreign Mission Society. He received his call-up letter from the French Army almost immediately. However the gentle giant who loved the Sermon on the Mount was not sent to the battle front. His assignment, in a prison camp for civilian aliens, required no shooting. Within a year, however, the Nazi *Blitzkrieg* had turned all of France into one huge prisoner-of-war camp! Four years of privation and humiliation tempered the steel in his character.

Soon after Paris was liberated, in August 1945, Vallade was able to recommence his mission as a priest. Sent to a working-class parish he was shocked by the alienation of laborers from the Church. He saw how much of his seminary training had been remote, far removed from work with ordinary workers. He sadly acknowledged the aptness of the new expression, "Pagan France", and began to have deep misgivings about comfortable Catholicism that had lost the masses.

Early in the 1950s he received orders to proceed to his real goal, the foreign missions. "Wary of ivory-tower Catholicism" when he landed in Japan, he spurned the offer of a two-year language course in Tokyo. He wanted to learn the language, he said, as he worked with the people. Assigned as a curate to the parish of Nishinomiya, he lost no time getting acquainted with the area. The city is close to Kobe, on the curve of Osaka Bay. The whole area was a prime target for "Devil" LeMay's incendiary raids. By the time of the surrender, August 1945, little more than an ashscape was left—and hundreds of thousands of workers, widows and orphans who were homeless. They built flimsy shelters from charred beams and heat-buckled scraps of tin. By the mid-1950s most houses, shops and factories had been rebuilt. However, as Vallade discovered, thousands still lived hand-to-mouth existences in leaky huts.

Parishioners responded to his appeal with a large quantity of tinned goods. Lugging a sackful on his back he hurried to the worst area. But he need not have hurried. The shanty dwellers refused his goods and turned their backs on him. He trudged home perplexed. Had LeMay's bombers killed and maimed so many that every westerner was still hated?

Someone in the rectory drew his attention to a Japanese magazine article on Ari no Machi no Maria, the professor's daughter who had bridged the chasm between "normal" citizens and the destitute. She had become "the heart" of a satisfied, hard-working group of "*bataya*". His informant reading the article for him explained "*bataya*", a word Vallade had never heard. *Bataya* were ragpickers, who lived from what they found in garbage cans and dumps, and were regarded as the lowest of the low. They are almost non-citizens! Yet in the photo they looked like very real people to the French priest. He was captivated by the smiling "Maria". Deciding to go and meet her and the Ants Town dwellers, he saved up the fare to Tokyo from his meager salary and was given time off by his pastor.

Satoko took an immediate liking to the big foreigner whose legs were not suited to the formal *seiza* style of sitting on the tatami floor of her small room. He insisted on following Japanese etiquette, bowed very low to her and in simple

Japanese explained how the Nishinomiya slum dwellers had refused his tinned goods. She replied: "Japanese don't like being beggars. If you want to be accepted and help them, show them how to make an honest living by setting up a ragpickers' group like us here at Ants Town. If you want to learn the ropes, maybe you should stay here awhile."

Matsui cut in sharply: "But if you do, you work and live like everyone else. There is no privileged class here!" Matsui was still mistrustful of foreigners and "people of religion" and continued aggressively: "To earn a meal in the common refectory you have to collect 100 yen's worth of scrap. And another thing, those fancy overalls and boots are out of place here. Wear simpler things if you want to work with us!" Satoko tried to tell the priest, with her smile, that Matsui had a good heart despite his brusqueness. Anyhow the Boss turned up then and said the priest was welcome and could sleep in the children's study-chapel. It would be wonderful to have Mass each day.

Vallade wasted no time in beginning his apprenticeship. He was given a shoulder basket and set out to gather scrap. Late in the day he returned with a full basket, rather pleased with himself. However the man on the scales told him much of what he collected wasn't saleable! His load came to sixty yen, not enough for an evening meal! He refused Satoko's offer of a meal with a shrug, saying he would do better tomorrow. He went off to the river bank, saw some dandelions, picked them and put them in a bottle on the altar. His casual acceptance of no supper won him supporters. There is a saying most Japanese know: *bushi wa kuwanedo taka yoji*. A samurai values pride more than food. The next day he was given tips on what to look for and where and collected 300 yen's worth of scrap. He laughed heartily as he ate with the others that night.

He stayed a month and ate breakfast with Satoko and Matsui most mornings after Mass. Matsui came to accept him and the three would discuss the "philosophy" of ragpicking. They agreed that the destitute were helped only if their dignity was valued and respected. Each was a person, a son or daughter of God, unique and of absolute worth. Until society took its obligations to the poor more seriously, dustbin sifting was a way many destitute could earn a living, if they worked as a community. This also helped society, by reusing paper, cardboard, bottles, scrap-iron etc.—rather than burying it all in the ever-widening disposal dumps that took up precious land. Without knowing the word, they were highlighting the need of recycling.

Vallade gradually came to understand how Satoko had changed Matsui, who confessed that his first ideas about humanism and helping the poor were inadequate. First, they lacked the essentially spiritual vision of human dignity flowing from each person's absolute value as a child of God. Matsui's original approach had also been too angry, and consequently counterproductive. He had lashed out at authorities and the affluent for not helping his work for the homeless. There is a saying: you can be an angry prophet only if you are prepared to do much praying and fasting. Satoko's example had shown him that the truly effective way, in the long run, is to base your life and work for the poor on love. Then the poor sense they are respected and valued as persons, and not used to implement an ideology. Also, people who can help the poor are gradually attracted to do so. "Her femininity", Vallade concluded, "played a profound part in Matsui's return to believing life was meaningful and indeed precious."

When Satoko saw how committed to the poor the French priest was, she began to speak openly and share confidences. This allowed him to see how "the love, dynamism and courage, so evident in her life, sprang from her love of God. God's will was the center of her very existence. Because she believed God wanted her to be a member of the Ants community, all the consequences appeared simple to her." Someone drew Vallade aside, however, and told him that Satoko's parents wanted to send her to a hospital or sanitarium where "she would recover and be more effective". He decided to make this suggestion. She replied: "Well, if the good Lord wants to cure me, I am waiting here in Ants Town. I do believe it is here he wants me to be, with my family." Ants Town had become her only family.

Most of the month Vallade was there Satoko was bedridden, but this seemed no longer to bother her. "She always smiled when people came and seemed perpetually grateful." She did secretarial work, writing Matsui's articles in legible script, doing accounts, etc., but she thought her main job was just to be there and pray. Vallade remarked on how simple her prayer life was. All she seemed to use was the Gospels, a Mass book and her rosary. "She possessed a very attractive sweetness of disposition," he noted, "but also great strength of purpose." Only on later visits would he learn of her interior trials and sufferings.

One day over breakfast she laughed and said: "Your novitiate is over. You have passed all tests!" She had had several long discussions with the Boss and Matsui, and they decided Father Vallade should begin an Ants Town back in Nishinomiya. He was a little flattered when she told him but protested he had neither money nor land. "That doesn't matter", she replied. "Just put your trust in Jesus and begin." They would help him by allowing one of their most trusted families to go to Nishinomiya with him to pioneer the venture. Losing them, and especially their teenage daughter who had drawn very close to Satoko proved very painful. Satoko told Matsui: "I now appreciate the sentiments of a mother when her eldest daughter goes off to marry. I can now better understand the pain Mary suffered when Jesus went off. It would seem that love and pain become inseparable companions here below."

Father Vallade came and stayed in Tokyo Ants Town on three occasions, each time staying a month. He used to sleep on the tatami floor in the chapel, and Satoko made sure she was always up in time to attend his Mass, even though unwell. Satoko advised him on how best to help destitute Japanese and asked his advice on spiritual matters.

He carries vivid memories of his many talks with her that gave him glimpses "of a great soul". She obviously benefited, he came to see, from an upbringing in an aristocratic family proud of its one thousand years of history—and from a classical education in Oh-in, a school steeped in *Nihon-teki* culture. Three powerful streams, Confucianism, Shintoism and Buddhism, nurtured her for her first twenty-one years. The waters of baptism, fortunately, did not stem those other streams, but blended them into one harmonious spirituality. Her faith and life became, he said heroically Christian. Every obstacle was washed aside by her one, all-consuming passion, to follow the will of God. That guided her safely between the whirlpool of Charybdis and the rock of Scylla, to use an image from Western classical mythology. The destructive rock was a Christian faith so restricted that it denied truth and grace in the faith and morality of her ancestors. The fatal whirlpool was the compromising of her total faith in Jesus. The resulting Christian humanism of Satoko "saved Matsui from the frustration that his mere humanism led him to".

Another harmonious blending that Father Vallade came to admire was a "sweetness joined with great strength". Her very attractive femininity and optimistic faith in "the good God" calmed and eventually changed Matsui's judgmental harshness and wilfulness. Satoko, in Father Vallade's experience, never lost her smile. However he came to discover she had disciplined herself to smile serenely despite physical pain, inner distress and sometimes spiritual darkness. She had tremendous faith in prayer and yet God tempted her sorely in not answering her prayers! God gave her an ever-present and painful consciousness of the dire needs of the poor, not just in Ants Town but in the other slums of Tokyo, throughout Japan and in poverty-ridden countries like the Philippines. She had a tremendous urge to go out among the destitute of Japan and the world—but God refused to give her even the mediocre health necessary to fulfil her vision. Father Vallade came to see the pain that this apparent contradiction caused her. It is not a new problem; it is an anguish that is obvious in so many of the Psalms—"Why, Lord? How long, Lord?" are constant cries from psalmists' lips.

Before she died, Vallade continues, she came to a great peace in knowing that God's will for her was to "lie in bed looking at the cracks in the ceiling" of the shed that was her home. The latter became her "beloved pilgrim hut", like the huts of Bashoo, Saigyo, Kenko Hoshi and so many other Japanese who lived frugally while travelling in quest of the Absolute One. She did influence the whole world, Vallade adds, but only after she died. Matsui's two books about her, the stage and radio plays and the Shochiku movie took her "heroic witness of God's view of the poor" throughout Japan. The Jesuits, Fathers Mathaix and de Vera and several other Westerners in Japan spread her message to Europe and America.

One look at the set of Father Vallade's jaw tells you he is a strong personality. Maybe that is why Satoko's strength of character appealed to him so much. She reminded him of the youthful Gallic saint for whom he had special love: Joan of Arc. Commenting on Satoko's blending of strength with "a gentleness and sweetness" he said: "This, I believe, came from Satoko's extraordinary love of the Virgin and her devotion to praying the Rosary."

Vallade eventually set up ragpicker communities in Osaka and Kobe. They joined Abbé Pierre's Emmaus International. The Tokyo Ants Town moved to its new site after Satoko's death, joined Emmaus International and set up a second community in Tokyo. The four Japanese communities of ragpickers helped set up Emmaus communities in Korea and the Philippines. As Japan became prosperous and jobs were easy to find, ragpicking ceased. Father Vallade opened the Kitahara Center in 1970 where he cares for the ragpickers who are too old to work and have no family to care for them.

Chapter 32

The Prayer of Smiling

In the skies above, stars.
In the fields below, flowers.
On human faces, smiles.

Saneatsu Mushakooji,
Japanese poet

One hot August day in 1954 Zeno turned up sweating pro-
fusely in his black serge habit, carrying something huge in a
furoshiki. He found Satoko in bed, helping Keiko and Akira
with their lessons. He cracked one of his customary jokes:
"Ain't left for heaven I see, so brung you work. Everyone
must be workin' till get travel pass to God's hometown!"
Zeno was always a tonic and she joined in his laughter at his
own humor. He plunked the object on the tatami mat with a
thud and took off the big *furoshiki* to reveal a three-foot-tall
cement statue of Mary of Lourdes. Maximilian Kolbe's last
act before leading Zeno and company to Japan in 1930 was
to go to the south of France to pray at Lourdes. Kolbe chose
the site on the outskirts of Nagasaki for their first monastery
because it would be easy to build a replica of the Lourdes
grotto on the mountainside running into their land. Friends
told Kolbe it was foolhardy to build his pioneer monastery in
so isolated a spot. Kolbe had replied: "If we look to Mary's
interests, she will look to ours." The central site the friends
suggested was obliterated in the nuclear blast in 1945. God,

as Zeno would say, "sees around corners!" Zeno had often shared stories with Satoko about Kolbe's love for Mary. It became an outstanding characteristic of the spirituality of Zeno and Satoko, too.

The Boss and Matsui accepted Zeno's gift and decided to build a Lourdes grotto right beside Satoko's room: "Mary of Lourdes will look after our Mary of Ants Town!" The Boss made sure the stone grotto was finished for an official blessing on August 29, the last Sunday of the Marian Year, 1954. It was hardly a masterpiece of architecture but Matsui could not help himself and planned a real stage show at the blessing, inviting the media. Good publicity to stop municipal eviction was ever a preoccupation with him.

The pastor and curate of Asakusa church celebrated a solemn High Mass for the crowd of well-wishers who came. Chief Justice Kotaro Tanaka and the president of the Japanese Chamber of Commerce, Aiichiro Fujiyama, sent telegrams. Matsui had various photogenic gimmicks including a cage of doves to release dramatically as the concluding "Lourdes Hymn" finished. But no sooner had they begun the hymn than the threatening summer storm burst right above them. Matsui, the reporters and the crowd rushed away for cover. Most of the ragpickers stood their ground beside the Boss, Satoko and Zeno. While thunder reverberated along the river and drumming rain soaked them to the skin, they sang the whole of the "Lourdes Hymn" including that appropriate stanza: "And the tempest-tossed Church, All her eyes are on thee. They look to the shining, Sweet Star of the sea. Ave, Ave, Ave Maria." Matsui later wrote: "All my fine plans for a media spectacular were washed into the river with the downpour. I was terribly disappointed, but not Satoko, Zeno and 120 ragpickers! I was chock-filled with human calculations. They were the true believers, the ones Jesus spoke of in Matthew's Gospel: 'I bless you Father, for hiding these things from the learned and the clever and revealing them to little ones.' "

For a second time in her life Satoko got soaked to the skin in Zeno's company. Those who knew her well speak of how profoundly the simple, almost illiterate Pole influenced her. He moved among the poor with the freedom of Brother Wind because he had become one of the poor—even at times sharing their lice and their grime. From Zeno she learned simple Franciscan trust in the Providence of the good Father who clothes the wild flowers and feeds the sparrows.

Zeno's example of good cheer and laughter reinforced a lesson Mother Angeles had taught. After Satoko had been baptized in the Mercedarian Sisters' chapel, the nun took her aside and made her a request. Congratulating Satoko on her beautiful smile she said a smile can be a prayer of trust in God ... and a real encouragement to others. Would Satoko promise God that she would always try to smile. Satoko readily agreed and together they knelt before the statue of Mary and asked her help in keeping the promise. There were times of darkness and pain when Satoko did not keep the promise. However in the final years of her life when she lived with the ragpickers, she kept it magnificently. It was something everyone remarked on after her death. The ragpicker priest Father Vallade came to understand her perhaps better than the others and knew how distressed she became at seeing society at large and the Christian Church in particular insensitive to the sufferings of the poor—not just in Japan but in the Third World nations. Her own inability to organize movements to help the destitute, and the seeming paralysis of energy among well-off Christians, caused her much inner turmoil. Yet she did not believe that inflicting her grief on others would help the situation! So she greeted everyone with a genuine smile and took her personal poverty and pain to her Lord in prayer.

The banks of the Sumida can be very cold and damp in winter and stiflingly humid in summer. No one heard Satoko speak of this. Matsui, however, was not as serene. He sometimes flew into tantrums, shouting in frustration, throwing sheafs of documents to the floor. He said she would seem to agree with him, nodding sympathetically but not uttering a word. When his fury was spent she would quietly gather up the papers, putting them in order—and getting him back to his job in hand without opening her mouth. He confesses she had by far the stronger character. She did an enormous amount of secretarial work for him and the Boss. There was much paperwork in being responsible for two hundred citizens in a Japanese town.

On one occasion Matsui became so fed up with the people of Ants Town and their enemies in City Hall that he told her he was quitting for good. He would leave them all to their stupid selves. There was a meeting that night, and he would drop his bombshell then. She was very sick in bed when he told her, and she nodded sympathetically. He marched into the meeting that night and saw her sitting with the others. The stubborn fool should be in bed, he muttered to himself, and went over to tell her off. As he reached her, she pressed a metal crucifix into his hand and, looking into his eyes said: "I have been praying for you." He was startled at the heat in the crucifix. He did not resign but after the meeting ordered someone to take Satoko's temperature. It was 104°F!

Chapter 33

One Frail Grain of Wheat

In late December, 1957, a sympathizer in municipal head-quarters told Matsui that a decision had been reached to burn Ants Town down in the coming January and disperse the community. Matsui had often told authorities that the community would gladly vacate Sumida Park if a suitable living site were given them, close enough to the city to allow them a livelihood by ragpicking. Now, in freezing midwinter, their cause suddenly seemed doomed.

Matsui swore to himself in frustration for he could think of no one left to turn to. He had no new stories for his old allies of convenience, the journalists. For nine years a magnificent social experiment had survived against all odds, at tremendous personal cost to people like the Boss, Satoko, Tsukamoto and his wife Keiko, and dozens of others who had helped the ragpickers out of the despair of postwar Japan. These good people and their children were now to be cast out in the name of civic progress!

Calling the Boss to Satoko's room, he glumly broke the news. Satoko immediately annoyed him by a recitation of the past. God had helped them out each time and would help them again! "God", she said, "will always be on the side of people who are working for true justice." He suggested she take a closer look at all the places in Japan and around the world where injustice was crushing little people! Matsui terminated the discussion abruptly, disappointed by the contribution of pious platitudes.

He stormed out of Ants Town in search of someone with more practical ideas but spent a fruitless day, returning late and bone weary. There was a letter from City Office awaiting him. In quite hostile language it ordered him to appear before the section chief next morning, explaining why several hundred people were living on a large section of a city park without any authorization. He swore and threw the letter to the floor. He hadn't eaten since midday but his rage destroyed any desire for food.

He sat down at his rickety desk and began writing furiously, arguing that the municipality had an obligation to these people. With Satoko he had compiled figures on the homeless of Tokyo, and on how much money the ragpickers had made from city refuse. Ants Town showed what could be done to solve the problem of Tokyo's destitute and deserved praise and gratitude.

He knew this was their last chance. He kept scratching out sentences, rephrasing them, crumpling up pages and starting again. By the time he had a document to his satisfaction it was very late. He would do a fair copy with *sumi* ink and brush, but first he deserved a shot from his bottle of "onion whiskey". He poured a very generous amount and downed it. After the fiery sensation subsided and his tenseness gave way to a pleasant glow, he put his head on the desk "for a couple of minutes' breather".

He woke with a start at the 6.30 A.M. call to get ready for community prayer! The first thing he noticed was that his precious document was gone! He rushed out of his room to find the Boss where he knew he would be, in Satoko's room. The Boss was always up before most and called on Satoko ten minutes before morning prayer. He checked that she was all right and said her greeting smile "made him feel good all day".

Matsui heard the Boss talking with bedridden Satoko and came in, murder written on his face. He was about to speak when he saw his document on the tatami beside her bed. Next to it, in her distinctive brush strokes, was a copy of the same document. He demanded an explanation. Satoko said she saw his light burning very late. She had heard about the document from the Boss and knew he would like it done formally in brush strokes, so brought it back to her room and did it.

He looked at the lengthy document, so finely redone and snapped: "You could hardly have had any sleep last night. Don't you think that is irresponsible, given your state of health?" She was no longer surprised or upset at his mood swings, understanding his highly strung, artistic temperament. Instead she was sympathetic, knowing all the disappointment he met in work that brought him few personal rewards. So she just smiled and told him he had worked himself to exhaustion for them all, and that she could easily make up for a little lost sleep. Too long in bed was her problem, not too little! She laughed and the Boss guffawed. Matsui was not amused and told them so. There was every likelihood that the section chief would turn him down today and then they, and the children and the old folks, would be out on the streets.

Satoko, sitting up in bed, bowed deeply, apologizing for upsetting him with flippancy on so serious a day. She took her rosary from beside her pillow, put it in his hand and placed her hand over it. "Sensei, please carry this rosary with you today. It was blessed by the Pope and carried to Lourdes. I will spend the day until you return from the City Office praying to Maria-sama. She has always helped us and will help us in this crisis. Please just go and put our case peacefully and refuse to get upset, no matter what."

On his way by bus to the City Office Matsui read the beautifully written document. He was startled, though, when he came to the end. She had added a personal message for the section chief. If the authorities drove the people from

Ants Town without helping them find another site for their community, she would sit in front of the City Office fasting and praying until they found a place for the Ants or she died. Matsui was thunderstruck.

He strode into the section chief's office with her rosary clenched in one hand and his briefcase in the other. Bowing stiffly, he launched straight into his appeal. "I have come, not as a chance representative of Ants Town to argue with a high city official. You and I are two human beings brought together by God's Providence. I want to state unequivocally, right here at the beginning, that I am ready to give my life to secure an alternative site for the people of Ants Town. I have been able to make this decision because there is in Ants Town a young woman who has written a message for you. She has made a solemn promise to fast until death for Ants Town. Her name is Satoko Kitahara and she has written this book, *The Children of Ants Town*, which I leave with you.

"It is not just the people of Ants Town we are prepared to die for. We are prepared to struggle and die for the poor and powerless everywhere. You may despise us as a ragtag collection of vagrants, powerless to back up such a sweeping claim, indeed utterly impotent to accomplish anything."

He stopped talking and carefully laid the rosary on the official's desk. "This rosary with its image of the Crucified does not just mean we are Christians. No, it is the rosary of a young woman prepared to fast till death for love of the people in Ants Town. Her great love has made our community unique, unique maybe in the whole world. One day her name will be known throughout the world, I assure you. Her example will win freedom for poor people everywhere!"

Matsui took up the rosary and clenched it in his fist again. He flipped open his briefcase, took out the document she had rewritten last night, and began reading it as if he were reading to the assembled National Diet. "In Tokyo, a city of seven million there are seven thousand homeless people. Seven hundred thousand others are living in poverty. You in the government have failed to come up with any solution to all this. The people of Ants Town have found a solution—in what is thrown out as garbage! If just 20 percent of the city of Tokyo's garbage were utilized, billions of yen would be raised annually. The money needed to purchase a new site for Ants Town, and to house Tokyo's seven thousand homeless, is under your nose! Don't just burn us out. Help us to keep helping ourselves. Use your authority to find us a new site where we can continue making an honest living by collecting scrap. *And* send us your other homeless and we will teach them how to make a living, too!

"If you refuse to help us, she will come and sit outside this City Office praying and fasting until she dies, because she cares for the good people that you authorities dismiss as mere vagrants. One sick woman will stand up for them against all you power brokers and so-called civil servants! I beg you, sir, consider well the consequences of your decision." Leaving the book she had written on the section chief's desk in the hope that he might read it, Matsui rose, bowed stiffly and left.

Some nights later the Ants celebrated their ninth Christian Christmas. Matsui found himself pensively listening to the ragpickers singing "Silent Night". The words were gentle: "Round yon Virgin-Mother and Child, Holy Infant so tender and mild." The hands that held the candles were rough, and the ruddy faces reflected in the candlelight were in stark contrast to artists' ideas of Mary and the Christ Child. "Some of the faces were like caricatures in comic strips, or the faces of brigands and witches in those tales from ancient China! There were sweet faces, too. Some of the children could have stepped out of the pages of beautiful fairy stories like *The Blue Bird of Happiness*. In that sea of contrasting faces one stood out, Satoko's, framed in her thin white veil."

The procession started. The Boss led the way, dressed in the Santa Claus suit Satoko had sewn for him, carrying a sack full of presents. The pageant wound its way through Ari no Machi and stopped in front of the Lourdes grotto, where life-size shepherds made of papier-mâché knelt worshipping the Child laid in a manger. Cardboard sheep, rabbits and birds crouched beside the crib.

Matsui strained his eyes to identify a well dressed couple who stood apart in the shadows. Ah, Satoko's parents! Faithful to the unspoken understanding they rarely came to see their daughter. Matsui comments: "There were many among the Ari no Machi dwellers without a 'normal' family member they could turn to in need. Out of sensitivity to their feelings Satoko and her parents saw precious little of each other. After a few words with their daughter that night the parents turned to go home. They saw me, bowed and said: 'We just wanted to see how she is. She is very happy— and it is the love of you people here that is responsible for her recovery.'" Matsui walked with them to the gate of the settlement.

He suddenly went cold all over as he thought of their suffering if the City Office burned Ants Town down. He knew without a shadow of doubt that Satoko would go to the City Office and sit exposed to the weather and refuse any food. In this winter cold she would not last ten days! Would it require her death for the officials to have a change of heart?

Their farewell broke his terrible reverie. "Thank you so much for all you have done for our daughter. Thank you, thank you", they called, bowing deeply and disappearing into the darkness of Sumida Park. He stood there whispering to himself: "If you wish to be my disciple you must give up father, mother, wife and children, brothers and sisters, yes, and even your life. Unless you take up your cross and follow me you cannot be my disciple."

He quoted it in the old *bungo-tai*, the classical Japanese translation. He preferred that to modern translations because it carried nobility and otherworldliness, like the Kabuki plays he had loved from childhood. A denouement to the contest between City Office and Ants Town was fast rushing up with every possibility of the heartbreaking pathos of a classic Kabuki tragedy. A shudder passed over him as he contemplated Satoko's death by starvation, and her parents' grief— and his own position. Her death would mean his, too. He would not be a man if he did not join in her fast.

Chapter 34

Until They Dry up Like Tulip Bulbs

When she heard of the City Office plan to burn them out in early January, Satoko did a lot of praying. She had struggled before making her decision about fasting to death. Would it be suicide? She decided it would not be, because Jesus said in his Last Supper discourse that there is no greater love than laying one's life down for friends. Matsui says it was the death of Father Kolbe in Auschwitz that impressed her very much and set her thinking about those words of Jesus. Zeno had given her a pamphlet about Kolbe when he first met her and added other graphic details from his own experience and that of Kolbe's fellow Franciscans and Auschwitz inmates. Given its importance to Satoko, a brief retelling of the saga is appropriate here.

In 1936 Kolbe was recalled from Japan to head the huge Polish monastery and media complex he had begun in the 1920s. In 1937 Pope Pius XI published his encyclical letter, *Mit Brennender Sorge*, delineating the fundamental irreconcilability of Catholicism and Nazism. Kolbe used his wide circulation papers, magazines and radio station to spread the message in Polish. Hitler invaded Poland on September 1, 1939, and within a month the Gestapo arrested Kolbe. On May 28, 1941, he was transferred to Auschwitz, inmate No. 16670.

On the last day of July 1941, a fellow prisoner in Block 14 escaped. Lagerführer Karl Fritzsch, the man who first used Zyklon B gas to exterminate prisoners, had everyone from Block 14 lined up. He told them the standard punishment for an escape: ten of their number would be stripped naked and locked up in a bunker, without food or water, "until they dried up like tulip bulbs". One of the ten that Fritzsch casually pointed to with his baton was Franciszek Gajowniczek, a sergeant in the defunct Polish Army. He had joined the Underground after Poland's surrender, been betrayed to the Nazis by an informer and sent to Auschwitz.

"My poor wife and children", Gajowniczek cried aloud as he was gun-butted from the ranks. Suddenly Kolbe stepped out and walked slowly toward Fritzsch. Kolbe was emaciated, his eyes were sunken and his body carried the marks of whippings and bootings. The guards turned their guns on him and the other prisoners stared in disbelief. No one had dared break ranks before. "What does this Polish pig want?" snapped Fritzsch.

"I am a Catholic priest and want to die in place of that man with a wife and children. I am old and have no family", replied Kolbe. The Lagerführer obliged. Kolbe and the other nine were stripped and gun-butted into the starvation bunker, Cell 18. It was fierce midsummer.

Bruno Bergowiec, an inmate whom the SS made undertaker, accompanied the guards to the starvation cell each day. He testified on oath during the process leading to Kolbe's beatification by Paul VI in 1971: "Father Kolbe would lead the condemned in fervent prayers and in hymns to the Virgin.... Sometimes they became so absorbed in prayer they did not notice the guards enter.... After seven days they were so weak they could only recite the prayers in a whisper.... Though the others now lay on the floor Father Kolbe stood or knelt ... a look of serenity on his face.... I overheard one guard say: 'I've never seen anyone like him. Sometimes I had the impression I was in a church!'

"The willpower of the weaker ones began to crumble and they begged the SS guards for a little water. They would only get kicks in the groin.... Father Kolbe had a special gift of comforting them. When someone fell into despair and began screaming and cursing, he would calm him down."

"The SS screamed at them to stop praying, but to no effect. Kolbe above all disturbed them. When he looked at the SS they would shout: 'Keep your eyes to the ground. Don't you dare look at us.'"

After fourteen days, only four were still alive and Kolbe alone was still conscious. The SS needed the cell for other "criminals". Hans Brock, a German jailbird the SS had released and put in charge of the hospital barracks, was sent in. He finished them off with a syringe of phenol. It was the afternoon of August 14, 1941. In the Catholic calendar it was the Eve of the Assumption of Mary into heaven, Kolbe's favorite feast. He had often preached on it as the sign and symbol of what will happen to all who die with faith and love. After Auschwitz was liberated, fellow Polish inmates spoke of the effect of the prayers and hymns coming from the starvation bunker. One of them, the well-known writer Jan Szczepanski wrote of Kolbe's heroism: "The long agony of dying became an act of reverence and respect.... Fritzsch was too narrow to perceive that the world of violence was defeated by one act."

Chapter 35

Enduring Like Pine and Bamboo

New Year's Day is the most important day in the Japanese calendar and work is taboo from January 1 to January 3 unless absolutely unavoidable. Every business, government office, school and home must be thoroughly swept and put into order before midnight, December 31. The preparation is completed with that Japanese panacea, the *o-furo*, the piping hot deep-bath. From between the stroke of midnight of December 31 till sunset on New Year's Day, over two-thirds of the population will visit a Shinto shrine to pray. Many will have waited up all night or risen before dawn to witness the first rays of the sun. *Kadomatsu* are seen outside many homes, offices and public buildings. *Kadomatsu* is a large ikebana-like arrangement of fresh pine branches and three pieces of newly cut bamboo. The pine in China and Japan is a symbol of endurance, fidelity and vitality. Its needles retain their deep green color and sharpness no matter how torrid the summer or bitter the winter. There is an old Chinese poem, quoted in Japan: "Pines in the snow are even greener." Bamboo is the symbol of endurance and fidelity. It can be lashed about mercilessly in a gale, or bent low under the weight of snow, but it never breaks! After the storm has spent its force, the bamboo stands as graceful as ever. It symbolizes the ideal woman, strong and gentle.

The City Office section chief to whom Matsui had given a copy of Satoko's book, *Children of Ants Town*, was too busy to read it before December 31. He spent most of

January 1 and 2 meeting the many who came to his home for New Year greetings. On January 3, however, he began reading her book. He had interruptions but kept reading, fascinated, until he finished it late that night. Suddenly he had doubts about his assessment of the ragpickers. Maybe they were not law-breaking malcontents who threatened public health but people as human and precious as his own wife, parents and children. The book told an extraordinary and moving story. But was it true, or was it propaganda to legitimize squatting on government property? Deciding to go and see for himself he telephoned Matsui to meet him at Ari no Machi the next day.

As his chauffeured car sped to Sumida Park he reread some pages of Satoko's book that had moved him strangely. It was the section written by Keiko Yoshida, a girl in her mid-teens, briefly telling her family's involvement.

Her father was a soldier in Manchuria during the war while she, her mother and two brothers lived with grandparents in Onomichi, on the Inland Sea. The year after the war finished everyone was overjoyed when the father suddenly turned up. He set about energetically to find work. His old job in the public service no longer existed so he tried his hand at hawking all manner of things—clothing, pictures, groceries, confectionery. No matter how long and hard he worked there was very little profit, certainly not enough to keep his family. Unwisely they decided that opportunities would be better in Tokyo. By the time they realized how wrong they were, almost all their money was gone. They moved to progressively seedier lodgings until they were turned out onto the streets, penniless and hungry. Roaming aimlessly they finally stumbled across a cemetery in Ueno for nameless air-raid victims. People had made shelters from grave posts and air-raid debris. No sooner had they settled into a kennel-like shelter than a downpour started and went on for three days.

Everything got wet and they thought they would go mad if they stayed there any longer. Stiff and famished they walked as far as the Sumida River. That night, still without food, they took shelter under Kototoi Bridge and almost froze. The father wished he had died like so many of his friends on the China battlefields. To see his wife and children reduced to such misery broke his heart.

As the bridge offered no real shelter they moved again. That's when the mother noticed diapers strung up to dry outside huts in Ants Town and became excited: "Look, *O-to-san*. Children are living there. Let's see if they won't give us a corner." Her husband was too demoralized to respond so she picked her way alone across the muddy ground.

Ozawa the Boss listened to shivering Mrs. Yoshida's tale of woe and decided people must move over to accomodate another family. Keiko, not yet in her teens and near fainting, writes of the joy of being given food and a futon to stretch out on. She had no school to go to so began ragpicking with her parents and two brothers the next day, the Boss having told several ragpickers to show them the ropes so they could earn their keep. They found ragpicking awfully humiliating but anything was better than starving. Keiko felt very frightened and confused until that evening when she met Satoko, "so beautiful, and smiling", and asking Keiko to tell her all about herself. Suddenly the little waif felt at home.

From then on, Keiko continued, she went to school, went on that summer excursion to the Hakone mountains, took part in collecting twelve thousand yen's worth of scrap for the October Red Feather Drive and was one of the Ants whom Tokyo's Governor Yasui took into his office and praised. Helped by Satoko she grew to love study and writing compositions.

At first, her mother and father spoke of "washing their feet" of Ari no Machi as soon as they had a proper place to go. However, as the place changed under the influence of Satoko, they changed, too, and began to discover real friends among the two hundred or so who now lived there. Her mother started volunteering for the dirtiest jobs like cleaning out the pit toilets. Her father began saying he would like to help other Ants Towns start up for homeless families. Under the influence of Satoko Sensei they all began going to Sunday Mass, took instructions and were now baptized. She herself had chosen the baptismal name of Cecilia, the patron saint of music.

She concluded her story with a plea. "Almost daily, homeless people come to this settlement for help. We are still poor but we live in peace, attend school, have a little bathhouse and children's room for study, recreation and prayer. If any of us get sick we are cared for. Ants Town has become a place where there is real joy. Yet every so often the rumor spreads that officials are about to come, burn our buildings down, turn us out on the streets and order us to stop ragpicking. Whenever these rumors start up my father and mother sit up late worrying. We are not asking anything exorbitant, they say.... We just want to be left with our good friends here, starting each day with prayer and making our living by honest work.

"Kitahara Sensei, pray for us. Please ask Almighty God to help us and our little community, and allow this peaceful way of life to continue. Please ask Mary to pray that we won't be driven out into that misery we knew before we were taken in by Ari no Machi. We will pray for your health, Sensei, so that you can continue your work for the afflicted of the whole world."

The driver stopped the shiny City Office car as close as he could to the ramshackle settlement that looked so ugly in the watery winter sunlight. The chief alighted and placed his highly polished shoes carefully on the muddy ground and gingerly walked to the rickety fence. He was surprised to see a tasteful *kadomatsu* of pine and bamboo. The book plainly stated that the dwellers of Ants Town were not lazy or misfits or malcontents but decent people uprooted by the war. The writer, Satoko Kitahara, claimed that Ants Town was a very successful sociological experiment in community, and saw a certain ecological nobility in dustbin sifting!

A tense Matsui greeted a section chief who had come to meet him on his own ground, determined to ferret out the truth even if it took him all day in this warren of ragpickers. He returned the book to Matsui with a blunt challenge: "It's a great story but how much of it is fiction?" Matsui, accustomed to mistrust from officials, replied testily: "It is 100 percent true!"

"Right oh, Matsui-san, where is the girl Keiko who wrote one of the stories?"

Matsui smiled: "Let's go and meet her. That's her mother over there sorting scrap." The city official gazed at Yoshida-san, the once-desperate mother who had said: "There are diapers on the line over there.... Maybe there's a corner for us." He noted the quick, tidy way she sorted the scrap, and looked carefully at her face. The ragpicker woman had preserved a definite refinement. "May I offer you a cup of tea before we meet Keiko and any others you wish to see?" invited Matsui.

A sharp nor'easterly was blowing across the cold Sumida, penetrating the section chief's overcoat and he was glad of the shelter of Matsui's strange quarters. As he sipped hot green tea he became conscious of an organ playing and young people singing. "Who is that?" he asked.

Matsui replied: "The children. They do a lot of singing on school holidays."

The visitor had an ear for music and listened intently. "They're good", he conceded.

"Yes," agreed Matsui, "and maybe that is Keiko on the organ. Satoko taught her to play nicely. Let's go and meet them."

In the course of that morning the section chief spoke with Keiko, the children and Satoko; he saw Ari no Machi from the inside and discovered it had been honestly described in her book. When he was alone with Matsui he took his hand, shook it vigorously and said: "I am deeply impressed. Good things have been happening here and I did not know it. I promise you I shall do my utmost to find an alternative site for you people when this land is reclaimed as a city park. I have strict responsibilities as a public official, but I give you my word that I shall work with might and main to find a humane solution acceptable to all."

Matsui said good-bye to the city car with profound bows, abandoning his customary rigidity, and went straight back to tell Satoko and the Boss that the immediate crisis had been averted. Tears came into Satoko's eyes. Without thinking, she responded with Zeno's gesture—she took her beads in her hand and held them up to Matsui. Then she bowed deeply and kissed the crucifix.

Chapter 36

Let My People Go

After Christmas the cold had intensified and Satoko's condition steadily deteriorated. For the first time in her life she did not follow the time-honored Japanese custom of sending out Nengajo, New Year greeting cards. However she did write a letter to the City Office suggesting that a practical solution to the problem of finding a new site for Ants Town was only about four miles away—land reclaimed from Tokyo Bay. As the city sprawled out in all directions the municipal authorities had been filling in the west side of the bay with anything suitable for landfill, including garbage. This made extensions of Haneda airport possible. Let the people from Ants Town build new dwellings on some of the reclaimed area, she suggested.

Ants Town's new friend, the section chief, contacted the department responsible for the reclaimed land. He was told they could have first option on Lot No. 8, an area just filled in, not very far south of Ants Town, and large enough for two hundred people to build on. They would sell it cheaply—twenty-five million yen! That was about $25,000.00, which would be much more today. "A marvelous site", said Matsui, "but an impossible dream! We are like the Israelites pursued by the Egyptians, but Tokyo Bay won't miraculously open up for our escape!" Satoko pulled her dressing gown tight and got up. She took the *sumi* stick, poured some water and made Chinese ink. Then she took her brush, wrote "twenty-five million yen" on a strip of paper and pasted it to the wall. Getting back into bed she held up her rosary to Matsui and said: "God has never let us down yet! Let's pray for twenty-five million yen."

Zeno heard she was unwell and called on her. Her little room soon rang with his laughter. Growing serious he asked how she was. "I have not received that ticket to paradise yet, as you can see, Zeno-sama. There is so much still to be done, and I have no desire to escape my share of work. However, I am ready to go the moment He calls." Satoko told him of the 25 million yen and he said he would join in their prayers for the money. Satoko thanked him and so did her mother. The latter had come as soon as she heard of her daughter's worsening health.

With a mother's instinct she knew it was serious and begged her daughter to let them take her to a TB specialist's hospital. Satoko thanked her for her concern but reminded her that there were other sick people in Ants Town who could not go to such a hospital. They had to be content to line up in an outpatients department. She was taking medicine but it would be wrong if she received special treatment that other Ants Town dwellers could not have. However Satoko allowed the mother to come as often as she liked, which was something new.

Father Taeki Chiba brought her Communion. He or the curate Father Miyauchi did this regularly when she was bedridden. Years later Father Miyauchi still spoke of the extraordinary supernatural atmosphere around Satoko at prayer. Taking her Communion was a great boost to his own faith. She had other visitors, too, members of one of Japan's "New Religions", who promised a miraculous cure if she joined. Satoko's mother grew annoyed at their high-pressure visits and marvelled at Satoko who heard them out patiently, and thanked them for their concern. She said she respected their faith. All true faith had a noble purpose, she added, but she was perfectly content as a disciple of Jesus.

The mother was distressed that the meals brought to Satoko from the common kitchen were so plain. Her daughter was insistent, however, that she eat what everyone else had in Ants Town. Other sick people there did that and so would she. When relatives like the Satos or friends brought cake, confectionery or fruit Satoko accepted the gifts with thanks. However when they left she divided the presents into little packets for the Ants Town children "who are still young and need extra nourishment". Satoko was getting no better so on February 18 her mother asked the Boss's permission to sleep with her each night. The Boss, who loved and even venerated Satoko, readily agreed.

On January 22 the section chief telephoned Matsui to come and see him about an important development. Matsui went to Satoko's room first to tell her something big was in the air. Satoko had had a bad night and spoke only with difficulty. Matsui told her not to talk but just pray. She smiled and held up the rosary that was almost always in her hand now.

The section chief met Matsui with a beaming face. The department in charge of land reclamation agreed to lower the price by almost half. Several organizations, including the Catholic archdiocese of Tokyo and several prestigious universities, had become interested in Ants Town. They promised to cooperate financially if the Boss and Matsui could find a new piece of land at a reasonable price. The department handling reclaimed land was told this, and agreed to installment payments on terms that Ants Town could meet.

Matsui could hardly believe the price drop and the amazing terms of payment. He sped back to Ants Town and straight to Satoko's room. "We've done it, Satoko; we've done it, and it's thanks to your prayers! Now all you have to do is ask God to get you well so we can plan the new Ants Town and move into it. We'll get someone to drive you to see the new place as soon as you're a little better."

Satoko replied very deliberately: "No, that will not be necessary. God has granted us everything we've asked of him. That is enough."

"He has heard all our other prayers," replied Matsui, "so now we shall ask him to get you well again."

Her mother and the doctor were also in the room with Satoko and Matsui. The three noted that she replied to this with a simple No! Some time later they discussed the same impression each took from this: she refused to agree because she had offered her life to God as the one thing she had left for the Ants Town community. The doctor was a man of no religion but was deeply moved by his intuition.

During her illness children coming back from school or ragpicking would stop outside the window of her room, asking her when they could see her. She replied each time that she could not see them yet but was thinking of each one of them. Her aunt Kyoko called to see her that same day, January 22. Satoko's voice was weaker but no one suspected how bad she was.

Kazuko also came, to wash Satoko's hair and give her a sponge bath. As she began the sponging she was suddenly shaken by a terrible presentiment: she was preparing Satoko's body for burial! Despite her efforts, tears began trickling down her cheeks. Satoko saw this and said: "O-nee-san (Elder sister), every single prayer has been answered, every one. I am so happy." That reassured Kazuko and she dismissed the strange foreboding.

When the sister had finished and prepared to go home, Satoko asked her to stay on ... maybe even sleeping in the room with her mother and herself that night. It was strange for her younger sister to make such a request, she thought, but she said it was impossible, as she had to get supper and breakfast for her husband and children. Maybe tomorrow night. Satoko thanked her and asked to see her husband, too, and wondered aloud when their father would be back in Tokyo from the university conference. He was now President of the Takasaki University of Economics.

Satoko's mother wished her husband was back from the conference, too. She had begun feeling apprehensive some days before when Satoko tore her diary into small pieces. When her mother asked why, Satoko simply said it "no longer served any purpose". Her anxiety increased when Satoko refused to go along with Matsui-Sensei's enthusiastic suggestion to ask God for a return to health. The mother's name Ei means Feminine Excellence. Her deepest reserves of excellence were demanded as she stayed silent beside a daughter who persisted in doing humanly absurd things, for a faith she did not share.

Satoko did not sleep well that night, nor did her mother. At about 1:00 A.M. Satoko saw the mother was awake and murmured: "I wonder if Father will get here. I feel so weak. I think I am close to the end of my strength."

At 7.30 A.M. the mother was quietly tidying the room for breakfast when Satoko asked for a glass of water, drank a little and said how good it tasted. The mother took her temperature and received a shock. Excusing herself for a moment, she went to Matsui's room and asked him to telephone the priest and the doctor. When she returned to the room Satoko was saying the Rosary limply, seemingly lost in prayer. At about ten minutes to eight she slipped into a coma and within minutes stopped breathing. Father Chiba arrived, and gave her the last anointing. The doctor arrived and verified her death. The cause: kidney failure, from a nephritis infection that was presumably tubercular in origin.

Satoko's aunt Kyoko Sato laid her out in the white dress her mother fetched from home. It was the dress Satoko was baptized in and had hoped to wear when she took her vows in the Mercedarian convent as a bride of Christ. Kyoko surrounded the coffin with white lilies, the ancient Christian symbol of virginity. Ants Town was stunned and begged Satoko's family to allow them to conduct the wake and funeral. The wake is a very public and important affair in Japan. The body is kept in the home where the sliding walls are taken out to allow a continuous stream of mourners to pray before the corpse, burn incense as a mark of belief in the afterlife, and comfort the family. The mourners will include the whole neighborhood and representatives of associations, schools, businesses, etc. connected with the bereaved family. Normally a very public figure like Professor Kitahara, president of a university, would hold a very solemn wake in his home or even use a large hall. The Kitaharas, however, agreed that Ants Town was Satoko's real home and the obsequies would be held there.

Ants Town was shocked but there was a deep-down sense of peace. The Japanese ideograph for death expressed this aptly: 死 in which there are three component parts. ヒ originally 𠤎 means old person—seated due to being too feeble to walk about. 𠄌 is the old person dead and buried under the ground. 歹 is an abbreviation of the ideograph for moon. Death plunges its victim into darkness, just as the sun disappears and the world is gripped by darkness. But then the moon rises and bathes the earth in a new and beautiful light—a symbol of the soul of the deceased going into a new realm of existence. Satoko's sudden death plunged Ants Town into grief but there was a consolation they held on to with certainty—she was home in heaven.

At that time in Japan it was strictly against Catholic regulations to have a funeral Mass outside a church. Father Chiba asked Archbishop Doi could he have the funeral Mass in the grounds of Ants Town and the Archbishop said yes and that he himself would be present. The diminutive prelate held Satoko in high regard. He met her soon after she went to

Ants Town, after Matsui succeeded in getting that first article in the Asahi newspaper about "Father Zeno building a
church in Ants Town". Zeno's superiors were used to his
quaint ways but thought this time there would be stern questions from the cathedral about this unauthorized church.
Satoko accompanied Zeno when he went to explain to the
Archbishop and apologized for being called Father when he
was "just an ignorant Brother". The Archbishop smiled, said
Zeno and Satoko were very pleasing to the Lord and added
that Zeno had more right to be called Father by poor people
"than most of us!"

The funeral Mass was held in Ants Town in front of the
Lourdes grotto on Saturday, January 23, at 11:00 A.M. The
two hundred ragpickers were up in front with Satoko's parents, sisters and relatives. The sky was overcast and it was a
bitterly cold day, but about four hundred other people came.

Nuns found themselves sitting next to Yakuza, Japan's
notorious gangsters. Some of Matsui's movie-world friends,
who were now well-known stars, turned up. The governor
of Tokyo and nationally famous actor Hisaya Morishige were
among the many who sent telegrams. Media people came in
force. The latter might have their doubts about the irascible
Matsui but they accepted Satoko as a genuine saint. One edi-
torial likened her to Dr. Schweitzer of Africa. Other newspapers described her as an heroic witness against the new
selfishness and materialism that was invading Japan.

She was buried beside her brother and sister in The Garden of Souls Cemetery, Tokyo. Priests, religious and other
people, some of them non-Christian, began praying to her.
Some claimed remarkable recoveries from illness, due to
her intercession in heaven. In 1975 Archbishop Shirayagi of
Tokyo began an official investigation into her reputed holiness. Many believe it would be very encouraging if a lay-
woman, who called Catholics to a more serious commitment

to the impoverished masses of the world, were canonized. Japanese Christians, who are fewer than 1 million in a population of one hundred twenty million, would be especially pleased—Satoko was so *Nihon-teki*.

The ragpicker priest, Father Vallade, sees her as an "ambassador for the homeless", calling Christians back to Christ's vision of a Church that would identify with the poor. Satoko did not criticize nuns, brothers and priests. However, she did note that people living in fine buildings and wearing good clothes—even if religious habits—were so often unable to cross the gap that separates people like ragpickers and destitute refugees from "normal" society.

Chapter 37

Wabi, Mu and the Gospels

Satoko became a cult figure in Japan, especially after her death. Newspapers and magazines, both secular and religious, stage productions and radio plays, school readers, even songs and a comic book held her up as a heroic model. Within a month of her death the cinema giant Shochiku began preliminary work on a movie that was screened in theaters across the land. Called *Ari no Machi no Maria*, it won several international awards. The February 1990 issue of the prestigious intellectual magazine, *Bungei Shunju* gave short sketches of "the fifty women who most moved the heart of the Japanese nation during the sixty-two-year reign of the emperor (Hirohito)". Satoko was one of the fifty. Why has this totally Christian woman such appeal in a nation where Christians are less than 1 percent, and Catholics less than 0.5 percent?

Part of the answer is surely this: her life and death are filled with what the Japanese refer to as *wabi*. There seems to be no equivalent word in any other language. Japanese tell you wabi cannot be understood—it must be "felt" in the heart. The ideograph for wabi gives an important clue to its meaning: 佗 It is a combination of three ideographs: イ which means person (being an abbreviation of 人), ⼍ or ⼍, which means the roof of a house. (When the Chinese first devised ideographs well over three thousand years ago, a house had a flat roof, with a big rock or log on top to anchor it.) Under the roof, that is inside the house, is ヒ, originally written ヒ a person sitting. This was chosen to represent an old person who cannot walk about but has to sit, as previously pointed out in the ideograph for death. So the wabi ideograph means: (the feelings of) someone looking at a feeble, old, house-bound person. Because of the latter element, the adjectival form in Japanese, wabi-shii means wretched, miserable, desolate. However, Japanese poets in medieval times began using the noun wabi in a highly specialized sense. After all, when the old person one is looking at is a much-loved grandparent, for instance, one sees a great inner beauty beneath the sere and feeble body. Wabi now came to mean the living inner glow within human and nature phenomena that appear merely wretched to the unenlightened.

I shall attempt to explain only one aspect of wabi, the "human" aspect that impinges on the Satoko story. I have neither sufficient space nor confidence to elucidate fully this highly esthetic and profound reality of Japanese experience. Anyone seeking a deep understanding of the Japanese heart, however, must make a specialized study of wabi, and of its look-alike sister, *sabi*, by reading the great Japanese commentators. One modern commentator, Daisetz Suzuki cites an example of wabi taste in a poem by thirteenth century Ietaka Fujiwara: "There are people who only wait for cherry blossoms. What about the grass already thrusting through late winter snow in their mountain village?" People who only notice showy beauty dismiss a snow-covered landscape as desolate and not worth a second look. They miss the more subtle and nobler beauty of "the life impulse within the wintry desolation", as Suzuki puts it.

The greatest of the haiku poets, Basho, wrote poetry full of wabi in his little hut on the banks of the Sumida. Many of his nature settings are desolate and even "wretched": a storm raging over a bleak heath, a young monkey shivering in winter drizzle, a lone crow on a withered bough in autumn twilight, turbulent waves on a wintry sea. Such scenes made him confused and melancholic when he was a young man. They were sad reminders that everything in nature, and in human life, is uncertain and cursed with impermanence. The cherry blossoms quickly fall, leaving only poignant memories.

But, spurred on by a great yearning for tranquillity of heart, he read the spiritual poets like Saigyo, the twelfth-century samurai-turned-Buddhist monk, and entrusted himself to the discipline of the Zen monk Butchoo. These holy men taught him to see, with "the eyes of the heart", the Absolute, hidden behind all phenomena. They gave no name or definition to the Absolute because that weakling called human intelligence can grasp only what is limited and finite. Sometimes his Buddhist mentors referred to the Absolute as the Law, sometimes as *Mu*, No Thing. The Absolute is utterly beyond the "things" humans know but is totally different from "nothing". Because we could fall forever into the Absolute and never reach the bottom, sometimes the word used was *Ku*, the Void, like the void of the limitless sky.

When Basho experienced the reality of this Absolute, this Law that is the origin of all true laws, this all-merciful One, his heart was flooded with peace and joy. All the sadness, brokenness and impermanence of human life, and of nature around him, took on a transcendent meaning and unity. Everything became holy. He looked back on the pain, frustration and loneliness of the hard roads he had travelled, and suddenly it all appeared as worthwhile and very good. The difficult parts of the journey deepened his compassion for fellow wayfarers.

In his short masterpiece, *The Narrow Road to the Deep North*, Basho devotes a page to a night spent at an inn while on his journey to the far north. Through the thin shooji screen wall separating his room from theirs, he listened to two prostitutes bewailing their fate. His heart was assailed with sadness at "their sorry plight ... making fickle love each night". In the morning they saw he was a Buddhist monk and with tears in their eyes begged him to take them to the holy shrine at Ise. With regret he said he could not do this, telling them to trust in their Savior (Buddha). "For a long time after I left them behind", he continues, "my heart overflowed with pity, and I could not get them out of my mind."

He took his brush and wrote a haiku, a seventeen syllable poem: *Hitotsuya ni* (five syllables) *Yuujo mo netari* (seven) *Hagi to tsuki* (five). "Under one roof with prostitutes. Hagi flowers and the moon!" The hagi is a small shrub. Its flowers appear but briefly in autumn and are soon cut down by the chill north winds that usher in winter. For that reason the hagi had become the poetic symbol of impermanence, weakness, impotence—those things that made the prostitutes' lives so unhappy. However, gliding serenely above all the sadness, wretchedness and impermanence was the peerless harvest moon, sign of the all-merciful, all-unifying, ever-constant Absolute. In contemplating this, Basho was freed from the forlornness that assailed him.

When Satoko lived there three centuries later, the Sumida ran past a wretched slum. Her ragpicker children were abused and despised like those daughters of poor farmers who were sold to brothels in Basho's time. Like the poet, she too was able to see an inner glow beneath the grime, in humble hearts very open to love. That vision preserved her peace and strengthened her resolve.

Satoko found great *wabi* beauty in the Christmas story, and taught Matsui, the Boss and the children to see it, too. In the wretched homelessness of the Child and his Mother lay the very way to the home that would last forever. Following *unsui* Zeno's lead she taught Ants Town how to celebrate Christmas as a true story happening now. Then they became shepherds and even Wise Men discovering the Mother and Child on the banks of the Sumida. Not too far away in the

Tokyo Carmel, Japanese nuns silently spread the same incarnational message in the Christmas cards they painted—a Holy Family, with Japanese faces and almond-shaped eyes, looking out onto snow-covered hills and peasants' huts suffused with wabi beauty.

For Satoko the Lourdes grotto in Ants Town was more than a reminder of the first Catholic church she entered— in Yokohama where she was deeply moved by the image of Mary conversing with Bernadette. Again with Zeno's help she came to see Lourdes as a modern reenactment of the Christmas event. The rock grotto from which the Mother of God spoke in the local dialect to poorly educated, asthmatic, poverty-stricken Bernadette, was a contemporary Bethlehem cave. The glow in the grotto came from the light in the cave. It was for Satoko the fulfillment of the quest for wabi beauty of her Shinto priest and shrine-maiden ancestors. Satoko like Bernadette was stricken with ill-health but both saw no contradiction in praying for others to be healed while seeking no personal cure. For both women, sickness, interior darkness and an early death had lost their terrors. Indeed these things took on a rare spiritual beauty in the light that shone from what first appeared as a dark, wretched place—called Golgotha.

Matsui had come to appreciate wabi early in life through his father, a well-known writer of kabuki plays. When Matsui readied a room, in the Ants Town shed, for Satoko to come and live in, he made it three meters by three meters [about ten feet by ten feet], the precise size of a tea hut. That was no coincidence. In *The Tales of the Heike*, written in early medieval times, mention is made of the "an", the hermit hut to which the Empress Dowager retired. Kamo no Chomei in the thirteenth century wrote one of Japan's literary classics about this popular ideal of retiring alone to such a Buddhist hermit hut. In the sixteenth century this idea was incorporated into the tea ceremony hut—which the teamasters called "a hermit's hut in the middle of the city". The tea ceremony, which has had and continues to have a profound influence on Japanese tastes, is essentially a spiritual experience. One goes into the almost-bare tea hut to empty one's heart of arrogance, anger, impurity and distraction—to "wash the eyes of the heart". Then one has a vision of wabi beauty—not just in the tea hut but in the mundane sights of everyday life. A simple pot of tea shared at home with one's family can become beautiful and holy.

Basho highly appreciated this philosophy, or rather theology! Commenting on Sen no Rikyu, the sixteenth-century proponent of the wabi tea hut he says this "way" teaches one to "follow nature and befriend the four seasons. Everything seen becomes a flower.... One who does not see the flower is akin to a barbarian!" Basho loved his own little hut by the Sumida where he wrote poetry that has led many to discover the Absolute present everywhere. Yet he saw himself simply as "a little monk in a wind-torn robe". Satoko discovered joy in her littleness, similar to Basho's, in her little "an" on the same riverbank. She rejoiced to see so much of her nation's culture fulfilled in the Gospels that had taught her to discover "the Kingdom of God already within you".

In 1973 Shiroo Takagi, a well-known Japanese playwright, wrote and directed an operetta, staged in the famous Takarazuka Theater, which is not far from the Osaka airport. Called *The Town Where Stars Fall* it was a ninety minute production in sixteen acts, based on the life and death of Satoko. It won great audience acclaim and at a press interview Takagi said: "In my thirty years with the Takarazuka Theater I have never before seen such enthusiasm and emotional involvement on the part of the players."

Takagi's interest in Christianity came very unwillingly. Some years before, he was setting out on a trip to Europe and told his eleven-year-old daughter he would bring her back whatever she wanted. She replied: "I would like a bottle of Lourdes water." He was flabbergasted and suggested all kinds of other things that Europe had to offer a child. All to no avail. There was only one thing she wanted!

So he changed his itinerary in France and in a bad mood dragged himself all the way down to Lourdes. This had an unforeseen result. "For the first time in my life I prayed! My prayer was answered in a way I personally regard as miraculous! After trying to keep God at a respectable distance for several years by promising him I would one day be baptized, I was shocked into action when Jesuit Father Takemiya accused me of dilly-dallying because of intellectual pride."

He took instructions and was baptized. He does not regret it. However he has a strong complaint: "Christianity in Japan is so heavy with western cultural baggage." This is where he found the life of Satoko refreshingly attractive. She was a Japanese of the Japanese. In the lengthy research he did before writing his operetta, he said, he was also delighted to discover she was someone who had plenty of big faults at the beginning—such as the intellectual pride and vanity that so often accompanies a wealthy, aristocratic upbringing. However, when she freed herself of these defects after a long struggle, that classical upbringing resulted in a very *Nihon-teki* young woman. The ragpicker priest Vallade, who helped Takagi research his operetta, makes the same point: Satoko's background of Confucianism, Shintoism and Buddhism became fertile soil for Christian seed. There is something vital at stake here, which goes a long way to explain why so few Japanese are Christians.

Pope John XXIII said someone without a knowledge of history is like a person without a memory—an incomplete person. The preachers who converted Greece and Rome to the Christian faith (and thereby prepared the way for Christendom of the thirteenth century) had an optimism about the great Greek philosophers and their Roman commentators. These Christian missionaries rejoiced to find so much truth and good already present there. They accepted this as coming from God, the Source of all truth and good. Saint Justin is a case in point. Born of non-Christian Greek parents, he studied the classic Greek philosophers in Ephesus. When he discovered the Gospels just before A.D. 135, he brought to the baptismal waters all the truths he had found in his much-loved Platonistic philosophy. He spoke of these pre-Christian truths as "seeds of the Logos", the Logos being the Son of God. He died a martyr in Rome in A.D. 165, having won over many leading personalities to the Christian faith. The majority of the great Christian apologists of those seminal times followed his lead.

This thing almost happened in the Far East under Jesuit Matteo Ricci. Cultural-baggage fundamentalists, however, won the day and Ricci's flourishing Chinese mission was destroyed. Vatican II leaves no Catholic in doubt that Ricci's (and Justin's) missionary methods are authentic missionary methods for Catholics. This is what Shiroo Takagi is talking about.

When the Catholic bishops of East Asia met in Tokyo, March 1979, they reflected on the new Vatican II thinking and called on their followers to go out to non-Christian compatriots "in sustained and reflective dialogue ... and in prayer, which will teach us what we can receive from them, what the Holy Spirit has taught others to express in their religious books, in a marvelous variety of ways—different perhaps from our own, but through which we too may hear his voice, calling us to lift our hearts to the Father. At the same time we will find an opportunity to share with them the riches of our own Christian heritage."

When Protestant-Catholic dialogue increased in tempo, Catholics learned a great deal from Anglicans and Protestants.

A far more central place for Bible reading is one of a dozen examples that could be cited. Reverend Joseph Neville Ward was a Methodist clergyman who became very interested in ecumenism in England. He decided the best way to understand other faith traditions was to try praying like them. He experimented with the Rosary and was very surprised at how biblical a prayer it became for him. One result was his incisive book on the Rosary, *Five for Sorrow, Ten for Joy*.

Early this century in the United States a young man with very few tangible assets set out to found a publishing firm. He thought this would be the best way to proclaim the uncompromising Calvinist faith that he treasured. He was William B. Eerdmans and the company he founded and which bears his name, flourishes to this day. His son, named after his father, has inherited the same Calvinist faith. He believes, however, that the Holy Spirit is speaking to all the churches today through ecumenical "signs of the times". This convicton is reflected in Christian books he is publishing that carry much broader perspectives than the Calvinist books brought out by his father. An example that is to the point here is *Mary for All Christians*, the work of John Macquarrie, one of today's most respected theologians in the Anglican Communion.

It is not just Anglican and Protestant writers who are taking a fresh look at Mary—or, as a number point out, taking a look at the devotion to Mary found in Reformation figures like Martin Luther. In recent years many Protestant and Anglican faithful have gone on pilgrimage to Marian shrines like Lourdes or Fatima and have commenced saying the Rosary regularly. I would hope that the Christian witness of Satoko makes Christians of other denominations think about the fruits of the Holy Spirit that are evident in her life, a life in which prayer to Mary, especially the Rosary, was one outstanding characteristic.

BIBLIOGRAPHY

Allyn, John. *The 47 Ronin*. Tokyo: Charles E. Tuttle, 1970.

Bashoo, Matsuo. *The Narrow Road to the North*. Translated by Nobuyuki Yuasa. U.K.: Penguin, 1966.

Bessing, Maria, Robert J. Nogosek, and Patrick H. O'Leary. *The Enneagram*. Denville, N.J.: Dimenslow Books, 1984.

Brackman, Arnold C. *The Other Nuremberg: Tokyo War Crimes Trials*. New York: Quill, 1987.

Bush, Lewis. *Japanalia*. Tokyo: Okuyama, 1956.

Chesterton, G. K. *St. Francis of Assisi*. 25th ed. London: Hodder and Stoughton, 1946.

Chesterton, G. K. *The Everlasting Man*. New York: Image Books, Doubleday, 1955.

Cronin, Vincent. *The Wise Man From The West*. London: Readers Union, 1956.

de Roo, Joseph R. *2001 Kanji*. Roppongi, Tokyo: O.F.M. Language School, 1980.

Guillain, Robert. *I Saw Tokyo Burning*. London: John Murray, 1981.

Hammarskjöld, Dag. *Markings*. New York: Knopf, 1979.

Hammitzsch, Horst. *Zen in the Art of the Tea Ceremony*. New York: E. P. Dutton, 1988.

Hardy, Richard P. *The Life of St. John of the Cross*. London: Darton, Longman and Todd, 1987.

Inoguchi, Nakajima and Pineau. *The Divine Wind*. New York: Bantam, 1960.

Japan, The Official Guide. Tokyo: Japan Travel Bureau, 1958.

Lyons, Phyllis I. *The Saga of Dazai Osamu*. California: Stanford University Press, 1985.

Macquarrie, John. *Mary for all Christians*. Michigan: Wm. Eerdmans, 1991.

Millot/Bair. *Divine Thunder*. Mayflower Books. Hertfordshire: St. Albans, 1974.

Morita, Akio. *Made in Japan*. New York: Signet (N.A.L. Penguin), 1986.

Naito, Hatsuho. *Thunder Gods*. Tokyo: Kodansha International, 1989.

Ono, Sokyo. *Shinto: The Kami Way*. Tokyo: Charles E. Tuttle, 1962.

Ravier, André. *Lourdes: Land of The Gospel*. Lourdes: L'Oeuvre de la Grotte, 1965.

Reischauer, Edwin O. *Japan, Past and Present*. Tokyo: Charles E. Tuttle, 1962.

Schurhammer, Georg. *Francis Xavier* Vol. IV, Japan. Rome: Jesuit Historical Institute, 1982.

Sen XV Soshitsu. *Tea Life, Tea Mind*. Tokyo: Weatherhill, 1979.

Seven Stories of Modern Japan. Sydney: Wild Peony, 1991.

Story, Richard. *A History of Modern Japan*. Harmondsworth, U.K.: Penguin, 1987.

Suzuki, Daisetz. *Zen and Japanese Culture*. Bollinger Series. Princeton: University Press, 1973.

Tea in Japan. Edited by Paul Varley, and Isoa Kamakura. Honolulu: University of Hawaii Press, 1989.

Toland, John. *The Rising Sun*. New York: Bantam, 1971.

Ueda, Makoto. *Matsuo Bashoo*. Tokyo: Kodansha International Paperback, 1982.

Ward, Joseph Neville. *Five for Sorrow, Ten for Joy*. Cambridge, Mass.: Cowley Press, 1985.

We Japanese. Hakone: Fujiya Hotel, 1950.

SOURCES IN JAPANESE

Kitahara, Kinji, "Ari no Machi no Kodomotachi, by Satoko Kitahara," in *Maria Satoko wo Shinobite*. Tokyo: Yaegaku Shoboo, 1971.

Mainichi. *Shoowa Shi (Shoowa 20)*. Tokyo: Shinbunsha, 1983.

Matsui, Tooru. *Ari no Machi no Maria*. Tokyo: Shunju Sha, 1984.

Matsui, Tooru. *Zeno Shinu Hima Nai*. Tokyo: Shunju Sha, 1966.

ACKNOWLEDGMENTS

I wish to express my gratitude to those who helped me tell Satoko's story for the English-speaking world. I was greatly helped by the following people in Japan: Tooru Matsui, who allowed me to interview him, despite his illness. Kazuko Takagi, who told me much about her younger sister Satoko and their family. Father Tony Glynn, S.M., his parish staff and the Ladies League at Tomigaoka Church, Nara, for invaluable help with Japanese sources. Sister Hamada and Community, Sacred Heart Convent, Tokyo, for putting me up and putting up with me while I did research in Tokyo. Setsuo and Terue Narasaki, and Sachiko Yamato also provided valuable assistance, as did Mayor Eizo Nishida of Nara and the Conventual Franciscans in Tokyo, and in Rome through Father E. Piacentini. Finally I am indebted to Provincial Sister Imaizumi for Hokkaido research, and Sisters Kishiwada and Yukawa for tireless co-ordinating work.

People in Australia who helped were, firstly, Toni Josephs, who typed the whole Ms. and put it on discs. She and her husband Jack gave many valuable suggestions and practical help. Father Garry Reynolds, S.M., Provincial of the Marist Fathers, Australia, provided the opportunity to research and write the book. Father Jim Murphy, S.M., proofread the Ms. and made very helpful suggestions. Brother Joseph McMahon, F.M.S., and Brother Brendan Neilly, F.M.S., and the community at St. Joseph's College, Hunter's Hill, where I was chaplain were very supportive. Dr. Sakuko Matsui, of the East Asia Study Department, Sydney University, helped me greatly with things Japanese. Rieko and Ken Nakai, a couple dedicated to improving Japanese-Australian understanding, gave much practical support. Also Dr. Greg and Mary Ann Knoblanche, Roma O'Donnell and Drs. Padraic Grattan-Smith, Sr. and Jr. For the translation of a three-hundred-page document on Satoko in Italian I am indebted to Dr. Lou and Cathy Gallo, Julie Drury, Teresa and Cathy Amoia, Tony De Tullio, Teresa Larcher, Silvana Toia, Joseph and Eunice Spangaro. Rosaleen McVittie helped considerably concerning the Urasenke "tea way".

These, and many other friends in Japan and Australia volunteered their help so that a modern Japanese woman could give her heroic witness to English-speaking people. She was an ambassador for the destitute. The present provincial of the Marist Fathers, Father Tony McCosker, S.M., has agreed that all profits from this book will go to help the destitute of the Third World, especially the people of the Philippines, with whom Satoko wanted to go and work.

It is fitting that this book originally should have come out in May. This is the month Satoko loved specially because in the Roman Catholic communion it is the month dedicated to Mary. This was also the month when she decided she could best follow Christ by becoming a ragpicker. May her prayers from heaven help us to live, ever more fully, Christ's love and practical concern for the poor.

May 1992, Marist Centre,
Toongabbie, N.S.W., Australia